FURNITURE TREASURY
(Mostly of American Origin)

THE MACMILLAN COMPANY
NEW YORK · BOSTON · CHICAGO · DALLAS
ATLANTA · SAN FRANCISCO

MACMILLAN AND CO., Limited
LONDON · BOMBAY · CALCUTTA · MADRAS
MELBOURNE

THE MACMILLAN COMPANY
OF CANADA, Limited
TORONTO

FURNITURE TREASURY

(Mostly of American Origin)

ALL PERIODS OF AMERICAN FURNITURE WITH
SOME FOREIGN EXAMPLES IN AMERICA
ALSO AMERICAN HARDWARE AND
HOUSEHOLD UTENSILS

BY

WALLACE NUTTING

FIVE THOUSAND ILLUSTRATIONS
WITH DESCRIPTIONS ON THE
SAME PAGE

IN TWO VOLUMES
VOLUME II

THE MACMILLAN COMPANY · NEW YORK
1948

CONTENTS OF VOLUME II

CONTENTS — *Continued*

FURNITURE TREASURY
(Mostly of American Origin)

1774. Carved Three-Legged Chair. Reputed To Have Been Brought from France, but Claimed To Be Made of American Woods. Carving and Molds Resemble Those on Chests. 17th Century. William B. Goodwin, Hartford.

1775. Three-Legged Chair, Rung Missing. Simple Type. Seat Set in as Panel. 17th Century. Fuessenich Collection.
1776. (Right.) Style of Corner Chair, but with Four Legs. 17th or 18th Century. Flayderman & Kaufman.

1777-79. Kitchen of Webb House, Wethersfield. Two Chair Tables. Quaint Wall Shelves with Rope. Early 18th Century. Colonial Dames.

1780. CROMWELLIAN. TERM APPLIED TO CHAIRS WITH THIS BACK. 1650–60. WILLIAM B. GOODWIN.
1781. (Right.) CROMWELLIAN. COVERED WITH ORIGINAL TURKEY WORK. 1650–60. MRS. FRANCIS P. GARVAN.

1782. CROMWELLIAN. NEW LEATHER. SMALL FINIALS A PUZZLE. FORMERLY THE AUTHOR'S.
1783. (Right.) CROMWELLIAN. UNUSUAL TURNINGS. BESIDES TURKEY WORK, THESE CHAIRS WERE UPHOLSTERED IN LEATHER OR FABRIC. 1650–60. WADSWORTH ATHENEUM.

1784. "Two Back" Turned Chair, Matches a Mushroom Arm. Restored Feet. 17th Century. Wadsworth Atheneum.

1785. (Right.) All Turned. Carver and Brewster Elements. 17th Century. Connecticut Historical Society, Hartford.

1786. Unique Chair Found on Cape Cod. 17th Century. Dr. Irving Lyon, Buffalo.

1787. (Right.) Wainscot, Carved Back. King Philip Chair. 17th Century. Martin House.

1788. Robinson Wainscot, Guilford, Connecticut. Seat New, Tape Loom Cut in Back Subsequent to Date of Chair. The Earliest Turnings. 1630–50. Wadsworth Atheneum.

1789. Rector Pierson Wainscot. Yale University. 1640-60.

1790. Governor Leete Wainscot. Wainscot Means Wagon Oak,
and Refers to the Paneling of the Earliest Chairs. 1640-60.
Stone House, Guilford.

1791. WAINSCOT, BANISTER BACK. THIS IS THE ONLY AMERICAN CHAIR SHOWN WITH TWO PANELS UNDER THE ARM. STRONG RESEMBLANCE OF ALL WAINSCOT ARMS. 17TH CENTURY. FRANCIS D. BRINTON.

1792. (Right.) WALNUT. UNIQUE ARM. PENNSYLVANIA CHAIRS, 17TH CENTURY TYPE, QUITE DIFFERENT FROM ANY OTHERS FOUND. J. STOGDELL STOKES.

1793. OAK, ONE NEW ARM. LONG ISLAND. 17TH CENTURY. WADSWORTH ATHENEUM.

1794. (Right.) CARVED OAK. POSSIBLY AMERICAN. 17TH C. DANVERS HISTORICAL SOCIETY.

1795. WAINSCOT, "SQUARE TURNING." FOUND IN VIRGINIA. AMERICAN WHITE OAK. FEET AND CREST RESTORED. ONLY EXAMPLE FROM THE SOUTH. BEFORE 1650. WILLIAM B. GOODWIN.

1796. (Right.) SIDE WAINSCOT. CROMWELLIAN EXCEPT FOR PANEL. 17TH CENTURY. J. STOGDELL STOKES, PHILADELPHIA.

1797. UPHOLSTERED ARM AND BACK, SCROLLED EARS. DIFFICULT TO DATE. J. STOGDELL STOKES.

1798. (Right.) WAINSCOT. DULLED DECORATION ON TOP RAIL. 17TH CENTURY. J. STOGDELL STOKES.

1799. MOST PERFECT BREWSTER TYPE. THERE ARE ONLY ONE OR TWO OTHERS. POSTS MORE THAN 2½ INCHES IN DIAMETER. 1640–60. MRS. J. INSLEY BLAIR.

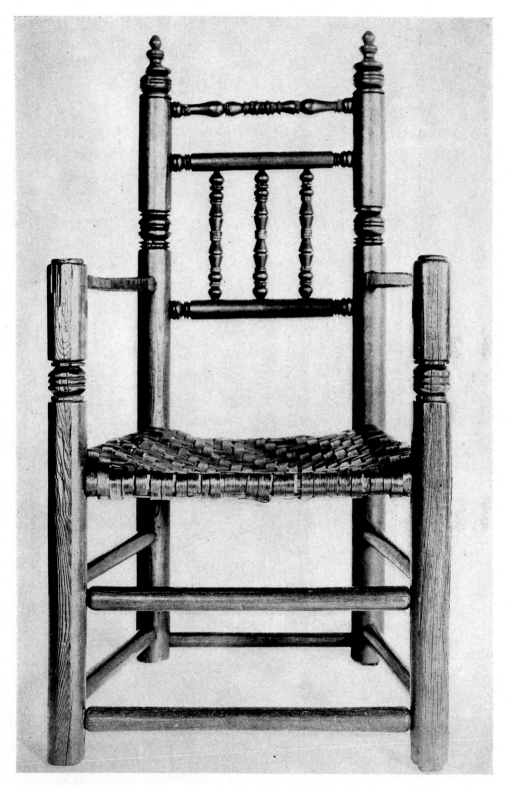

1800. GOVERNOR CARVER, GOOD FINIALS AND SPINDLES. ASH. BALLS ON FRONT POSTS LOST.
43½ INCHES HIGH. POSTS LARGE DIAMETER, 1 9/16 INCHES. 1640-60.
WADSWORTH ATHENEUM.

1801. GREAT CARVER, BEST BACK KNOWN. 1640–60.
WADSWORTH ATHENEUM.

1802. "Brewster," Original Balls. The Term Brewster Is Applied to Chairs Having Spindle Work below the Seat. 45½ Inches High, 23½ Inches Wide. Outside Width of Back 17⅜ Inches. Most Such Chairs Found in Massachusetts or Connecticut. 1640–60. Wadsworth Atheneum.

1803. A Slant-Back Carver, All Original. 1640–60. Pilgrim Chairs Were First in Ash, Then in Maple. George Dudley Seymour. Wadsworth Atheneum.

1804. Transition Brewster. Posts Somewhat Smaller. 1670–90. Turning below Seat not Found in the First Period in America. Present Ownership Unknown.

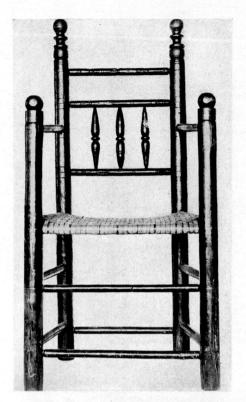

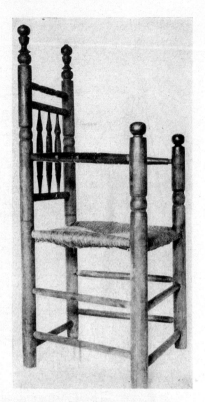

1805. Carver of Medium Weight. South Shore. Balls Restored. 1650–70. Wadsworth Atheneum.

1806. (Right.) High-Post Carver. Western Massachusetts. 48½ x 25. These Ash Spindles Are Shaky. 1650–70. Wadsworth Atheneum.

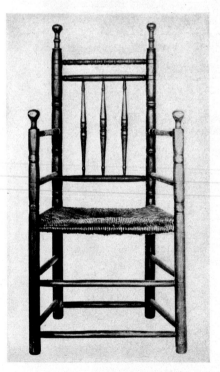

1807. A Light Carver. Balls Replaced. 1670–80. Wadsworth Atheneum.

1808. (Right.) Light Carver. All Original. 1680–90. Wadsworth Atheneum.

1809. Heavy, Initialed Carver. Maple. 47 x 24½. Back 18½ Inches. Depth
16 Inches. 1640–60. Wadsworth Atheneum.

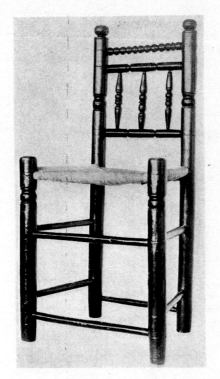
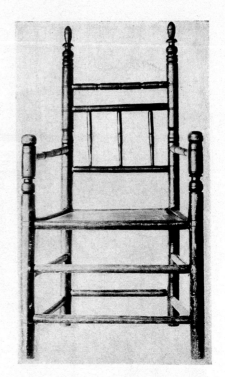

1810. SIDE CARVER. SPOOL-TURNED TOP RAIL. AUTHOR FOUND A SIMILAR CHAIR IN ENGLAND. 1660–80. WAS B. A. BEHREND'S.
1811. (Right.) LIGHT CARVER, POORLY SPACED SPINDLES. 1660–80. WADSWORTH ATHENEUM.

1812–13. PAIR OF SIDE CARVERS. 1665–80. CHAUNCEY C. NASH.

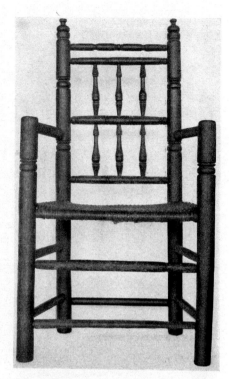

1814. "Miles Standish" Brewster. Badly Restored as to Feet and Balls in Front. 1630–40. Posts' Largest Diameter $2^{11}\!/_{16}$ Inches. Flattened Spindles. Side Spindles Not Original. Mrs. F. H. Lincoln, Hingham.

1815. (Right.) Two Tiers of Spindles. 1640–70. Balls Lost. Fuessenich Collection.

1816. Brewster Type, Dowels Run Through and Show as Knobs. 1630–50. Seat Composed of Spindles. Fuessenich Collection.

1817. (Right.) Double Tier of Spindles. 1640–70. Fuessenich Collection.

1818–19. A Pair of Side Carvers. Unusual Finials. 1650–70. J. Stogdell Stokes.

1820. Light Turned Carver. 1650.   1821. A Brewster. Dowels Protrude. 1640.

Wadsworth Atheneum.

1822. Great Slat Back, Winged. Flat Arm Rail. Turnings below the Seat Indicate
Later Date Than the Carver. 1670–90. Dwight Blaney.

1823. Semi-Brewster. Feet Pieced. 43½ x 26½. 1640–60. Wadsworth Atheneum. (All on Page.)
1824. (Right.) Pilgrim Slat Back. Fine Finials. 43½ Inches High. Post Diameter 2½ Inches.

1825–26. Mushroom Pilgrim Slat Backs. The Left a Child's Chair, the Right
a Semi-Brewster. Original Type of Mushroom. 1640–60.

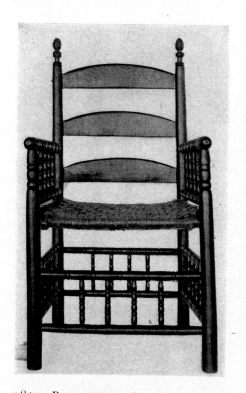

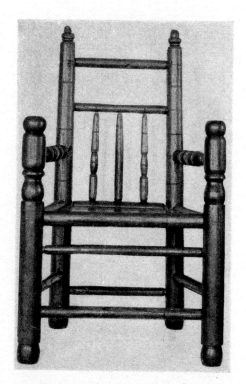

1827. PENNSYLVANIA SEMI-BREWSTER. PROBABLY OF LATER DATE THAN NEW ENGLAND EXAMPLES, OWING TO THE LIGHTER TURNINGS AND LATER SETTLEMENT. 17TH CENTURY. J. STOGDELL STOKES.

1828. (Right.) SPINDLES RUNNING INTO SEAT. FEET WRONG. AUTHOR CANNOT SPEAK WITH CERTAINTY REGARDING THIS CHAIR. 17TH CENTURY.

1829. PILGRIM SLAT BACK. 1650–70. WADSWORTH ATHENEUM.

1830. (Right.) PILGRIM SLAT BACK. LIGHTER, LATER. 1680–1710. WADSWORTH ATHENEUM.

1831. Heaviest, Perhaps Earliest Pilgrim Side Slat Back. New Hampshire. 1630–50. Wadsworth Atheneum.

1832. (Right.) Pilgrim Slat Back. Finials Probably Missing, Paneled Seat. 1640–60. John C. Spring, Boston.

1833–34. Pair of Side Pilgrim Slat Backs. 1680–1710. Wadsworth Atheneum.

1835. TURNED CORNER CHAIRS ARE NOW ENTERED UPON. A FINE EXAMPLE HERE WITH LARGER
TURNINGS IN THE UPPER THAN IN THE LOWER STRETCHER. 1700–1720. MARK HENDERSON,
NORWALK, CONNECTICUT.

In leaving the Pilgrim chairs, it is understood that the reason for the use of ash was that the turning could be roughed out by splitting from this wood. The material, however, was inferior to maple, and this fact was soon observed. The material of chairs of this period in England was generally oak. It has been found rarely in American Pilgrim chairs.

Maple is the most admirable wood for turning because it is strong and smooth. But much, if not most of the early maple was soft, growing in the lowlands. The sugar (rock) maple is stronger and harder and is much used today. But the softer maple answered all purposes and was easier to work. Apple wood supplies the finest material for smooth turnings, and was used for tool handles. But it is very hard, difficult to work, heavy, and often gnarled.

1836. A Turned Corner Chair with an Attached Drinking Arm Which Swings Down. 1700–30. Clifford S. Drake, North Hampton, New Hampshire.

1837. (Right.) Corner Chair with a Double Lap, and a Wide Flattening of Arm. Reported as from New England. Maple Except Oak Top Rail. 1700–20. J. Stogdell Stokes.

1838. Corner Chair, Unusual. All Original. 1700–20. Mark LaFontaine, Springfield, Vermont.

1839. (Right.) Corner Chair with Crude Dutch Feet. A Scrolled Slat Back. Most Interesting. 1710–30. William F. Hubbard, Hartford, Connecticut.

1840. ROUNDABOUT. ONE SPANISH FOOT. UPPER BACK IS PURE DUTCH. 1720. HARRY V. WEIL.

1841. (Right.) CORNER OR ROUNDABOUT WITH COMB. IN ENGLAND WOULD BE CALLED BARBERS'
CHAIR. 1700–20. G. WINTHROP BROWN.

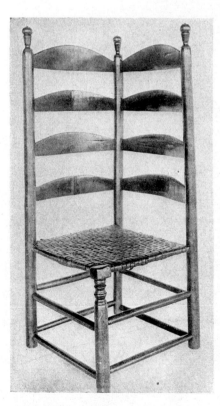
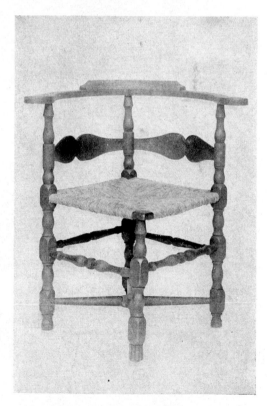

1842. TWO BACKS AT RIGHT ANGLES. COURTING CHAIR. 1700–20. ARTHUR W. WELLINGTON.

1843. (Right.) X STRETCHER. THE COMBINATION OF OUTSIDE AND CROSS STRETCHERS MAY BE
UNIQUE. 1700–20. L. G. MYERS.

1844. One Spanish Foot. 1720. H. W. Erving.   1845. Foreign. 17th Century. Geo. S. Palmer.

1846. Burgomeister, Walnut, 25 x 33. 17th or 18th C. Mrs. Francis P. Garvan.

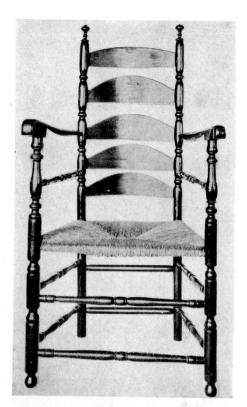

1847. FIVE BACK, MAPLE. ROLLED ARM. 1710–20. ESTATE OF J. MILTON COBURN.
1848. (Right.) FIVE BACK, ROLLED ARM, INTERMEDIATE SPINDLE. 1710–20. HENRY S. STEARNS.

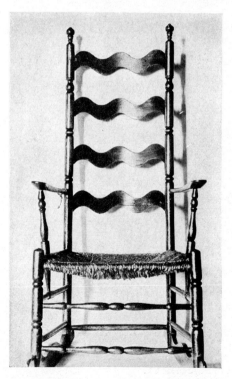
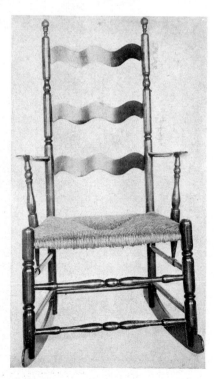

1849–50. SERPENTINE BACKS. DOUBLE BEARING ARM. CONNECTICUT TYPE. 1710–40. LEFT, ESTATE
OF J. MILTON COBURN; RIGHT, G. WINTHROP BROWN.

1851. FIVE BACK, SAUSAGE AND BALL TURNED. A HIGH TYPE. DELICATE INTERMEDIATE SPINDLE. 1710–30. GEORGE DUDLEY SEYMOUR.

1852–53. Sausage Turned, Rolled Arm, Five Back. Followed by Four Back with
Scrolled Slats. 1700–20. Wadsworth Atheneum.

1854. Three Slat, Designed for Rollers Behind. Front of Arms Apparently Cut
Off. 1700–20. Was B. A. Behrend's.

1855. (Right.) A Name Chair with Cherub Carving and Applied Knobs on Back.
Foreign or Pennsylvanian. Early 18th Century.

1856. A Well-Turned Five Back. Flat Arm Rail. Balls instead of Rolled Arm. 1700–10.

1857. (Right.) Four Back. Candle Posts. Tin Caps Restored. 1710. Wadsworth Atheneum.

1858–59. Webb House, Wethersfield. Fine Ball Foot, Pennsylvania, Parlor Table.

The author thought it a fine plan to perpetuate celebrated Connecticut houses in the wall paper. Because this was a bit different from the conventional, the present owners have obliterated the work.

1860. Square Posts, Tenoned Rungs. Date Uncertain, Also Origin.
1861. (Right.) Sausage Turned, Four Back, Intermediate Spindle. 1700-20.
Wadsworth Atheneum.

1862. Turned Four Back, Side. Fine Finials. 1710-20. Wadsworth Atheneum.
1863. (Right.) Double Bearing Arm, Probably Connecticut. 1710-30.
Wadsworth Atheneum.

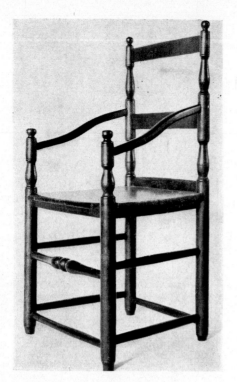

1864. Maple and Ash, Seat Pine. Southern Connecticut. 34¾ x 20¼ x 16.
Perhaps Early 18th Century. Chester E. Dimick, Gales Ferry, Connecticut.
1865. (Right.) Short Banisters, Side Chair. Origin and Date Doubtful.

1866. Original Rocker, with Posts Turned for That Purpose. Early Rockers
Always Pinned, Not Nailed. 1700–25. Wadsworth Atheneum.
1867. (Right.) High Desk Chair. Four Sets of Rungs Including Seat. 1710–40.
Wadsworth Atheneum.

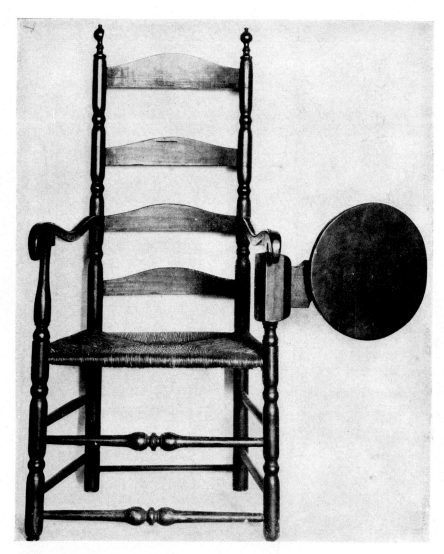

1868. Four Slat Back with Drinking Arm, Which Tilts. A Hollow Box Which Swings Carries Arm. 1720–30. R. P. Pauly.

1869–70. Carved Embroidery Yarn Holder To Be Connected by Ropes. Hickory. 1680–1700. Wadsworth Atheneum.

1871-72. New England Slat Backs. The Turning Is the Same in the Posts with Very Slight Variation. Stretchers on Chair at Right, Sausage Turned. 1700-20. George Dudley Seymour.

1873. A Potato Boiler. H. W. Erving.

1874. Heavy Cast Griddle. Pennsylvania.

1875–76. A Five Back, Very High. Sausage Turning. On the Right a Four Back with Graduated Spacing. Sixteen Identical Stretchers. 1700–10. Formerly the Author's.

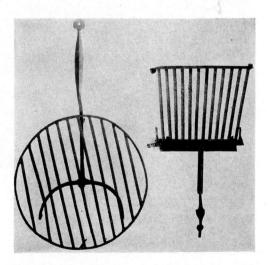

1877–81. Gooseneck Broiler, Swivel Broiler, Broiler with Hollowed Grids and Spout To Save Juices. Whirling Toaster, Double Pothook.

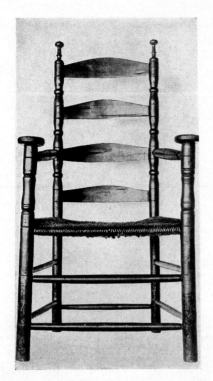
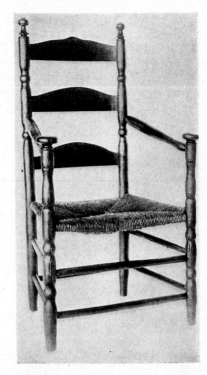

1882. LARGE MUSHROOM, FINIALS TOO SMALL. ARMS SLIGHTLY SLANTING. 1700–20.
WADSWORTH ATHENEUM.

1883. (Right.) SLANT OF ARM VERY MARKED. 1700–25. WADSWORTH ATHENEUM.

1884. GROUPING OF AUTHOR'S COLLECTION. WADSWORTH ATHENEUM.

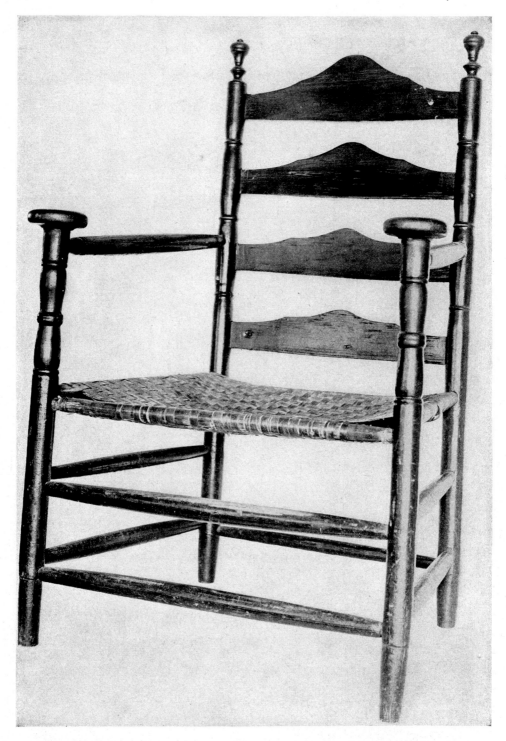

1885. Great Mushroom Chair, Posts in One Piece, Tops 4½ Inches Diameter. Giant Size. Connecticut Origin. 1700–20. Wadsworth Atheneum.

1886. SMALL MUSHROOM. THE POSTS ARE ALWAYS TURNED IN ONE PIECE, THE MUSHROOM NEVER BEING DOWELED ON. SUCH A DOWEL WOULD RENDER A CHAIR SUSPICIOUS. 1700. MRS. W. B. LONG, BOSTON.

1887. Three Wide Slats. Onion-Shaped Mushrooms. Two Other Chairs Like It Are Known. Also a Side Chair, All Probably by the Same Maker. Mrs. J. Insley Blair.

1888. Elaborately Turned. Salamander Back. Origin: This Style
Found in Canada, Vermont, and New Hampshire. Rare; Sought After.
1720–30. Mark M. Henderson, Norwalk, Connecticut.

1889. Chair with Elements of No. 1888. Two Bearing Arm. 18th Century. I. Sack.
1890. (Right.) Five-Back Pennsylvania Arm. Rockers Not Original. 1710-40.

1891. Loom Stool with Reel, Pennsylvania. The Head Is Shown in Another Picture. Tulip Decoration. William B. Montague, Norristown.

1892. LIGHT PENNSYLVANIA ARCHED SLAT BACK. BULBOUS FEET RESTORED
PROPERLY. 1720-50. AUTHOR'S FORMER COLLECTION.

1893. FIVE SCROLLED BACKS. BALLS OF FEET RESTORED. 1710–30. FRANCIS D. BRINTON.
1894. (Right.) FIVE SCROLLED BACKS. SIDE. THIS TYPE HAS GOOD FRONT STRETCHERS. FEET
HAVE LOST PART OF BALLS. 1710–30. NEWARK, DELAWARE.

1895–96. AN ARM AND A SIDE CHAIR MADE TO MATCH. ARM HAS MUSHROOM. PROBABLY
NEW ENGLAND. 1710–30. HARRY L. F. LOCKE, HARTFORD.

1897–98. Beautiful Examples, Four and Five Backs. The Former with Somewhat More Brilliant Turnings. Pure Delaware Valley Type. 1720–30. J. Stogdell Stokes.

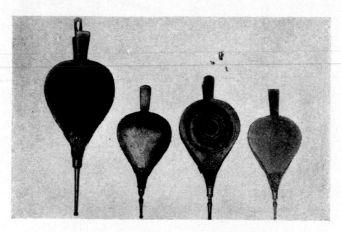

1899–1902. Four Pairs of Bellows, Stenciled or Decorated with Turning. 18th Century.

1903. FINE TYPE PENNSYLVANIA SIX BACK. CABRIOLE LEGS IN FRONT. THESE WERE MADE WITHOUT BRACKETS. 1720–30. J. STOGDELL STOKES, PHILADELPHIA.

1904. (Right.) SIDE CHAIR, PROBABLY BY SAME MAKER, AND MADE TO MATCH THE PRECEDING. EXCEEDINGLY RARE. 1720–30. FRANCIS D. BRINTON, WEST CHESTER, PENNSYLVANIA.

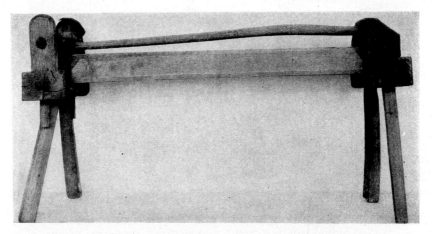

1905. A FLAX BREAKER. 18TH OR EARLY 19TH CENTURY. USED TO LOOSEN THE FIBERS OF THE FLAX BEFORE HATCHELING. WADSWORTH ATHENEUM.

1906. CHAIR WITH TREADLE FOR OPERATING FLY SWITCH. LATE 18TH CENTURY. CONTRIV-
ANCE FOUND IN OTHER INSTANCES. THOUGHT TO HAVE BEEN INVENTED BY FRANKLIN.
1907. (Right.) FINE PATTERN, PENN. SIX BACK. BOTH, J. STOGDELL STOKES.

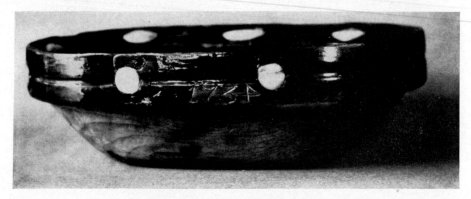

1908. A BOWL DATED 1734; TURNED WOOD WITH DECORATIVE INSERTS. W. B. MONTAGUE.

1909. A FIVE BACK, TWO BEARING ARM, ORIGINAL ROCKER. PLACED HERE FOR CONVENIENCE. THE AUTHOR'S. EARLY 18TH CENTURY.

1910. (Right.) ROLLED ARM, SQUARE POST, SPINDLE BACK. APPARENTLY IN A CLASS BY ITSELF. 18TH CENTURY. W. F. HUBBARD, HARTFORD.

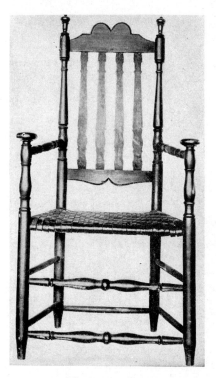
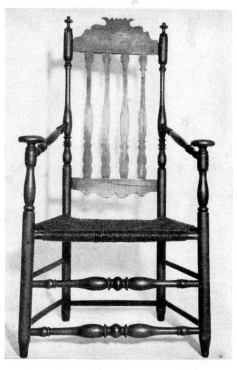

1911. MUSHROOM BANISTER BACK. TURNED ARM. 1700-20. WADSWORTH ATHENEUM.

1912. (Right.) BANISTER BACK MUSHROOM, ARM STRONGLY SLANTED, AND TURNED. FINE TYPE. 1700-20. DR. AND MRS. J. M. BIRNIE.

1913–14. Spanish Foot Banister Back. Not a Pair. Large Front Stretcher Is a Mark of Style. 1700–10. Wadsworth Atheneum.

1915–17. A Toaster, a Loaf Sugar Cutter, and a Huge Pair of 17th Century Oak Hinges. Wadsworth Atheneum.

1918. Reversed Banister Back. 1700–10. Mrs. John M. Holcombe, Hartford.
1919. (Right.) Banister Back, Dutch Carved Top Rail. 1700–1725. N. Cushing.

1920. Three Banister Back, Feet Missing. Beveled Top Rail. Initial W. Maple. 1710. 40½ x 19½ x 13½. Katherine N. Loring, Wayland, Mass.
1921. (Right.) Attractive Connecticut Type. Reeded Banister, Arched Bottom Rail; Wild Rose Top Rail. 1710–30. Fuessenich Collection, Torrington.

1922. SPANISH-FOOT SIDE CHAIR, CARVED STRETCHERS IN TOP
AND BOTTOM RAILS DIFFERING IN STYLE. WELL CARVED IN
MOLDED SCROLLS. 1700–20. FORMERLY THE AUTHOR'S.

1923. Spanish Foot, Carved Top Rail. The Feet of Spanish Chairs Usually Have Glued-On Toes, as It Was Practically Impossible To Work the Leg Otherwise. 1700–10. Was B. A. Behrend's.

1924. (Right.) Reversed Banister Back. 1710–30. George S. McKearin, Hoosick Falls, New York.

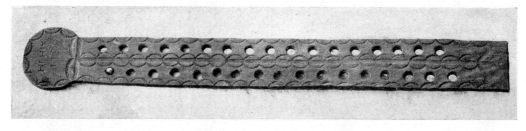

1925. An Article Whose Use Is Not Certain. Perhaps for Spit Bearing. Initialed and Dated 1799. Wm. B. Goodwin Has a Similar Iron. Wadsworth Atheneum.

1926. BANISTER BACK; ROCKERS SHOULD BE REMOVED. STAR CARVING ON ROLL OF ARM. 1700–30. MRS. NILES LEWIS PECK, BRISTOL, CONNECTICUT.

1927. (Right.) FIVE BANISTERS, CARVED RAIL, SPANISH FEET. RAM'S HORN ARM. 1700–10. HELEN T. COOKE, WELLESLEY.

1928. SADDLE BACK, REEDED BANISTER ARM. NOT ORIGINALLY A ROCKER. FINE LARGE STRETCHER. 1710–20. FORMERLY THE AUTHOR'S.

1929. (Right.) A SPINNING CHAIR. SEAT VERY HIGH. 18TH CENTURY. FORMERLY THE AUTHOR'S.

1930–31. A Well-Turned Reeded Banister, and Neatly Turned Four Back with Doubled Foot. 1700–10. J. Stogdell Stokes.

1932. Ball and Chain. The Stone Has Spiral Strips Welded about It. Probably for a Gate or a Bucket Balance. Unique. Fuessenich Collection.

1933. HEART AND CROWN REEDED BANISTER, INTERMEDIATE SPINDLE. A GOOD TYPE. 1700–30.
GEORGE DUDLEY SEYMOUR, WADSWORTH ATHENEUM.

1934. Reversed Banister Back. Less Comfortable, but Perhaps Thought More Decorative. 1700–20. Side Chairs To Match. E. C. Hall, Longmeadow, Massachusetts.

1935. (Right.) Banister Back, Double Bearing Arm. 1710–30. Mark LaFontaine.

1936. Banister Back, Scalloped Top Rail, Spiraled Arm. 1710–30. Geo. S. McKearin.

1937. (Right.) Five Reeded Banisters, Heart and Crown Rail. Arm, Which Looks as if Superimposed, but Probably Original. 1710–30. James Davidson, New London.

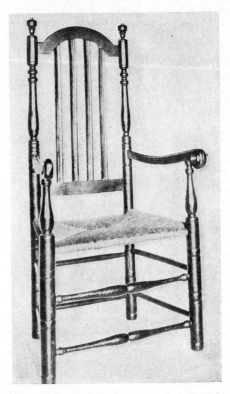

1938. Five-Banister Back, Rolled Arm, Winged Top Rail. 1710–30. L. G. Myers.
1939. (Right.) Banister Back, Pierced Arm Roll. 1710–30. James N. H. Campbell.

1940. Banister, Carved Rail. 1700–10. The Split Spindle Should Line with and Dupli-
cate the Post, as Here. Brooks Reed.
1941. (Right.) Five Banister, Rolled Arm, Ogee Top Rail. 1710–20. Was B. A. Behrend's.

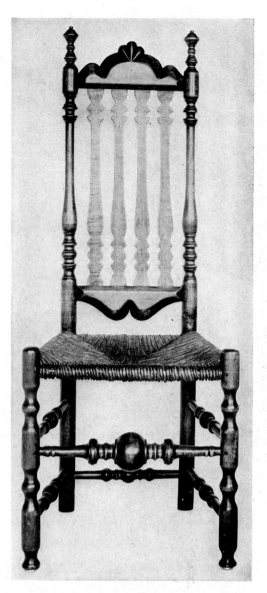

1942. Side Banister, Day Bed Back. 1700. Arthur W. Wellington, Weston.

1943. (Right.) Beveled Rails, Strongly Turned Banisters. Fine Stretcher. 1700.
G. Winthrop Brown.

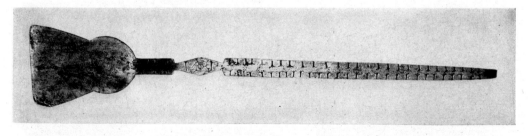

1944. Decorative Flapjack Turner. Pennsylvania. 18th Century. Wadsworth Atheneum.

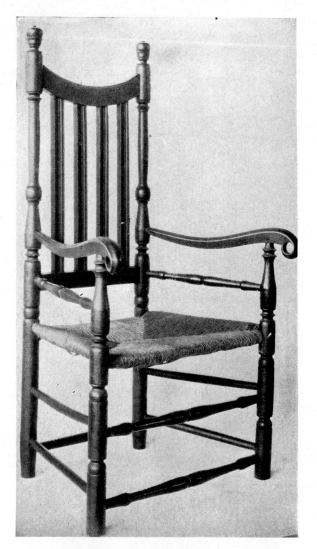

1945. SADDLE-BACK, REEDED BANISTER, INTERMEDIATE STRETCHER. PIERCED ARM ROLL. CONNECTICUT TYPE. 1700–20. J. STOGDELL STOKES.

1946. (Right.) BANISTER WITH SUNRISE TOP RAIL. GOOD FINIALS. 1700–20. RHODE ISLAND SCHOOL OF DESIGN.

1947–52. TWO WOODEN TRENCHERS. LARGE AND SMALL. A DOUBLE-FACED PLATE FOR THE MEAT AND DESSERT COURSE. A GOPHERING IRON. TWO COVERED DRINKING MUGS BUILT OF STAVES. WADSWORTH ATHENEUM.

1953. REEDED BANISTER. DAY BED BACK, GRACEFUL ARM, GOOD STRETCHER. THIS CHAIR AND
THE NEXT ARE FROM THE SAME SET, AND THEIR CRESTS FOLLOW EXACTLY THE TYPE OF THE PENN-
SYLVANIA DAY BED. THE INFERENCE IS THAT THEY WERE MADE TO ACCOMPANY A BED WITH THE
SAME TURNINGS.

1954. (Right.) SIDE CHAIR, SAME DESIGN. 1710–25. BOTH, J. STOGDELL STOKES.

1955. A DOUBLE-ENDED CULINARY FORK, TWISTED HANDLE. AT AN
ANCIENT INN SOUTH OF BETHLEHEM. 18TH CENTURY.

1956. WALNUT, "SQUARE TURNED" POST. PENNSYLVANIA. LATE 17TH C. J. STOGDELL STOKES.

1959. Rayed Spindles above Banisters. 1720–40. J. Stogdell Stokes.
1960. (Right.) Side Banister, Unique Carved Rail. Was in First Church of Framingham.
1700. Maple and Ash. The Edgell Chair. Stanton D. Loring.

1961. Hatchel Block on a Stand with Cover. Late 17th or Early 18th Century. Katrina Kipper.
1962. (Right.) Turned Frame with Tilting Board, Adjustable. Use Not Known. Flayderman & Kaufman.

1957. (Opposite.) Winged Scrolled Back. Shaped Arm. The Hayloft, Whitemarsh, Pennsylvania.
1958. (Opposite.) (Right.) Oak, Paneled Seat. The Type of This Chair Is Very Much Like the
Wainscot or Cromwellian, Except for the Back. 17th Century. New Jersey. J. Stogdell Stokes.

It should be generally understood that the turned chairs of which we have shown many dating from 1690–1720 are maple, unless we have specified to the contrary. Maple was the readily available and excellent wood for this purpose. We get into walnut or fruit wood for fine chairs about 1700. And before 1690 ash persisted to some extent, though maple is usual after 1650.

1963. LEATHER BACK. BUILT IN THE STYLE OF THE CANE CHAIRS, EXCEPT FOR THE UPHOLSTERY. 1700–25. WADSWORTH ATHENEUM.

1964. (Right.) LEATHER BACK WITH RABBETED CURVED RECESS TO TAKE LEATHER BACK. 1690–1710.

1965. Walnut, Five Leg with Finial. Said To Have Been Made by Early Knickerbocker
Craftsmen. 1690–1700. J. Stogdell Stokes.

1966. (Right.) High and Middle Stretcher Well Turned, as Well as Posts and Side Stretchers.
A Large Chair, Peculiar Arm. 1690–1700. J. Stogdell Stokes.

1967. Graceful Arms and Peculiar Stretchers. None in Front. Face of Arms Is
Molded. Not in Leather. 1690–1700. Howard Reifsnyder, Philadelphia.

1968. (Right.) Spanish Foot, Side Chair. 1700. Flayderman & Kaufman.

1969. Leather Back, Carved Top Rail. 1690–1700. Wadsworth Atheneum.
1970. (Right.) Cane, Back and Seat Original. This Scroll Sweeping Inward at the Feet Is Called English. 1690–1700. Wadsworth Atheneum.

1971. Spiraled, Leather Back. Flemish Scrolls on Top Rail. Beech. Feet Restored. 47½ x 18½ x 17. 1690–1700. William B. Goodwin.
1972. (Right.) Leather Back. Slipper Chair. 1690–1700. Mrs. F. P. Garvan.

1973. FLEMISH SCROLL AND STRETCHERS, RAM'S HORN ARM. FIRST OF A CLASS OF CANE CHAIRS, AS THIS WAS ORIGINALLY. 52 x 24½ x 21. MAPLE. 1690–1700. E. B. LEETE COMPANY.

1974. (Right.) SPANISH FOOT, CARVED SIDE. 49½ x 17½ x 14. PAINTED WITH A DESIGN OF LEAVES COVERING ENTIRE CHAIR EXCEPT BACK. CANE VERY FINE. 1690–1700. CLIFFORD S. DRAKE.

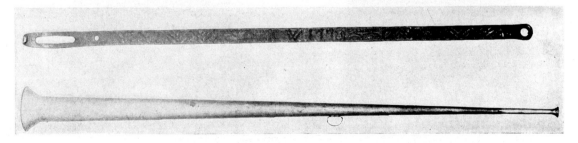

1975. LONG DOOR BAR, DECORATIVE DESIGNS. DATED 1778.
1976. COACH HORN, 18TH CENTURY.

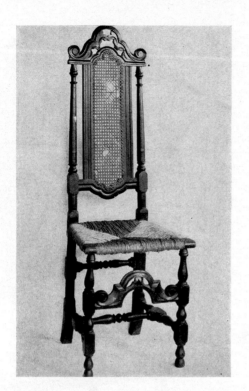

1977. Ball on Foot below the Pear. 1690–1700. Rudolph P. Pauly.
1978. (Right.) Oak, Panel Back. Pennsylvania. 1690–1710. J. Stogdell Stokes.

1979. A Handsome Shape, Ram's Horn Arm, Stretcher Repeated in Crest Rail. Rare.
1690–1700. Helen T. Cooke.
1980. (Right.) Top Turning, English Type, Fine Crest. 1690–1700. Flayderman & Kaufman.

1981–82. A Flemish Side Chair and an Armchair with Flemish Back and Carved Arm. Fruit Wood. This Phrase Covers Apple, Pear, Sometimes Cherry. 1690–1700. Edward C. Wheeler, Jr.

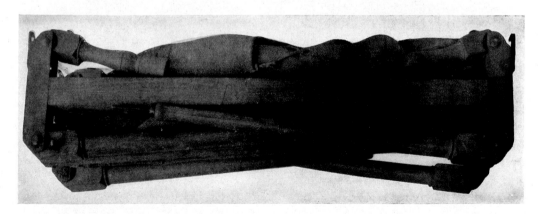

1983. A Complete Full-Sized Bed! It Proves That Our Ancestors Knew How To Economize Room. 18th Century. Adolph Breitenstein, Providence.

1984. Fully Carved Flemish Mode. The Arm Here Is in the Flemish Scroll
as Well as the Leg. Crest Rail Similar to, but Not Identical with,
Stretcher. 1680-1700. H. W. Erving.

1985. Flemish Chair, Arm Supports Not Carved. Elaborately Carved Stretcher and Crest Rail. 1690–1700.
Extremely High, 57½ Inches. Wadsworth Atheneum.

1986–92. Knockers. Palmer Collection.

1993. FLEMISH SIDE CHAIR, FULLY CARVED. IN THE SIMPLER CHAIRS THE BACK PANEL IS NOT CARVED ON THE SIDES. 1690-1700. STANLEY A. SWEET.

1994. (Right.) FLEMISH SCROLL REPEATED ABOUT THE BACK. 1690-1700. EDWARD C. WHEELER, Jr.

1995-2001. KNOCKERS FROM PALMER COLLECTION. COLONIAL AND EMPIRE PATTERNS.

2002. SPANISH FOOT, RAM'S HORN ARM, TURNED STRETCHER, SHAPED BACK PANEL. 1700–20. WADSWORTH ATHENEUM.

2003. FLEMISH SIDE CHAIR, FULLY CARVED. 1690–1700. MRS. JOHN MARSHALL HOLCOMBE.

2004–10. KNOCKERS FROM PALMER COLLECTION. BIRD AND OTHER PATTERNS.

2011. English, Flemish Type. Legs Quartered Outward. Crosshatching on Square at Back. 1690–1700. Mrs. Francis P. Garvan.

2012. American Flemish Often Called Charles II. The Crest Rail Is Imposed. It Is Not so Good as When Mortised between the Posts, but It Is More Beautiful. Beech. 1690–1700. Mrs. Francis P. Garvan.

2013–19. Knockers from Palmer Collection. The S Type.

2020. Spanish Foot. Two Cane Panels in Back. Remarkable Outward Rake of Back Leg.
1700. Wadsworth Atheneum.

2021. (Right.) American Flemish Chair. Legs Angle Outward. Molded Seat. 1690–1700.
Mrs. Francis P. Garvan.

2022–28. Knockers from Palmer Collection. Shell, Lyre, and Pear Types.

2029-30. Pair of Flemish Scrolled, Side Chairs. Were, of Course, Originally Caned Alike. Good Carving. 1690-1700. Francis Hill Bigelow, Cambridge, Massachusetts.

2031. Spanish Foot, Ram's Horn Arm, Shortened so that Post Sets Back from the Front Post. 1700–20. Stanley A. Sweet.

2032. FLEMISH SCROLL ARMCHAIR. ARM SUPPORT TURNED. TOP RAIL MORTISED, IN MORE SECURE AND EARLIER METHOD. FINE RAM'S HORN ARMS. 1690–1700. J. WINTHROP BROWN.

2033-34. A PAIR OF BEAUTIFUL CHAIRS. THE CREST RAIL IMPOSED. THE BOTTOM STRETCHER BETWEEN THE SIDE STRETCHERS IS ALSO SCROLLED. 1690–1700. EDWARD C. WHEELER, JR.

2035. Reversed Scrolled Foot. Back Panel with Reeds outside the Scroll. 1690–1700.
Edward C. Wheeler, Jr.

2036. (Right.) A Chair Formerly in the Possession of the Author, in Which the Beautiful
Scroll at the Back Has Been Ruthlessly Covered Up in Part by an Upholstered Insert.

The material of these chairs, in England, is usually beech. In America it is rarely beech, often maple in the simpler examples, and generally fruit wood in the finer pieces. In construction these chairs are apt to grow shaky in time. Their high backs give a strong leverage. They are not built especially for comfort, but are highly decorative against the wall. They are naturally side chairs. There is a wide difference in the types. Particularly in the front leg, we have it running straight out from the seat and in all degrees of angles, until a full ninety degrees is reached.

2037–38. A Pair of Chairs, Arm and Side, with Reversed Scroll on the Foot. Fruit Wood.
The Armchair, as Often, Has the Seat Lower than the Side Chair. 1690–1700.
Edward C. Wheeler, Jr.

2039–40. Six-Pointed Star Looking-Glass Knobs. c. 1800. William B. Goodwin.

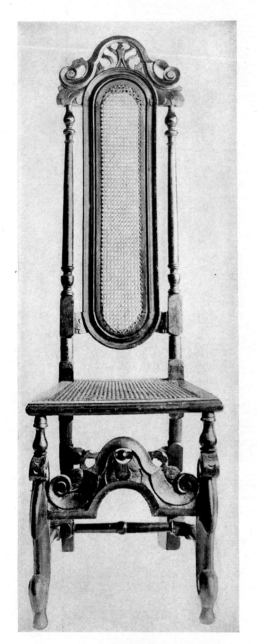 

2041. FLEMISH CHAIR WITH OVAL PANEL. A HANDSOME DESIGN. THE STRETCHER BELOW IS A TRUE ARCH. 1690–1700. EDWARD C. WHEELER, JR.

2042. (Right.) SPANISH FOOT, CARVED SIDE CHAIR. PANEL WITH SCROLLS AT THE TOP AND BOTTOM. A VERY GOOD EXAMPLE OF THE FOOT. THERE IS GREAT VARIETY IN THE SPANISH FOOT, AND UNLESS IT IS WELL DONE IT IS UNSIGHTLY. THE STRETCHER IS VERY EFFECTIVE. 1710–20. WADSWORTH ATHENEUM.

2043. Flemish Side Chair, Said To Have Belonged to
William Penn. Notice the Knob or Shoe under the
Scroll of the Foot. 1690–1700. Edward C. Wheeler, Jr.

2044-45. A Pair of Spanish Foot Chairs with a Touch of Carving in Interesting Leaf-Like Designs, Reeded Panels, Rolled Crests, Good Front Stretcher. 1710-20. Francis Hill Bigelow, Cambridge.

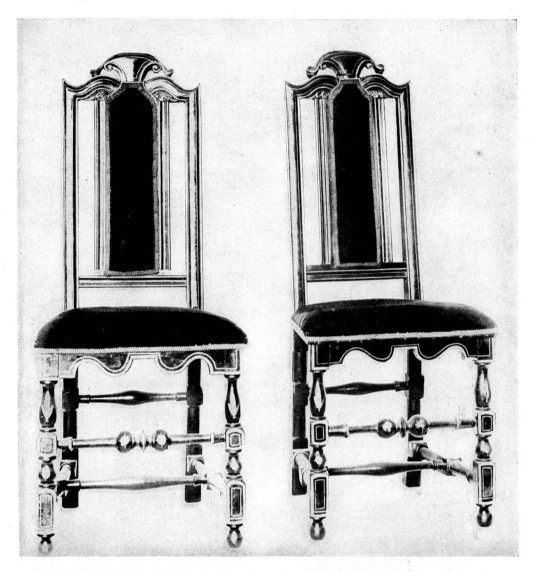

2046-47. A Pair of Turned Chairs with Interesting Backs. Scrolled Frames and Painted Decorations in Bands of Gold. Found at Salem, and Said To Have Belonged to Nathaniel Hawthorne, from Whose Former Residence They Came. The Motive at the Top Is Deftly Handled. The Molded Rails Stop on the Scrolled Panel. We Notice a Transition Here from the Turned Back Posts to a Suggestion of the Dutch Style, Which Is a Little Later. The Bottom Rails and the Side Rails of the Panels Are Reeded. About 1720.

The term side chair has been puzzled over for long. The plausible explanation is that it is a wall chair, to be used, that is, against the side of the room. But as there is no objection to placing an arm-chair against the wall, and no possible objection to withdrawing a moderately low-backed side chair from the wall, the name is not wholly explained. Perhaps it meant a chair readily drawn up against a table, without interference such as arms would offer. Is not that better?

2048. Spanish Foot, Wing Chair. Walnut. Style of Turning Earlier than the Dutch. 1700–20. Knickerbocker Origin. J. Stogdell Stokes, Philadelphia.

2049. (Right.) Queen Anne, Heavy Type. Walnut. Massachusetts. 1730–50. Estate of Harry Winthrop Weeks, Framingham Massachusetts.

2050. Queen Anne, Mahogany. Pad under Foot. 45 x 29½ x 20½. 1740–60. Dr. and Mrs. J. M. Birnie, Springfield.

2051. (Right.) Walnut with Carved Shell, Heavy. 1730–60. H. W. Erving.

2052. QUEEN ANNE, WALNUT. LEATHER COVERED. OF COURSE, THE ORIGINAL COVER MAY HAVE BEEN SOMETHING DIFFERENT. NO STRETCHERS. 1730–60. GEORGE S. PALMER COLLECTION.
2053. (Right.) QUEEN ANNE, WALNUT, LIGHTER LEG. WIDTH IN FRONT 29½ INCHES. 1740–60. ROBERT T. SMITH, HARTFORD.

2054. HIGH BACK, ROLLED ARM, NO STRETCHERS. 1740–60. PENNSYLVANIA MUSEUM, PHILADELPHIA.
2055. (Right.) BALL AND CLAW, NO STRETCHER, PLAIN KNEE. NOTE SHAPE OF BACK LEG. 1750–70. HELEN T. COOKE.

2056. WING OR FIRESIDE CHAIR, BALL-AND-CLAW FEET, RICHLY CARVED LEG. NO STRETCHERS. PECULIAR BREAK IN THE BACK. 1750–75. MAHOGANY. 48 x 36 x 24. FRANCIS D. BRINTON.

2057. (Right.) BALL AND CLAW, CARVED KNEE, KNOB FOOT BEHIND. 1750–75. I. SACK.

2058. ACANTHUS CARVED. LEG SIMPLY SWEPT BACK WITHOUT A KNOB. BELL-SHAPED SEAT, LIKE MOST PRECEDING. 1750–75. WILLIAM B. GOODWIN.

2059. (Right.) MAHOGANY, REUPHOLSTERED IN LEATHER. PLAIN EDGEWISE STRETCHERS. 1760–75. METROPOLITAN MUSEUM.

2060. Handsomely Carved. Knob Foot Behind. Wing or Easy Chair. 1750–75. Metropolitan Museum.

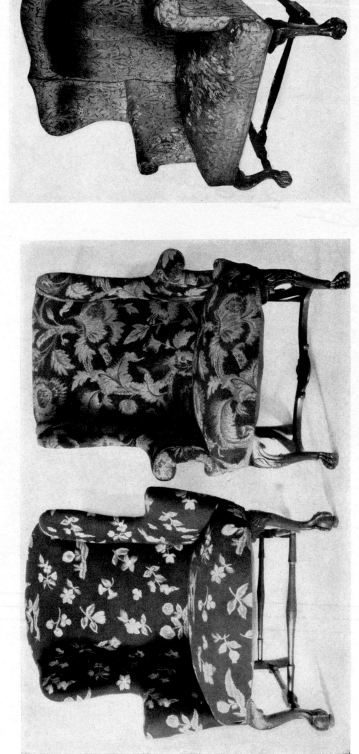

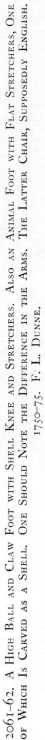

2061-62. A High Ball and Claw Foot with Shell Knee and Stretchers. Also an Animal Foot with Flat Stretchers, One of Which Is Carved as a Shell. One Should Note the Difference in the Arms. The Latter Chair, Supposedly English. 1750-75. F. L. Dunne.

2063. (Right.) Mahogany, Wing Chair with Stretchers. The Method of Breaking the Arm Back to the Whole Width of the Wing Is Here Shown. The Shape of the Arm of the Chair Preceding Is, However, More Fully Carried Out. 1750-75. I. Sack.

2064. Fully Carved on Legs, Front, Sides, and Arms, and Even the Feet Behind. 1750–60.
Howard Reifsnyder, Philadelphia.

This is one of the celebrated chairs, of which there are said to be five known, made as samples and bearing the attribution of Randolph, a Philadelphia maker, who showed himself by this work a supreme chair maker.

One notices the so-called animal foot. There is a carved effigy at the center of the skirt, and a diamond-cut background on three sides with dots in the corner of each diamond. The object of this work, like the cross-hatching or stippling, was to overcome the great difficulty of obtaining smooth surfaces in carving of backgrounds. When finished they would not reflect the light properly unless they were as perfect as a lens.

2065. A Chippendale Wing Chair with Straight, Fluted Leg. 1760–75. Sanderson Collection.

The straight-foot chair is a little later than the cabriole, and was in the later Chippendale manner. As to stretchers, there was variation in usage. Some of the finest chairs had no stretchers, and some of the simpler chairs had them. One notes three classes of arms, perhaps four: That which breaks as here. The earlier type also has a rounded seat and the arm rolls vertically and horizontally. In another type there is an unbroken straight line on the interior, and the arm may or may not roll both ways, but with a double roll vertical and horizontal we get the greatest variety of form.

WING CHAIRS

Otherwise called fireside or easy chairs, are characterized by great depth and are usually upholstered throughout. While we have shown one with Spanish feet, and others exist in that style, the finer types usually appear in the Queen Anne period or the Chippendale time. Perhaps more are found in the Hepplewhite time, but their lines are not so elegant. With the Sheraton there is a shifting of style, and the upholstered arm is omitted and, instead of the wing chair, we have what is often called in this country the "Martha Washington." A few round-back chairs appeared in the Sheraton time. They will be shown in that period, but not in a class by themselves. Of course, the steel spring is never found in old upholstery. Abundance of hair filling and feather cushions made up the depth that secured softness. The best wing chair is built almost like a ship and is a work of art. Nearly all the arms, however, became shaky in time, as their bracing without metal was very difficult. The wing chair and the roundabout, or corner chair, extended together through the same periods, except that in a later time the corner chair was almost an unknown quantity.

2066. A HEPPLEWHITE WING CHAIR. THE FRONTS ARE USUALLY STRAIGHT, AND THE ARM RUNS TO THE BACK AS HERE SHOWN. THE LEG BEHIND HAS NOT SO MARKED A RAKE AS IN THE EARLIER STYLE, AND ALWAYS ENDS IN A PLAIN FORM AS HERE. 1790–1800. WALLACE NUTTING.

2067. (Right.) A HEPPLEWHITE WING CHAIR WITH PEG FEET AND A MOST EXTRAORDINARY HEIGHT. NOTE THE SERPENTINE SHAPE OF THE WING AND THE UNUSUAL CONTOUR OF THE ARM, WHICH IS NOT THICK BELOW THE ROLL. 1790–1800. F. K. GASTON, NEW YORK CITY.

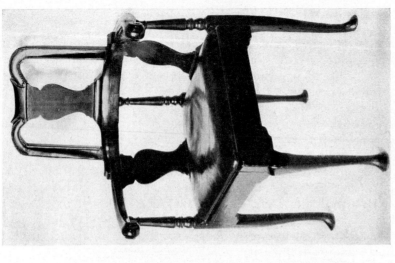

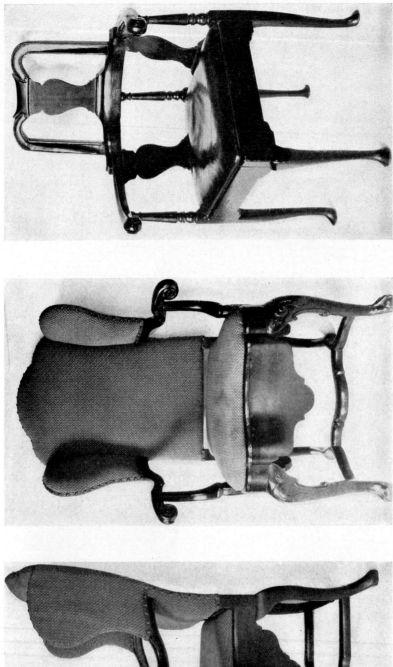

2068-69. A Side and a Front View of the Same Chair with a Scrolled Stretcher and Wide Skirt. The Wing Stops on the Arm. This Wide Skirt Is Found in Philadelphia and Baltimore. The Foot Is a Reduced Ball and Claw, and the Knee Is Carved with the Acanthus Leaf and the C Scroll. Walnut. Rare or Unique. 1730-60. Wallace Nutting.

2070. (Right.) With This We Enter Upon the Corner Chair, Beginning with the Dutch Type. Maple Chairs Have Been Already Shown. All Legs Alike in Their Feet, but Only the Front Corner Leg Is Pure Cabriole. The Back Has the Dutch Splat, and an Unusual Arm Which Rolls Downward Rather than Outward with Slight Carving. On the Back Is Superimposed a Pure Dutch Extension. 1730-50. John H. Buck, Hartford.

2071. A Corner Chair with Four Dutch Feet and Cross Stretchers. The Arm Rolls Outward as Usual, Instead of Downward. Virginia Walnut. Shaped Seat. Compare It with Seat on Bottom of Next Page. c. 1725. New England. H. W. Erving.

2072-73. Brasses of 1790-1800. Eagle and Serpent, and Post Boy. William B. Goodwin.

2074. FOUR LEGS SHAPED ALIKE WITH BALL-AND-CLAW FEET. TWO PIERCED, INTERLACED SPLATS. GOOD BACK. 1760–75. NATHANAEL G. HERRESHOFF, BRISTOL, RHODE ISLAND.

2075. (Right.) WALNUT DUTCH-FOOT CHAIR WITH WRIST, AND DEPRESSIONS SLIGHTLY RESEMBLING THE DRAKE FOOT. ARMS ROLL DOWNWARD. 1730–50. PHILADELPHIA TYPE. METROPOLITAN MUSEUM.

2076. SHAPE OF ARM AS LOOKED DOWN UPON. SQUARE-SEATED CORNER CHAIR. 1740–70. HELEN T. COOKE.

2077. THREE DUCK FEET, ONE CLAW-AND-BALL FOOT, WITH ACANTHUS CARVED KNEE. SQUARE SEAT. THE ARM OF THIS CHAIR APPEARS ON THE PRECEDING PAGE. 1740–70. HELEN T. COOKE.

2078. (Right.) MAHOGANY, THREE TURNED BUTTON FEET, AND ONE BALL-AND-CLAW FOOT; ACANTHUS CARVING. CROSS STRETCHER. 1750–75. FORMERLY THE AUTHOR'S.

2079. THREE STRAIGHT, ONE BALL-AND-CLAW FOOT. OGEE SKIRT. 1750–75. FLAYDERMAN & KAUFMAN.

2080. (Right.) WALNUT, SOUTHERN. THREE TURNED FEET, ONE BALL AND CLAW AND MARGINAL CARVED KNEE. 31¼ x 28 x 27. 1740–60. WILLIAM B. GOODWIN.

2081. Three Ball-and-Claw Feet, with Shells and a Depending Flower. Carved Splats. Cross Stretcher. 1760–75. Wadsworth Atheneum.

2082. (Right.) Mahogany, Three Ball-and-Claw and One Turned Foot. Scrolled Skirt, Pierced Splat, Square Seat. Connecticut. 1750–75. Robert P. Butler, Hartford.

2083. Curly Maple, Straight Plain Legs. Plain Splats. 1760–75. James Fenimore Cooper.

2084. (Right.) Straight Plain Leg, Pierced Splats. Mahogany. 1760–75. Est. Harry W. Weeks.

2085–86. This Page Is an Interlude, To Show a Series of Distinctive Chairs Found in New Jersey. These Two Chairs Have Nearly the Same Turning, and Are Pleasing in Outline, with Strong Local Feeling. Ball and Sausage Turning, Probably Early 18th Century. J. Stogdell Stokes.

2087. Spiral Turned Jersey Chair. Walnut. Cross Wicks. 1699. Described in the Records of the Pierson Family.

A number of these chairs, found in the same vicinity of this type, lead to the belief that they are native.

2088. (Right.) Local Jersey Turnings, About 1720–50. Both, J. Stogdell Stokes.

2089. A TRANSITION DUTCH MODEL WITH SPANISH FEET AND REEDED BANISTERS, RAM'S HORN ARM, FEET PARTLY WORN AWAY. UNUSUAL STYLE. 1700–20. HENRY V. WEIL.

2090. A LEATHER BACK, SIDE, TRANSITION DUTCH. MAPLE WITH STRETCHERS OF BEECH. 1710–20. FOUND IN HARTFORD. GEORGE DUDLEY SEYMOUR.

Whether a chair of the period be English is not always easy to declare. A slight difference in value. The wood of English pieces may be Virginian.

2091. A TURNED DUTCH CHAIR WITH AN EXTRAORDINARILY WIDE SPLAT. RAM'S HORN ARMS. 1700–20. KATRINA KIPPER.

2092. TRANSITION DUTCH, SPANISH FEET, PRETTY WELL WORN.
DECORATED IN GILT. 1710–20. EDWARD C. WHEELER, JR.

2093–96. TWO PAIRS OF KNOBS. THE LARGER WERE FOR ATTACHING TO SOME PIECE OF
FURNITURE. HENRY A. HOFFMAN, BARRINGTON, RHODE ISLAND.

2097. SPANISH FOOT, CHIPPENDALE BACK. AN INTERESTING COMBINATION OF STYLES FIFTY YEARS APART. 1730–40. J. J. SULLIVAN, WOODBURY, CONNECTICUT.

2098. (Right.) A SIMILAR CHAIR, BUT WITH VARIATION IN THE BACK AND LIGHTLY CARVED EARS. 1730–40. PYNCHON HALL, CONNECTICUT VALLEY HISTORICAL SOCIETY.

2099. SPANISH FEET WITH DUTCH BACK. 1710–30. FRANK A. ROBART.

2100. (Right.) SPANISH FOOT, MOLDED BACK STILES AND TOP RAIL. MAPLE. CONNECTICUT. c. 1720. H. W. ERVING.

2101. Spanish Feet, with Carved Saddle Back. 1720–30. H. P. Willis, Brookline.

2102. (Right.) Spanish Foot, Too Much Splayed. Ram's Horn Arm with Strong Twist. Carved and Pierced Back. 1710–30. Formerly the Author's.

2103. A Rare Type with Ribbed Arm Ending in a Spiral. Scrolled Skirt, Carved Saddle Back. 1710–30. Henry R. Davis, Everett.

2104. (Right.) A Side Chair of the Same Set and Belonging to the Same Owner.

2105–06. ARM AND A SIDE CHAIR OF A SET FORMERLY THE AUTHOR'S. BOUGHT IN PROVIDENCE. A RARE TYPE OF EARLY AMERICAN DUTCH. ONE SHOULD NOTE THAT THE ARMCHAIR HAS ITS SEAT A GOOD DEAL LOWER THAN THE SIDE CHAIR. 1720–30.

2107. A TURNED DUTCH CHAIR WITH EARS TURNING UP. 1710–30. FRANK A. ROBART.

2108. (Right.) TURNED DUTCH CHAIR WITH LARGE EARLY DUTCH FOOT SUCH AS WE FIND IN PENNSYLVANIA. GOOD STRETCHER. 1720–50. J. J. SULLIVAN, WOODBURY, CONNECTICUT.

2109. A Light Turned Dutch, Good Feet. 1730–40. Flayderman & Kaufman.
2110. (Right.) Chair with Somewhat Lighter Dutch Feet and Chippendale Suggestions in the Back. 1740–50. Morris Schwartz, New York City.

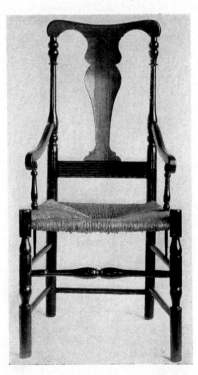

2111. An Arm with a Double Bearing on Seat and First Rung. A Back Found in New York and Pennsylvania. 1730–50. T. Belknap Beach.
2112. (Right.) A Turned Dutch Chair with Pierced Splat, Reversed. 1730–50. A. D. Barney, Farmington.

2113. WE ENTER UPON THE PURER, CONVENTIONAL TYPE OF THE QUEEN ANNE CHAIR, THE LATER PERIOD OF THE DUTCH STYLE. MARGINAL CARVING ON KNEE. 1740–60. FRANK A. ROBART.

2114. (Right.) A QUEEN ANNE ARM, WITH CARVED KNEE. THE ORIGINAL COOPER OF COOPERSTOWN LIFTED HIS WIFE IN THIS CHAIR INTO THE VEHICLE IN WHICH THEY DEPARTED FROM NEW JERSEY. SHE WAS TOO DISCOURAGED TO START. 1720–40. JAMES FENIMORE COOPER.

2115. A CONVENTIONAL DUTCH CHAIR WITH GOOD UNDERBRACING. THIS WELL-SHAPED SEAT IS SOMETIMES CALLED THE BELL PATTERN. RED WALNUT. 1720–40. H. W. ERVING.

2116. (Right.) PROBABLY SPANISH. 1720–40. SOPHIE HARRILL, KNOXVILLE, TENNESSEE.

2117. STYLISH DESIGN, BOLDLY CURVED ARM AND SHAPED SPLAT. THIS TYPE IS CALLED THE PARROT BACK. WALNUT. 42 x 27 x 20. 1725. FRANCIS D. BRINTON.

2118. (Right.) CARVED KNEE, PLAIN STRETCHERS, BACK WITH A MARQUETRY OUTLINE OF AN ANIMAL IN A SHIELD. ENGLISH. 1720–50. KATRINA KIPPER.

2119. A FINE TYPE OF PARROT BACK WITH ACANTHUS KNEE AND SPIRAL SCROLLED. SHAPED SEAT WITH SHELL. WALNUT. 1740–60. HOWARD REIFSNYDER.

2120. (Right.) A PARROT BACK, STRIKINGLY SIMILAR TO NO. 2117 ABOVE, EXCEPT IN THE FOOT. WALNUT. 1730–60. FORMERLY THE AUTHOR'S. METROPOLITAN MUSEUM.

2121–22. A Pair with Carved Drake Feet, Shell on Knee and Back, with Spiraled Scroll Six Times Repeated. American Walnut. Philadelphia. 1730–50. Metropolitan Museum

2123. Carved Drake Foot, Handsomely Scrolled Stretcher. Ribbed Arm Support, with Spiral Scrolled Knuckle. Philadelphia. 1730–50. Ætna Life Ins. Co., Hartford.
2124. (Right.) No Special Merit. Light Dutch Foot with Thin Shoe. 1740–50.

2125. Queen Anne, Virginia Walnut, Bell Seat, Overlapping Upholstery.
29½ x 21½ x 15¾. Connecticut. c. 1750. Robert T. Smith.
2126. (Right.) Slender Splat, Bell Seat. Cherry. 1740–60. J. Stogdell Stokes.

2127. Shaped Stretcher, Straight Front. Walnut. 1740–60. Wadsworth Atheneum.
2128. (Right.) Unusual Back Scroll. The Full Stretcher Scheme Appears Here
and in No. 2125. 1740–60. E. B. Leete Company.

2129. FULLY SHAPED ARM, CONCAVED ARM POSTS, OGEE SKIRT. CHERRY. 1730–50.
MRS. FRANCIS P. GARVAN.

2130. (Right.) SHELL ON SADDLE BACK. WALNUT. 1740–60. KATHERINE N. LORING.

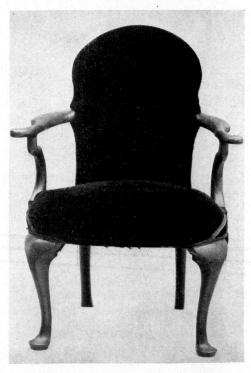

2131. ONE OF SET OF SIX, OGEE SKIRT. CREWEL WORK, ALL DIFFERENT IN DESIGN. PAINTED
INDIAN RED WITH FEATHER WORK. MAPLE. 1712. MADE BY THE SOUTHMEADS OF MIDDLETOWN.
WILLIAM B. GOODWIN.

2132. (RIGHT.) UPHOLSTERED, SHARPLY RAMPED ARM. 1740–60. METROPOLITAN MUSEUM.

2133. TRANSITION CHIPPENDALE. MAPLE. NEW ENGLAND. 1740–60. OPENWORK
SPLAT. H. W. ERVING.

2134. (Right.) QUEEN ANNE WITH PANEL BACK, CANED. MOLDED EDGE BACK POST.
SLIGHT CARVING ON RAILS. BEECH. NEW ENGLAND. 1720–40. H. W. ERVING.

2135. LEG OF QUEEN ANNE WING CHAIR. 1750–75. WM. B. GOODWIN, HARTFORD.

2136. (Right.) BALL-AND-CLAW FOOT IN THE QUEEN ANNE TYPE. 1740–60. I. SACK.

2137. Ramped Back Posts, Strongly Shaped Splat, Ball and Claw, Straight Front. Shell on Top Rail. 1740–60. Guy E. Beardsley, Hartford.

2138. (Right.) Fine Leg with Strong Acanthus Carving. Scroll in Bottom of Back into Which the Splat Enters. Carved Top Rail, Ramped Back. 1740–60. Samson Col.

2139. Openwork Splat, Carved Knee, Shell on Frame and Back. 1740–60. Morris Berry.

2140. (Right.) Ramped Back, with High Shell above Smaller Shell on Splat. Carved Knee, Peculiar Foot. 1740–60. Mrs. Francis P. Garvan.

2141–42. A Front and Side View. Animal Feet. Faces on Knee. Carved Saddle with Pendants, Foliage Carved Splat. 1720–40. English, Early Georgian. Walnut. Met. Mus.

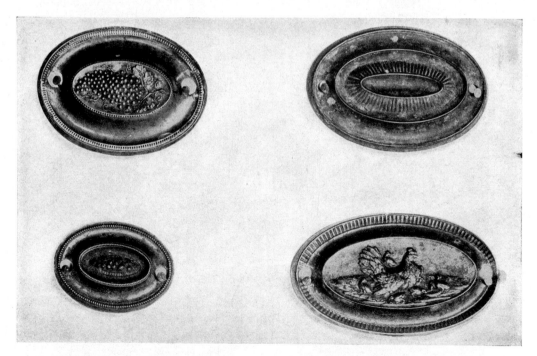

2143–46. A Series of Brasses of the Late Period. The Hen and Chickens Are Rarely Good. Rudolph P. Pauly.

2147. WALNUT. QUEEN ANNE, PHILADELPHIA TYPE, WITH RIBBED
ARM SUPPORTS, BALL-AND-CLAW FEET, SHELL ON KNEES AND CREST,
AND ROLLED SPLAT. 1740–60. PENNSYLVANIA MUSEUM, PHILADELPHIA.

2148-51. BRASS BELT BUCKLES. CONVENTIONAL. 19TH CENTURY. FRANK A. ROBART.

2152. A Philadelphia Queen Anne Arm, with Leg Carving Extending to the Ankle, Ball-and-Claw Feet, Ribbed Arm Supports, Shell on Top Rail, Supported by S Scrolls. Splat Carved. 1740–60. Metropolitan Museum.

The excellence and ornateness of the Philadelphia chairs have never been equaled in America elsewhere, though Baltimore produced some very excellent work, which is scarcely second in quality. The Pennsylvania arm post is somewhat hollowed on the inside, and is cut with two broad flutes which run together at the bottom and leave a rib between. The roll of the knuckle is also characteristic.

A characteristic of the Philadelphia chairs is that the side rail extended entirely through the post with its tenon and is wedged in. The construction was very solid, and is commendable.

2153. QUEEN ANNE ARM, WITH ACANTHUS ON KNEE, AND SHELL ON THE CONCAVE FRONT, AND TOP RAIL, THE LATTER SUPPORTED BY S SCROLLS. A PARROT-BACK SPLAT, VERY BROAD. THE ARM WE ARE ACCUSTOMED TO ASSOCIATE WITH A SLIGHTLY LATER PERIOD. IT IS QUITE DIFFERENT FROM THE PHILADELPHIA ARM, SWEEPING DOWN IN A SEMICIRCULAR CURVE, AND WROUGHT INTO A PRACTICALLY ROUND SECTION, AND SO MEETING AT RIGHT ANGLES THE ARM SUPPORT. 1750–75. PENNSYLVANIA MUSEUM, PHILADELPHIA.

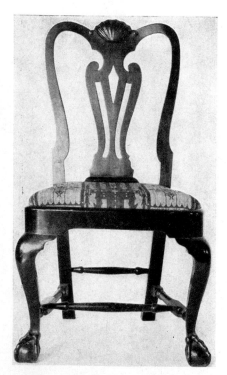

2154. A MAHOGANY SIDE CHAIR, QUEEN ANNE, WITH RAMPED BACK POST, CARVED KNEES, BALL-AND-CLAW FEET, AND SHELL AT TOP SUPPORTED BY S SCROLLS. SPLAT PIERCED WITHOUT CARVING. FULLY SHAPED SEAT. 1740–60. METROPOLITAN MUSEUM.

2155. (Right.) BRACED, BALL-AND-CLAW FOOT, QUEEN ANNE SIDE, WITH PIERCED SPLAT, RAMPED BACK POST, AND SHELL. 1740–60. G. W. H. SMITH.

2156. A SEAT IN CREWEL WORK ON HOMESPUN LINEN. A MRS. SOUTHMEAD OF MIDDLE-TOWN, CONNECTICUT, EMBROIDERED THE WORK. ABOUT 1720. WILLIAM B. GOODWIN.

2157. This Set Is the Pride of the Pendleton Collection, Rhode Island School of Design, Providence.

The class of chairs bearing the great name of Chippendale is the best known to the public as connoting a fine type of antique furniture. While Chippendale made all classes of furniture, he is best known in America by his chairs, his style book having been used largely by American cabinetmakers. Some of his designs were pronounced impractical, and some have not continued popular, as, for instance, those called Gothic, and Chinese. The question has also been raised whether the most intricate of the ribbon backs are in as good taste as the simpler forms. The genius displayed by Thomas Chippendale has never been surpassed, though in a different way Sheraton may rank with him as a designer. There are early types which suggest the growth of Chippendale designs from the Dutch, as, for instance, the celebrated chair above, the side chair of which is on the next page, and a settee of the same set appearing elsewhere. This carving is attributed to Grinling Gibbons, the greatest English name in that art. It seems wise to show a few English Chippendales to fill out and illustrate the style. Details will appear elsewhere. Gibbons died 1720, and if he did this work, the date establishes the earliest possible date of the set, which must, of course, be reckoned as Queen Anne.

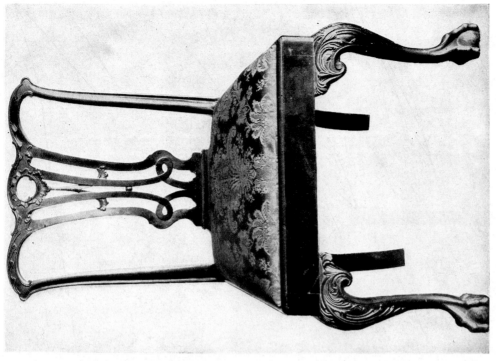

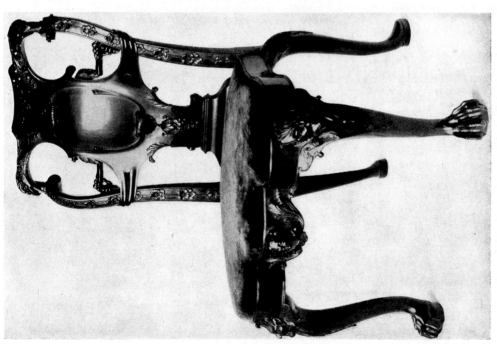

2158. A Side Chair of the Set Mentioned in the Previous Number. Grotesque Faces on the Knees, a Somewhat Mature Cherub on the Center of the Rail (Sometimes Called Benjamin Franklin!), a Large Plaque in the Splat Which Is Tied to the Posts and Held by Bird Claws. The Post with a Repeated Rose Pattern, Varying from Four to Five Petals, Is Rolled in a Fine Spiral at the Top and Grasped by a Bird's Beak, the Neck of Which Connects with the Saddle of the Top Rail. The Other Carving Details Include Shell, Pendants, and Sprays. The Back Leg Is Fully Shaped with a Dutch Foot, Whereas the Front Has the Animal Foot.

2159. (Right.) A Pure Chippendale Type, with Fully Developed Acanthus Knee and Delicate Pierced Splat, Lightly Carved, Dainty Foliage Sprays on the Back Rails and Around a Shield Shaped Opening. Leg Behind in a Plain Sweep. Metropolitan Museum.

2160–61. Two of the Exquisite Chairs Attributed to Benjamin Randolph. He Worked in Philadelphia and Reached the Climax in American Style. These Two and the Following Have the Spiral Foot Often Seen in France, and Found in Some of the Earlier Chippendale Chairs. Third Quarter 18th Century. Howard Reifsnyder, Philadelphia.

Some exception is taken by English critics to the plain shaping of the back legs. It is a question whether it is any better taste or as convenient to have a knob project like a toe or Dutch foot reversed, on the back leg. The old Latin proverb is pat here, that it is better not to dispute on the question of taste.

2162. ANOTHER CHAIR FROM THE SAME CELEBRATED SET, OF WHICH HOWARD REIFSNYDER HAS THREE. THIS EXAMPLE IS PERHAPS THE MOST ORNATE OF THE WORK ATTRIBUTED TO BENJAMIN RANDOLPH. SOME WOULD CALL THIS FOOT SCROLL A DOLPHIN FOOT. THE OWNER, H. W. ERVING, STILL BELIEVES THESE CHAIRS ARE ENGLISH, AND NO MAN SHOULD KNOW BETTER. IF ROCOCO IS IN ANY FORM ADMIRABLE, IT IS SO HERE. THE EXAMPLE IS SUPREME IN ITS SUPERB CARVING. MAHOGANY. c. 1750.

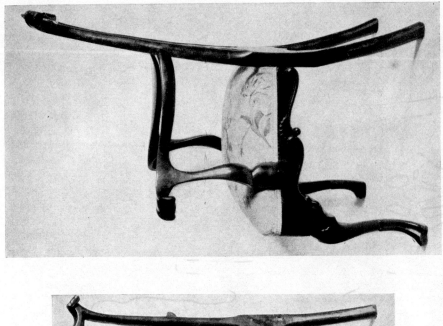

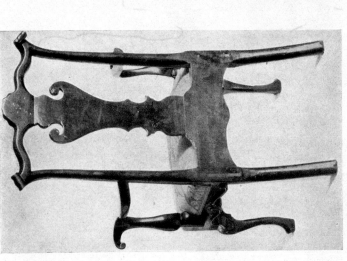

2163–65. Three Views of the Same Chair, Philadelphia School. Fluted Drake Foot, Shell Knee, Raised Marginal Carving, Shell on Center of Scrolled Skirt and Top Rail, Rolled Ears, Accentuated Parrot Back, Ribbed Arm Supports. Mahogany. 1750–75. Mrs. Francis P. Garvan.

Among the particular style marks of the Philadelphia type, is the oval section of the back leg, the long diameter being right and left. The splats also are usually very bold in their scrolled edges. In this example, there is a scrolling on the back rail at the bottom, which is most unusual, and the marginal raised carving extends on the sides, to the back leg. An English suggestion that these chairs are not to be viewed from the rear, is here shown to be without foundation.

Fourteen Chippendale chairs with Dutch feet now to be shown are more or less transitional, some also having a rounded front, showing the hold over of the Queen Anne influence.

2166. PROBABLY MADE IN PORTSMOUTH OR NEWBURYPORT. WALNUT. 34¾ x 22 x 17½. THE SEAT IS 14½ INCHES HIGH, SO THAT ONE MAY SAY THIS IS A SLIPPER CHAIR. 1740–60. CLIFFORD S. DRAKE.

2167. (Right.) STRAIGHT FRONT, DUTCH FEET, WITH STRETCHERS, LIGHTLY CARVED BACK. 1740–60. NATHAN CUSHING, PROVIDENCE.

2168. ALWAYS OWNED BY FABENS-MANSFIELD FAMILIES OF SALEM, ANCESTORS OF MRS. BEACH. 1740–60. MR. AND MRS. T. BELKNAP BEACH.

2169. (Right.) LIGHTLY CARVED. 38½ x 21 x 17. FROM PROVIDENCE. 1740–60. EST. HARRY W. WEEKS.

2170. ROUND SEAT, MAHOGANY. CARVED KNEE, SCROLLED BRACKET. FROM RICHMOND.
36¾ x 22 x 17. 1740–60. ESTATE OF HARRY W. WEEKS.
2171. (Right.) DRAKE FEET, RIBBED. 1750–70. WALLACE NUTTING.

2172. WALNUT. PHILADELPHIA. DRAKE FEET, RIBBED; SHELL ON CREST. 1740–60.
MRS. FRANCIS P. GARVAN.
2173. (Right.) DRAKE FEET, RIBBED, LARGE HANDHOLE ON TOP RAIL. MOLDED POSTS,
LIGHTLY CARVED EARS. 1740–60. MRS. FRANCIS P. GARVAN.

2174. CARVED BACK, STRAIGHT FRONT, WITH STRETCHERS, WHICH IN ALL THESE EXAMPLES
FOLLOW THE QUEEN ANNE STYLE. 1740–60. T. BELKNAP BEACH.

2175. (Right.) A WELL-SHAPED SPLAT, CARVED EARS AND SHELL. 39½ x 21 x 17. 1740–60.
CLIFFORD S. DRAKE.

2176–77. BASES SIMILAR, BACKS WITH CHIPPENDALE AND DUTCH ELEMENTS. ONE SQUARE, ONE
ROUND SEAT. 1740–60. C. SANFORD BULL.

2178. Cherry, 1740–60. Straight Front. No Carving. New England. H. W. Erving.

2179. (Right.) Foliage Carving on Splat, Below a Shell with a Pendant; Carved Ears. Walnut, 1740–60. 38 x 21½ x 15½. Dr. and Mrs. J. M. Birnie.

2180. Entering on the Pure Chippendale, We Have a High Ball-and-Claw Foot with a Shoe, and a Light Open Back, Carved Rail and Rolled Ears. 1760–75. I. Sack.

2181. (Right.) Knee Carving Extending on the Frame; Rolled Ears with Rope Molded and Shell Back, Carved Splat. 1760–75. Metropolitan Museum.

2182. Concaved Arm Support, Philadelphia Style, with Deep Skirt. Walnut. 1760–75. Met. Mus.
2183. (Right.) Very Handsome, Shell Ears and Foliage; Shell at Back. 1760–75. Met. Mus.

2184. Red Walnut, Shell on Front and Top Rails. One of a Pair. 1760–75. H. W. Erving.
2185. (Right.) Fluted Posts. Top Rail and Splat Unusual in Shape and in Carving.

2186. Quite Unusual in Carving, in Shape of Posts, Splat and Back Rail. 1760–75. I. Sack.
2187. (Right.) English, Mahogany, Fluted Posts, Gadroon Frame, Bell in the Carving of Back. 1760–75. Katherine N. Loring.

2188. Philadelphia, Dutch Underbracing, Carved Ears. 1760–75. Mrs. F. P. Garvan.
2189. (Right.) Philadelphia. Molded Posts, Carved Top Rail. Shaped Frame with Carved Ornament. Good Leg. 1760–75. Henry V. Weil.

2190. EFFECTIVE, BROAD SPLAT, BEADED POSTS. 1760–75. GUY E. BEARDSLEY.

2191. (Right.) PHILADELPHIA, RED WALNUT; LARGE. SHELLS ON KNEES, FRONT RAIL AND TOP RAIL. TYPICAL ARM AND POST. 1750–75. H. W. ERVING.

2192. CONNECTICUT. CHERRY. GRACEFUL, LIGHT STILES, OPENWORK SPLAT. CHARACTERISTICS OF AN ELIPHALET CHAPIN, SOUTH WINDSOR. CHAPIN MADE CHERRY DESKS AND HIGHBOYS ALSO. 1775.

2193. (Right.) RED WALNUT, NEW ENGLAND. SHELL ON HIPS, SEAT RAIL, AND TOP RAIL. OPEN SPLAT. 1750–60. H. W. ERVING (BOTH CHAIRS).

2194. FLUTED STILES; CARVED BACK. DECORATION ON MARGINAL CARVED FRONT RAIL. CARVED HIPS. HIP AND KNEE ARE TERMS FOR THE SAME THING. MAHOGANY. 1760–75. M. A. NORTON.

2195. (Right.) SHELLS ON SEAT AND BACK, FLUTED ROLLED EARS. 1760–75. MAHOGANY.

2196. LIGHTLY CARVED BACK, OPEN URN SPLAT, BALL AND CLAW; ACANTHUS KNEE. 1760–75. RHODE ISLAND SCHOOL OF DESIGN.

2197. (Right.) FLUTED STILES, FOLIAGE BACK, CARVED SPLAT, ACANTHUS KNEE. MAHOGANY.

2198–99. PHILADELPHIA. THIS ARM AND SIDE CHAIR ARE SUFFICIENTLY ALIKE TO SUGGEST THEY WERE MADE BY THE SAME PERSON AT AN EARLY DATE. THEY HAVE BEEN ATTRIBUTED TO SAVERY. THEY HAVE SOME DUTCH MARKS. ARMCHAIR 40 X 25 X 18. FRANCIS D. BRINTON. SIDE CHAIR, PERHAPS 1740–60. J. STOGDELL STOKES.

2200. UNUSUAL SPLAT, CARVED SHELL ON TOP. 1760–75. H. H. ARMSTRONG, HARTFORD.

2201. (Right.) NO CARVING EXCEPT BALL-AND-CLAW FEET. 1760–75. SIMPLE CHIPPENDALES HAVE GRACE AND POPULARITY.

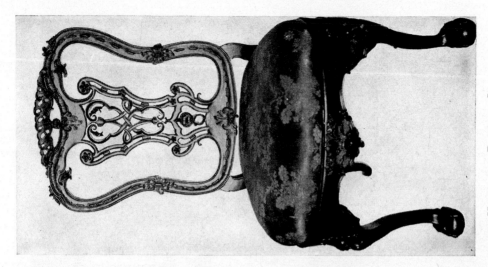

2204. Hispanic. Perhaps Inspiration of
the Dutch Chippendale and Hepplewhite.
Very Elegant. Walnut. 1740–60. The
Misses A. and E. P. Foster.

2203. English, Molded Cross Stretcher, Richly
Carved. Ears and Top Rail Very Fine. 1760–75.
The Misses A. and E. P. Foster.

2202. English; Mahogany. Engrailed Rail.
1760–75. The Type of Bracket (Which Is Always
A Separate Piece) Is a Good Design. I. Sack.

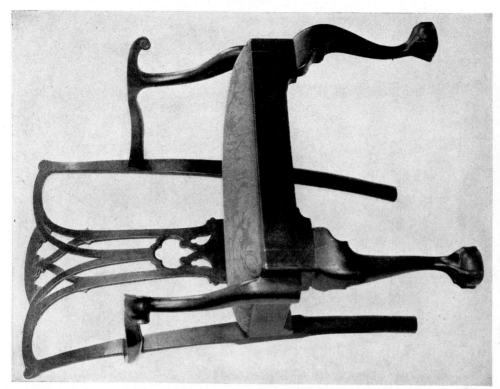

2205. Fluted Stiles, Shells on Top Rail, Seat Rail, and Knees. 1760-75. C. P. Cooley, Hartford.
2206. (Right.) Philadelphia Type, Shown in the Arm and Back Leg. 1760-75. Sanderson Collection.

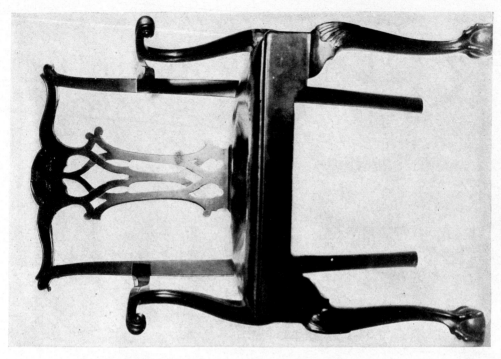

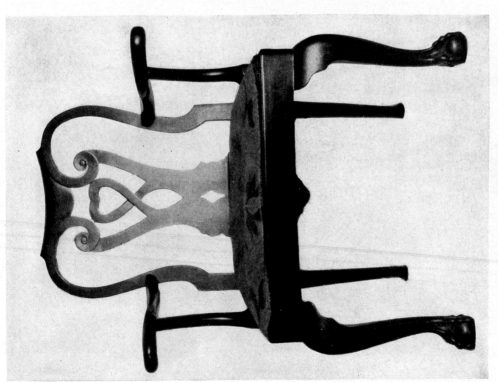

2207. Wide Swept Curve of Arm. Leg a Little Heavy in the Ankle. 1760–75. Morris Berry.
2208. (Right.) One of the Series of Chairs Collected by the Late Morgan G. Bulkeley, for Ætna Life Insurance Company, Hartford. Raised Margins and Rolled Ears on Back Rail. Shells on Knees. 1760–75.

2209. Good Leg. Unusual Motive. Arm Carved without Much Ramp. 1760-75. F. L. Dunne.

2210. (Right.) Shell Knee, Simple Ribbon Back, Sharp Arm Ramp. 1760-75. H. N. Campbell.

2211. Philadelphia; Walnut. Boldly Carved Shells. Good Ears. 41 x 21½ x 16. 1760-75. Francis D. Brinton.

2212. (Right.) Masonic Chippendale, with Many Emblems. Acanthus Knee, Boldly Ramped Arm, Fluted Pillar Stile. 1760-75. I. Sack.

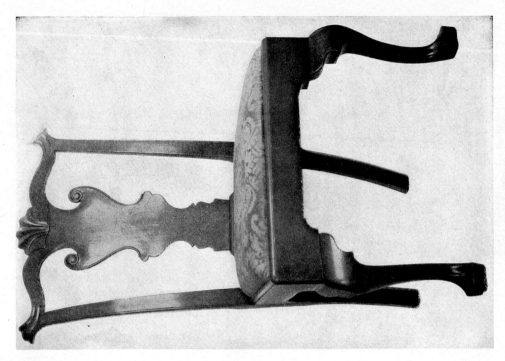

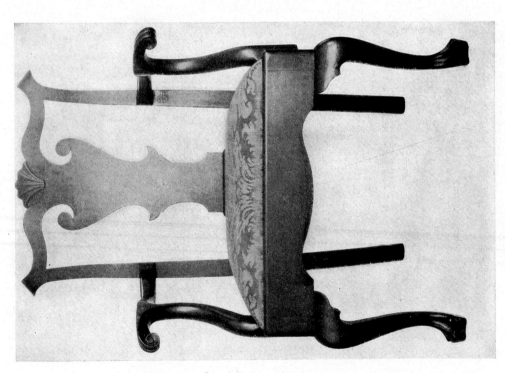

2213. Drake Foot, Philadelphia Arm. Top Rail with Shell and Plain Roll. Wide Splat. Walnut. 1760–75. Sanderson Collection.
2214. (Right.) Broad Splat with Raised Margin Ending in Scrolls. Fluted Rolled Ears, Drake Foot. Walnut. 1760–75. Sanderson Collection.

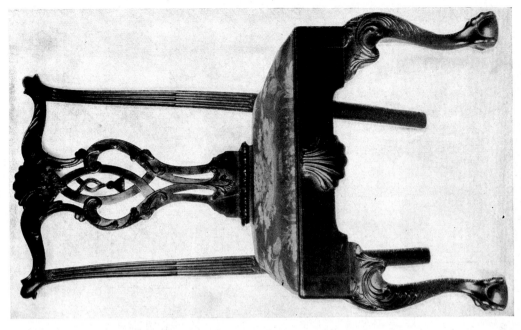

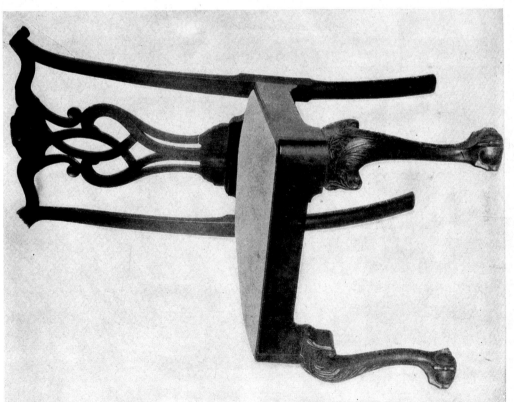

2215. Rolled Ear, Rope Carved Back with Shell. Fully Carved Back. Fully Carved Leg. Philadelphia Type. Mahogany. 1760-75. I. Sack.
2216. (Right.) A Specimen of Considerable Elegance. Mahogany. Stiles with Stop Flute. Rolled Ears, Shell and Scroll Back, and Foliage Carving on Splat. The Tassel Is the Only Element Which Seems Disconnected. Gadroon Mold at Base of Splat. Bought in Charleston, South Carolina. 1760-75. W. A. Hitchcock.

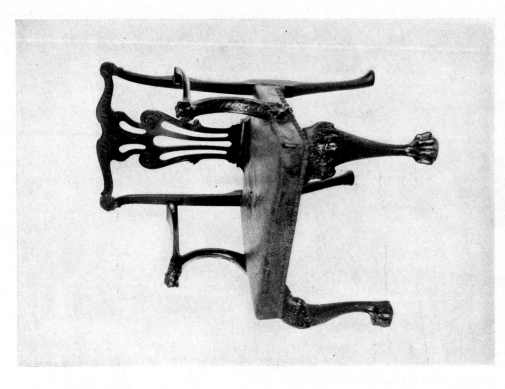

2217. Philadelphia Type. Boldly Ramped Ears. Unusual Shell on Seat Rail. Mahogany. 1760-75. Ætna Life Insurance Company, Hartford.

2218. (Right.) Animal Foot, Elaborately Carved Knee. Carved Arm Support and Knuckle. Shells on Ears, Foliage Carved Splat. Mahogany. English. 1760-75. Palmer Collection.

2219. Philadelphia Type. Ribbed Arm Support and Boldly Contoured and Rolled Arm Ending in a Carved Fluted Spiral. Fluted Stiles, Rope Molding, and Shell on Top Rail; Acanthus Carved Knees and Splat. 1760–75. C. P. Cooley, Hartford.

2220. Fluted Stiles, Shell Ears and Central Shell; Also Carved Central Foliage on Chair Rail. The Acanthus Knee Carving Is Extended Above on the Rails, and Similar Foliage Is Found on the Open Splat. Philadelphia Type. 1760–75. Howard Reifsnyder.

2221–22. An Oval and a Basket Pattern Brass. 1790 and 1810. Rudolph P. Pauly, Boston.

2223. Unusual Scrolled Bracing. Stiles Beaded on Both Sides, and Beading Carried around the Top. 1760–75. Metropolitan Museum.

2224. (Right.) Fluted Stile, Acanthus Knee, Plain Seat Rails, Open Back, Lightly Carved. Mahogany. Attributed to Savery. 1760–75. Mrs. Francis P. Garvan.

2225. Good Conventional Leg. 1760–75. Fluted Ears. Frank A. Robart.

2226. (Right.) Graceful Light Back and Legs. 1760–75. Katrina Kipper.

2227. Richly Carved. The Knee Has Great Elegance, and the Motive Is
Carried Up over the Rounded Corner of the Seat Rail. Engrailed Rail
Edge. Applied Ornament on Center of Rail Superfluous. Back Rail Carved
in a Complex Design. The Splat Is Quite Different in Style from Those
with Which We Are Acquainted. Chippendale School. Palmer Collection.
I. Sack. The Age Has Been Disputed.

2228. Mahogany, Probably English. Finely Carved. Back Stiles with Carved Rope Molding, "Ribband" Back. 1760–75. H. W. Erving.

2229. (Right.) Simple but Effective Chair with Good Parrot Back. Beading about the Stiles and Back Rail. 1760–75. Charles P. Cooley.

2230–31. Showing the Shape as Looked Down Upon of Two Carved Arms. The Former Is Found in New England and Pennsylvania, but Mostly Through the North. The Latter Has a Very Bold Outward Ramp with Much Grace, and Appears on Chippendale and Earlier Chairs. In This Case a Philadelphia Mahogany Arm, Owned by Mrs. Francis P. Garvan.

2232. A Well-Carved Chair, with Linen Fold and Tassel in the Splat, Carved Foliage on the Back, Including the Ears. 1760–75. Formerly the Author's.

2233. (Right.) Open Back, Shell Knee. Mahogany. Philadelphia. Mrs. Francis P. Garvan.

2234. Unusual Back with a Spray Carving at the Center of the Splat. Raised Marginal Line on the Back Stiles and Top Rail. 1760–75. Francis D. Brinton.

2235. (Right.) Dutch Underbracing, Lightly Carved Back, Graceful Lines. 1750–75. I. Sack.

2236. A Carved Rounded Ear. Molded Back Stiles. Graceful Legs, with Acanthus; Ball and Claw; Back Foot Shaped. 1760–75. English. Palmer Collection. I. Sack.

2237. (Right.) Dutch Foot and Underbracing, with Unusual Back, Possibly Dutch. 1740–60. Nathan Cushing, Providence.

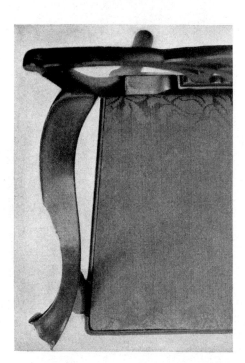 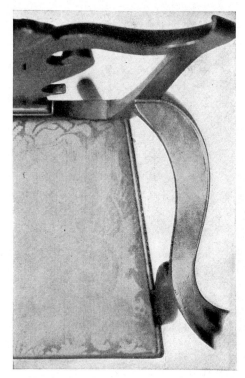

2238–39. Upper View of Two Arms of Chairs in the Sanderson Collection, Nantucket. Raised Marginal Lines. Chippendale Period.

2240. Inward Spiral Scrolled Feet, in Front and Behind. 1760–75. Data Mislaid.

2241. (Right.) Upholstered Chippendale, with Chinese Fret on Legs and Arm. 1760–75.

2242. Interesting Variant. Molded Stiles, Swept in Like a Hepplewhite Back at the Bottom. Delicate Chippendale Ball-and-Claw Leg. 1760–75.
Austin D. Barney, Farmington, Connecticut.

2243. (Right.) Transition Chippendale, with Hepplewhite Elements, Spade Foot, Richly Carved Splat. Mahogany. 39 x 20 x 15. 1780. Edward Bringhurst, Wilmington.

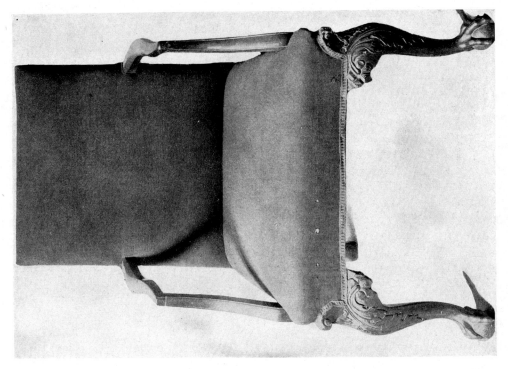

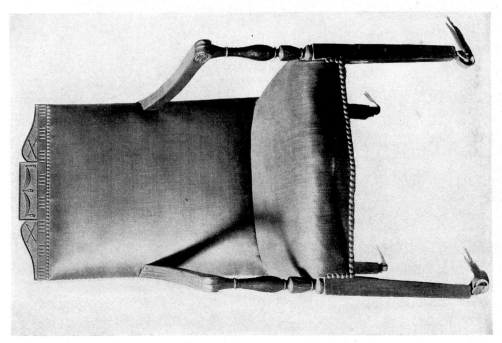

2244. Attributed to McIntire, of Salem. Mixed Elements. Graceful Arm Posts and Arm. 1790. Essex Institute.
2245. (Right.) Unusual Chippendale, Fully Carved Leg, with Extension on the Frame Ending in a Scroll. Back and Arms Much Like Sheraton. 1780. Essex Institute.

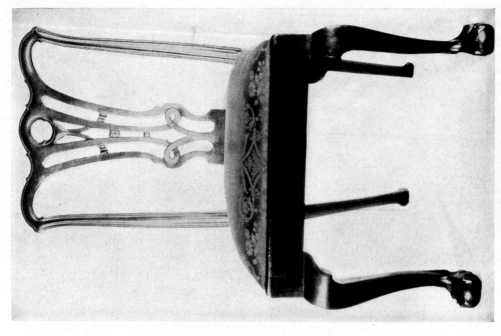

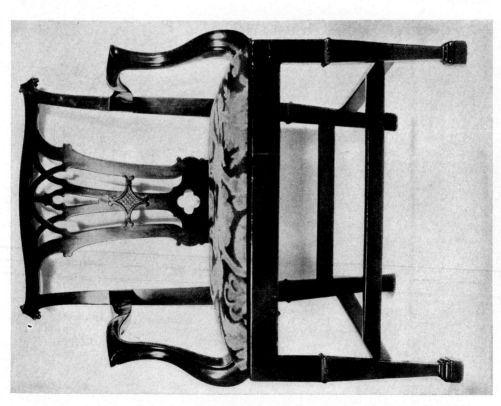

2246. A Transition Chippendale, with Spade Foot and Horizontal Band on the Upper Part of the Leg, Front and Back. Rare but Graceful Arm, Spiraled Rolled Ears. 1780. Charles P. Cooley, Hartford.

2247. (Right.) Molded Back Stiles, Light Open Splat. Plain Seat Rails. 1760-75. Charles P. Cooley, Hartford.

2248. ENTERING ON THE STRAIGHT LEG CHIPPENDALE, A CHAIR WITH LIGHT BRACKET IS SHOWN WITH MOLDED STILES AND CARVED BACK. 1760–75. NATHAN CUSHING.

2249. (Right.) ONE OF A PAIR, WITH CHINESE FRET ON LEGS AND OPEN FRET ON UNDERBRACING. 1760–75. FLAYDERMAN & KAUFMAN.

2250. PIERCED LADDER BACK, FLUTED AND LIGHTLY CARVED. 1760–75. WALLACE NUTTING.

2251. (Right.) PIERCED LADDER BACK. LEGS, ARM, AND STILES, FLUTED. 1760–75. ÆTNA LIFE INS. CO.

2252. Four (Pierced) Ladder Back, Lightly Carved. 1760–75. Ætna Life Insurance Company, Hartford.

2253. (Right.) Three Ladder Back. 26 x 31½ x 18. Ball-and-Claw Foot. Ladder Backs Are Unusual, and Those with Ball-and-Claw Foot Are Very Rare. 1770. Katherine N. Loring.

2254–55. Arm and Side Ladder Backs, Straight Legs with Molded Corner. Hollowed Seat. Lightly Carved, with Spiraled Ears. Part of a Set. 1760–75. F. L. Dunne.

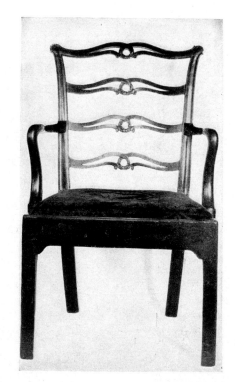

2256. A Three Ladder Back, Cherry, No Carving. Connecticut. 1770. H. W. Erving.

2257. (Right.) Like No. 2252, Except for the Absence of Stretchers, the Slip Seat, and the Brackets. 1770. Frank A. Robart.

2258. A Late Ladder Back, Found at Sherborn, Massachusetts. Maple. 36¾ x 19¾ x 15¼. The Ears Suggest the Date 1790–1800. Estate of Harry W. Weeks.

2259. (Right.) Connecticut. Cherry. Shaped Slats. Back Rather High. 1750–75. H. W. Erving.

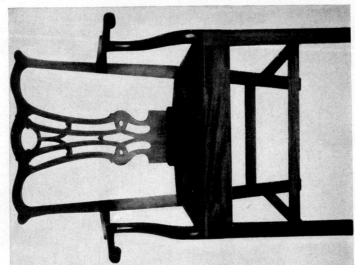

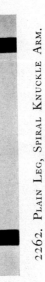

2262. Plain Leg, Spiral Knuckle Arm.
1770–75.
Ætna Life Insurance Company, Hartford.

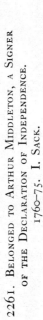

2261. Belonged to Arthur Middleton, a Signer
of the Declaration of Independence.
1760–75. I. Sack.

2260. English Arm, of Which Side Chair Has
Been Shown. A Restrained Arm Knuckle.
Katherine Loring.

2263. Chinese Chippendale. Mahogany. Triple Column Posts. Attributed to Philadelphia. c. 1776. 38 x 22 x 21. William B. Goodwin.

2264. (Right.) Chinese Chippendale, Bamboo Pattern. Unusual and Unpopular. 1770–75.

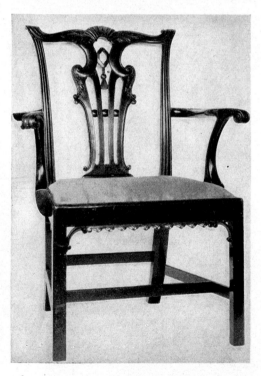

2265. Bracket on Frame, Concaved Arm Support. Handsomely Carved and Scrolled Arm. Fluted Back. 1760–75. The Misses A. and E. P. Foster.

2266. (Right.) New England. Cherry. Top Rail Carved. Slip Seat. Plain Legs and Stretchers. 1760–75. H. W. Erving.

2267. Mahogany. Ears Carved; Shell at Center. Front Legs Fluted. 1760-75. H. W. Erving.

2268. (Right.) Fluted Legs and Back Stiles. Delicately Carved Back. Found in Augusta, Maine. Mahogany. 37½ x 22½ x 18¾. 1760-75. Estate of H. W. Weeks.

2269. Plain Legs; Fluted Back Stiles and Top Rail. Back Carved with Foliage and Tassel. 1760-75. Mrs. Francis P. Garvan.

2270. (Right.) Connecticut. Cherry. Four Vertical Splats with a Tie. 1760-75. H. W. Erving.

2271. FLUTED, AND WITH CARVED BRACKETS, BACK DELICATELY CARVED. 1760–75.
THE MISSES A. AND E. P. FOSTER.

2272. (Right.) FLUTED BACK. GRACEFULLY AND LIGHTLY OUTLINED PIERCED SPLAT. CARVED
BACK. 1760–75.

2273–74. ARM AND SIDE CHAIRS OF A SET, FORMERLY OWNED BY THE AUTHOR. SLIP SEAT FRAME,
SHOWING THE METHOD OF PLACING THE SEAT. OPEN BRACKETS, LIGHT PIERCED SPLATS. 1760–75.

2275-76. Arm and Side Chair of a Set. Beaded Legs and Back Stiles. Carved Back. 1760-75. F. L. Dunne.

Chippendale's later manner was in the straight leg. This style could be quite plain, or ornate.

2277. Mahogany, with Fluting, and Gothic Back. 38 x 25 x 21. 1760-75. Mrs. Francis P. Garvan.
2278. (Right.) Fluted Throughout with Carved Brackets. Carved Top Rail and Delicate Molded Open Splat. 1760-75.

2279. (Above.) Fully
Carved Legs, with
Pendants and Panels.
Molded Feet. Carved
Brackets. Arm Post
Curved but not
Carved. Carved
Knuckles; Uphol-
stered Arm. 1760–75.
Morris Schwartz,
New York.

2280. A Brass of the
Early Empire Type on
a Chest of Drawers
in the Sanderson
Collection.

2281. Chinese Fret, Upholstered Arm. Plain Stretchers. Upholstered with a Chinese Pattern To Comport with the Style of the Carving. 1760–75. Charles P. Cooley, Hartford.

2283. (Opposite) Chippendale Widely Pierced Slats. 1770. W. Lanier Washington, Westport, Connecticut.

2283 A. Chippendale, Posts of Unusually Rich Design. Seat with Shaped Front and Carved on Three Sides. English. 1760–75. I. Sack.

2282. CHIPPENDALE, CHINESE RAISED FRET ON POSTS AND ARMS. 1760–75. I. SACK.

2284. Plain Rounded Ear, Interlaced Splat, Fluted Legs. 1760–75. Frank A. Robart.
2285. (Right.) Molded Back Stiles; Corner Mold on Legs. 1760–75. Morris Berry.

2286. Arm Scrolled as if One Piece, Carved Bracket, Beaded Corner Post, Fluted Back Rail, Gothic Four-Pillared Back, Connected by Diamonds. Carved Ears on Rail. 1760–75. H. W. Erving.
2287. (Right.) Lightly Built. Molded Back, with Carved Pendant. Rounded Ears, Carved Top Rail. 1760–75. Morris Berry.

2288. Very Deeply Scalloped Skirt. 1760–75. Morris Berry.
2289. (Right.) Mahogany. Unusual Fret on the Legs; a Carved X Back. Chamfered Underbracing. 36 x 21 x 20. 1750–75. Edward Bringhurst, Wilmington, Delaware.

2290–91. A Pair of Fluted-Leg Chippendales, with a Raised Line on Inside and Outside of Back Posts, Also across the Top. Carved "Ribband" Back. 1760–75. H. N. Campbell, Providence.

2292. VERY DELICATELY CARVED BACK. STOP FLUTE ON BACK STILES. 1760–75.

2293. (Right.) BACK CARVED WITH RAISED MARGIN, EXTENDING ALSO DOWN THE OPEN SPLAT. CARVED FOLIAGE AND INDENTED ROUNDED EAR. PLAIN LEGS. 1760–75. KATRINA KIPPER.

2294. GRACEFUL, LIGHTLY CARVED BACK, BACK POSTS CARVED AND FLUTED. 1760–75.

2295. (Right.) ONE OF A PAIR, FOUND IN CONNECTICUT. MAHOGANY. VERY LARGE. FLUTED BACK. UNUSUAL SPLAT. 1760–75. JAMES DAVIDSON.

2296–97. WELL-CARVED ARM. PLAIN SEAT RAIL. CHAIR ON RIGHT WITH EXTRAORDINARY WIDE SPLAT, AND DEEP SCALLOPED SKIRT. 1760–75. ÆTNA LIFE INSURANCE COMPANY.

2298–99. THE FORMER WITH SOLID, THE LATTER WITH OPEN BRACKET ON LEG. VERY WIDE SPLAT ON THE FORMER, AND GROUPED REEDS WITH A TIE ON THE LATTER. SEMICIRCULAR ARM. 1760–75. ÆTNA LIFE INSURANCE COMPANY, HARTFORD.

2300. Daintily Spiraled Ear. Openwork Splat. 1760–75. Estate of H. W. Weeks.
2301. (Right.) A Good Shell. Fluted Ears; Complicated Splat. 1760–75. Wadsworth Atheneum.

2302. No Carving, but a Graceful Pattern. 1760–75. Robert T. Smith, Hartford.
2303. (Right.) Very Unusual Splat, of a Motive Which Perhaps Was Not Intended To Be Analyzed, or with Some Significance Unknown. 1760–75, H. W. Erving.

2304. Upholstered Arm and Back, Fluted Legs and Arm Support. Mahogany. 42 x 26 x 22. 1750–75. C. Sanford Bull.

2305. (Right.) Straight Leg and Plain Curved Arm, Upholstered. Chippendale, as Are All on This Page. Now Upholstered in Leather. 1760–75. I. Sack.

2306. Upholstered Arm. Chippendale Fret on the Foot and Legs. 1760–75.

2307. (Right.) Like the One Above, Except for Bracket on the Frame, and the Width, Which Is a Little Greater. Mahogany. 38 x 27½ x 22. 1760–75. Dr. and Mrs. J. M. Birnie.

2308. A Very Common Chair in America Is the Transition Chippendale-Hepplewhite. The Feature Is the Chippendale Splat with a Back Rail Resembling the Top of a Shield, or with Taper Legs. The First Chair Is Not in That Class, Really Belonging to the Chippendale, with Straight Legs Having No Taper. Fluted Arms. 1760–75. H. W. Erving.

2309. (Right.) Dutch Foot, Chippendale Back. 1750–60. Ætna Life Insurance Company.

2310–11. Transition, Belonging to Helen T. Cooke and Charles P. Cooley, Respectively.

2311A. A Raised Fret, Chippendale, Upholstered Arms. Molded Feet. 1760–75.
Howard Reifsnyder, Philadelphia.

2312. One of Mahogany Set. Massachusetts. 36½ x 21½ x 19. Bellflower Motive.
2313. (Right.) Double Wheel Back, Taper Leg. 1780–90. Estate of H. W. Weeks.

2314. Mahogany. Connecticut. 1780–90.
Robert T. Smith, Hartford.

2315. Handsome Urn Back. 1780–90.
Morris Berry.

2316–16A. Graceful Outlines. Probably Made To Go Together. 1770–80. Mrs. Alexander Armstrong, Baltimore.

2317. From Winthrop, Massachusetts. 1780–90. Estate of Harry W. Weeks.

2317A. Molded Back. Hepplewhite Posts and Top. 1780–90. Morris Berry.

2318–18A. Martha Washington, but Owing to the Taper, Square Feet, Belonging to Hepplewhite Mode. One Molded, One Plain Arm. 1790. Mrs. Francis P. Garvan.

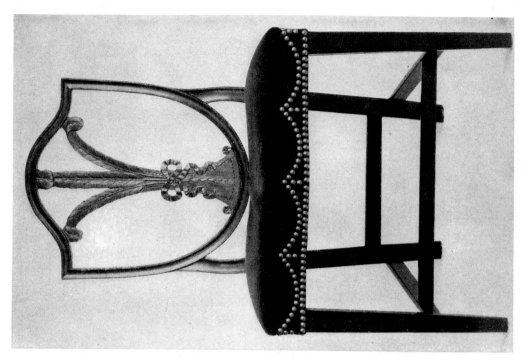

2319. Shield Back, with Inlaid Urn and Carving. Pendant Inlays on Legs and Bands Near the Foot. Fluted Arms and Back and Top Rail. 1790. Metropolitan Museum.

2320. (Right.) Three-Feather Back, from Set Always in the Fabens-Mansfield Families, Salem, Whose Descendant, Mrs. T. Belknap Beach, Owns Six.

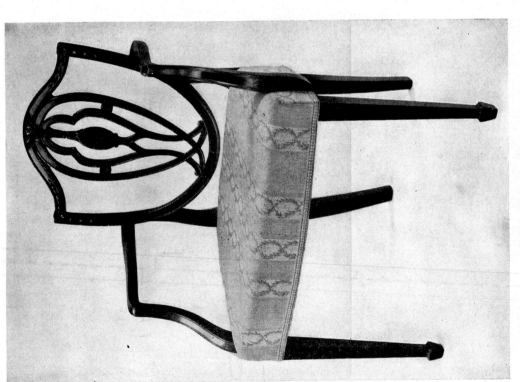

2321. FOUR FEATHERS AT THE CREST, PENDANTS AT THE CORNERS, INLAY ON ARM. RAISED EDGES OF BACK LATHS AND MAIN FRAME. BEADED ARM RAILS. 1790. METROPOLITAN MUSEUM.

2322. (Right.) THREE FEATHERS AND GRACEFUL DRAPERY. FLUTED LEGS, 1790. SANDERSON COLLECTION, NANTUCKET.

2325. Side Chair of No. 2323. 1790.
I. Sack.

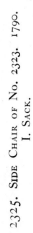

2324. Turned and Carved Arm Support. 1790.
Edward Bringhurst.

2323. Arm, with Spade Foot, Three-Feather
Back and Inlay. 1790. Shaped Seat. I. Sack.

2326. Inlay at Apex and on the Three Ovals of the Banisters. All Frame Members Fluted. 1790.

2327. Five-Sheaf Banisters Tied by Carving at the Center. Three-Feather Crest. 1790. Morris Berry.

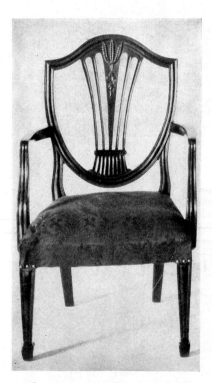

2328. Three Feathers with Pendant, Frame Fluted Throughout. 1790. F. L. Dunne.

2329. One of Ten, Slightly Carved. Annapolis. 1790. Joe Kindig, Jr., York, Pennsylvania.

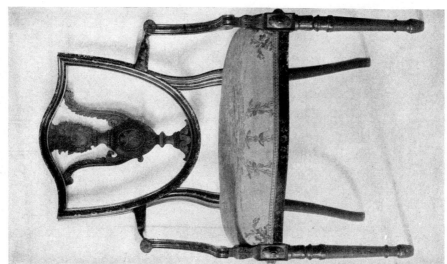

2330. An Exquisite Back of Urn and Drapery. 1790. Once the Author's.

2331. Beautiful and Rare Design. 1790. Mrs. Francis P. Garvan.

2332. An Elegant Design, Painted. Adam Brothers' Motives. 1790. F. L. Dunne.

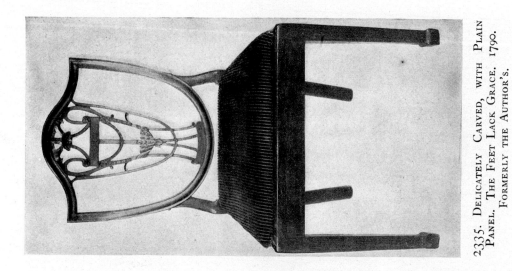

2335. Delicately Carved, with Plain Panel. The Feet Lack Grace. 1790. Formerly the Author's.

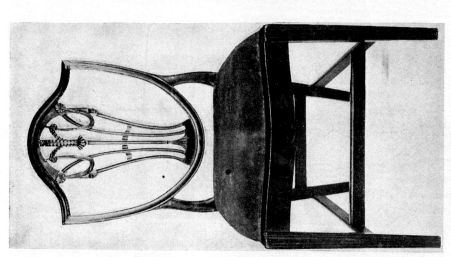

2334. Three Feathers and Drapery. Shaped Front. 1790. Formerly the Author's.

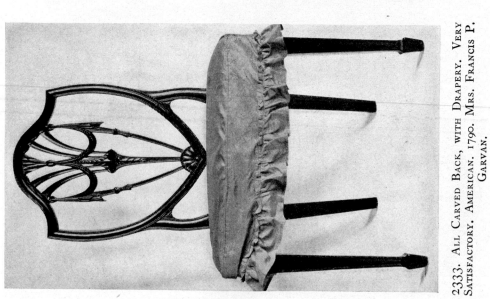

2333. All Carved Back, with Drapery. Very Satisfactory. American. 1790. Mrs. Francis P. Garvan.

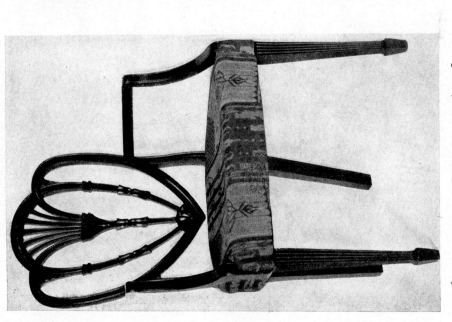

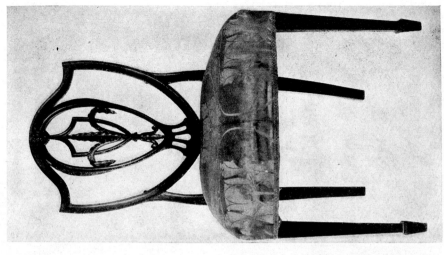

2336. Reeded Legs, Conventional Arm, Intersecting Shield Back. 1790. G. W. H. Smith.

2337. Intersecting Shield, Fluted Legs. 1790. G. W. H. Smith.

2338. Three Feathers, and Foliage on Top Rail. 1790. Formerly the Author's.

2339. THE RHODE ISLAND TYPE, ATTRIBUTED TO GODDARD & ENGE. A CONSIDERABLE NUMBER KNOWN; SOME WITH HOLLOWED SEAT AS HERE, OTHERS WITH FLAT SEAT. 1790. T. BELKNAP BEACH.

2340. (RIGHT.) FINELY CARVED URN, ALL FRAME MEMBERS FLUTED. 1790. HOWARD REIFSNYDER, PHILA.

2341. FINELY CARVED LEG AND ARM, WITH THE SAME MOTIVES CARRIED AROUND THE BACK. CURVED ARM JOINS THE BACK WITH CARVED LEAF. MONTREAL. 38 x 23¼ x 20½. 1790. CLIFFORD S. DRAKE.

2342. (RIGHT.) SHAPED AND MOLDED FRONT, GRACEFUL ARMS, MOLDED, AS WELL AS THE SHIELD BACK. PIERCED BANISTERS. 1790. F. L. DUNNE.

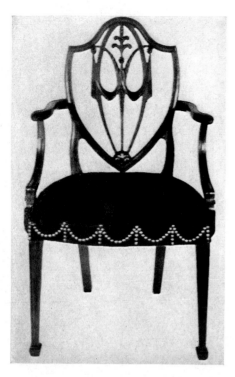 

2343. FIVE FEATHERS. BACK WITH HIGH RAMP. NEW ENGLAND. 1790. I. SACK.

2344. (Right.) A SIDE CHAIR OF THE SAME SET. THESE HARMONIOUS CHAIRS WITH THEIR DRAPERY AND REEDED LEGS, AND SPADE FEET ARE VERY SATISFACTORY.

2345. ONE OF THE CONNECTICUT SENATE CHAIRS. PENDANT INLAY ON THE LEGS, CARVED URN WITH ROSETTES ABOVE. FLUTED ARM AND BACK. 1790. GUY E. BEARDSLEY, HARTFORD.

2346. (Right.) CANE SEAT, CARVED, GROOVED, AND SHAPED FRONT RAIL; GROOVED BACK. 1790.

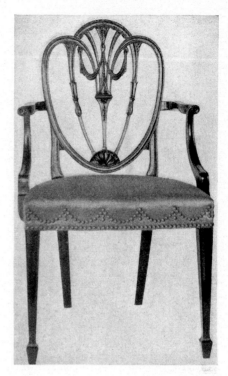

2347. BACK WITH INTERSECTING CURVES, CARVED DRAPERY, AND TIES ON BANISTERS. 1790. THE MISSES A. AND E. P. FOSTER, HARTFORD.

2348. (Right.) ARM CHAIR OF THE SAME SET. DELICATE CARVING, SPADE FOOT, ROSETTE AT INTERSECTION OF ARM WITH POST. 1790.

2349. FIVE FEATHERS, BACK FULLY CARVED, PLAIN TAPER FEET. 1790. PENNSYLVANIA MUSEUM, PHILADELPHIA.

2350. (Right.) THREE FEATHERS AND PENDANT OF HUSKS. 1790. PENNSYLVANIA MUSEUM, PHILA.

2351. FIVE CURVED BANISTERS, SLIGHT CARVING, MOLDED FRAME. 1790. FORMERLY THE AUTHOR'S.

2352. (Right.) THE CURVED BANISTERS ARE DONE ON THEIR LOWER SECTION WITH AN IMBRICATED CARVING, AND FLUTED ABOVE. INTERSECTING WHEAT EARS ON THE CREST OF THE SHIELD.

2353. FIVE BANISTERS TIED NEAR THE BASE AND DIVERGING FROM THAT POINT. FULLY MOLDED FRAME. 37½ x 21 x 18. 1790. ESTATE OF H. W. WEEKS (ALSO FOLLOWING).

2354. (Right.) FULLY FLUTED FRAME. INLAY AT BASE OF THE SHIELD. 37½ x 21½ x 17½. 1790.

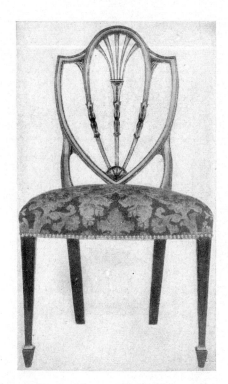

2355. THREE FEATHERS, FLUTING AT BASE OF SHIELD. SHIELD FULLY MOLDED, PLAIN LEG. 1790. H. H. ARMSTRONG, HARTFORD.

2356. (Right.) FINE SHIELD BACK. AMERICAN. MOLDED LEG AND BACK. MAHOGANY, AS ARE ALL WE HAVE SHOWN. 1790. H. W. ERVING.

2357-58. ARM AND SIDE. AMERICAN. INLAID AT CENTER, RAISED MARGINS, PLAIN LEG. 1790. HENRY V. WEIL.

 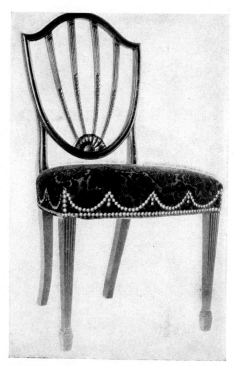

2359. Five Banisters Carved, No Stretchers. Molded Back. 1790. Formerly the Author's.
2360. (Right.) Mahogany. Connecticut. Four Carved Splats or Banisters, or Reeds. Reeded Legs, Spade Foot. 1790. H. W. Erving.

2361. Fluted Legs and Lower Back Stiles, Inlay at Base of Shield. Mahogany. Formerly the Author's.
2362. (Right.) Shield Formed by Intersecting Curves, Fluted Legs, Molded Back.

2363. A Delicately Shaped and Fully Carved Arm and Leg. A High Back. The Chair Usually Going under the Name "Martha Washington." 1795. Estate of H. W. Weeks, Framingham. 47½ x 25¼ x 20. Provenance: Groton, Massachusetts.

2364–65. Knobs for Looking-Glass, Dove on Pedestal. Early 19th C. Wm. B. Goodwin.

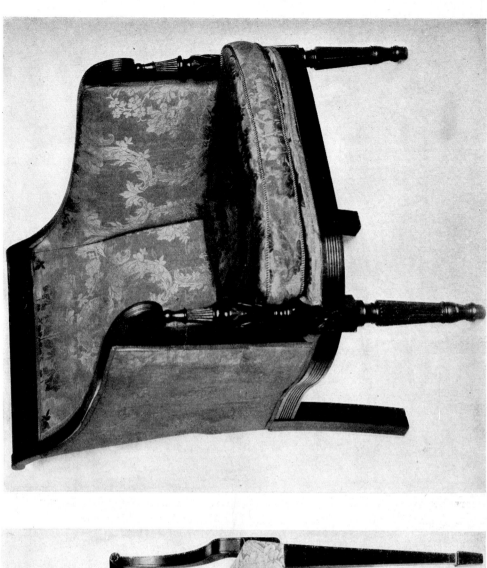

2366. A Chair Which Could Be Classed as Adam. The Banisters Terminate in Fan Carvings, Making Pointed Arches, or What Is Often Called a "Cathedral" Top. Legs Taper More Sharply than Usual. Rosettes in Front on the Arm. 1795. Sanderson Collection.

2367. (Right.) The Sofa Motive Shortened To Form a Chair. It Has the Same Incurve of the Arm, over the Post, That We Find in Many of the Sofas. The Purpose of This Is, in Part, to Conform with the Curvature of the Seat Rail. Reeded Posts and Frame, with Carving on the Post Urn, Straight Back Carved on the Roll. Rare. 1795. Edward Bringhurst, Wilmington.

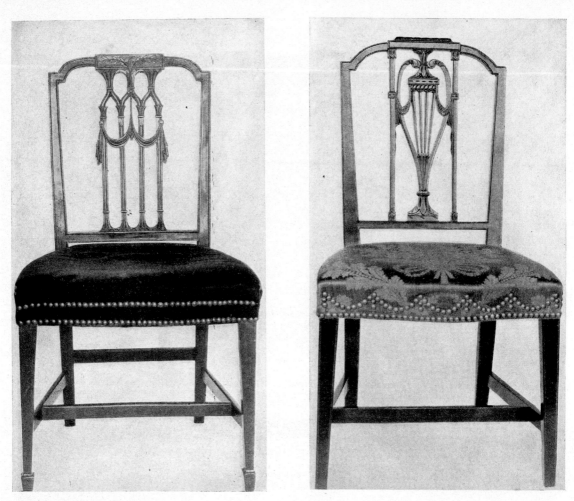

2368. FOUR BANISTERS OR SPLATS, TIED TOGETHER BY FESTOONS, AND POINTED ARCHES. 1795. HELEN T. COOKE.
2369. (Right.) HANDSOME URN BACK. 1795. THE MISSES A. AND E. P. FOSTER.

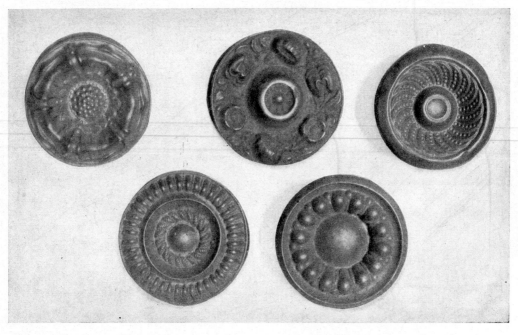

2370–74. EMPIRE KNOBS FOR CHESTS OF DRAWERS. 1825. F. A. ROBART.

2375. THE CARVING OF THE RACQUET BACK IS TOO FINE FOR EFFECTIVENESS IN A SMALL PICTURE. CHAMFERED BACK LEGS. 1795. EDWARD BRINGHURST.

2376. (Right.) A SIMILAR CHAIR, BUT WITH VARIATIONS. 1795. PENNSYLVANIA MUSEUM, PHILADELPHIA.

2377. "CATHEDRAL" BACK FORMED OF INTERSECTING CURVES. FESTOON ON TOP PANEL, FLUTED LEGS, NO STRETCHERS. 38 x 21½ x 18½. 1795. ESTATE OF HARRY W. WEEKS.

2378. (Right.) AN ARMCHAIR WITH DIAMOND PATTERN LATTICE, VERY LIGHT. 1795. FRANK A. ROBART.

2379-80. A Pair of Chairs with Urn and Scroll Back, Set in a Rectangular Form. We Have Here the Turned Leg without Reeding. 1795. Howard Reifsnyder.

2381. American Sheraton. Lightly Carved. 1795. Mrs. Francis P. Garvan.

2382. (Right.) Turned and Reeded Legs, Painted Decoration on the Finely Carved Arm. Carved Diamond Lattice Back. 1795. G. W. H. Smith.

2383. DESIGN OF DRAPERY CONNECTING THE CENTRAL PILLAR WITH THE SUPPORTING SIDE PILLARS. HUSK PENDANT. HOLLOWED SEAT. 1795. HELEN T. COOKE.

2384. (Right.) ONE OF SIX, WHICH ONCE BELONGED TO BENJAMIN FRANKLIN. 37 x 21 x 18. DELICATELY CARVED. 1785. FRANCIS D. BRINTON.

2385. A DELICATE AND TASTEFUL BACK. LIGHT CHAIR, NO STRETCHER. 1795.

2386. (Right.) GAILY AND WELL DONE WITH ROSES AND DAISIES. 1795. G. W. H. SMITH.

2387. "Cathedral" Back, Clustered Column Reeds. 1795. Formerly the Author's.

2388. (Right.) Four Detached Splats, All Carved. Fluted Back and Legs. 36½ x 21 x 18. 1795. Estate of Harry W. Weeks.

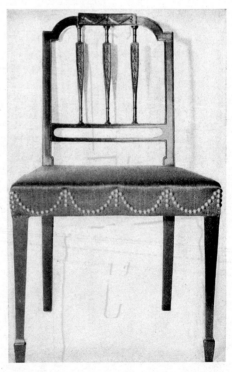

2389. Patera above Urn, Carved Back, Reeded Legs, Straight Feet. 1795. Estate of Harry W. Weeks.

2390. (Right.) Unusual Design. Three Carved Arrow Splats. Festooned Rail. Henry A. Hoffman, Barrington, R. I.

2391. Handsome Back, Carved Urn, Three Feathers. 1795. Helen T. Cooke.

2392. (Right.) Detached, Parallel Reeds, Fluted Frame. 1795. E. B. Leete Company.

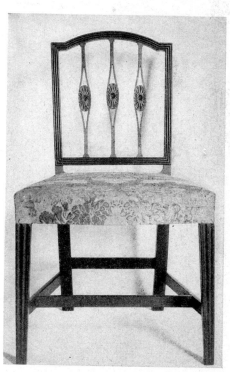

2393. Arched Back, No Carving, Very Simple. 1795. Wallace Nutting.

2394. (Right.) Massachusetts Origin, from Wayland. Shuttled Reeds with Carved Ovals. Reeded Back, Fluted Legs. 36 x 15½ x 18. 1795. Clifford S. Drake, North Hampton, N.H.

2395. Central Reeded Banister, Fan Shaped at the Top, and Crossed by a Festoon. Fluted Legs. Stretchers. 1795. Pennsylvania Museum, Philadelphia.

2396. (Right.) Lyre Back, Turned Legs. 1795. Morgan B. Brainard, Hartford.

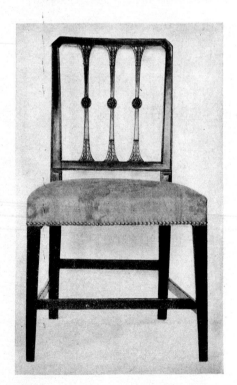

2397. Simple Back with Chamfered Corners, Three Splats with Rosettes and Spreading Carved Top. 1795. The Misses A. and E. P. Foster.

2398. (Right.) Adam-Sheraton. Turned and Reeded Back Post, and Banisters. Turned and Reeded and Carved Legs. 1795. Very Harmonious Chair. Pennsylvania Museum, Phila.

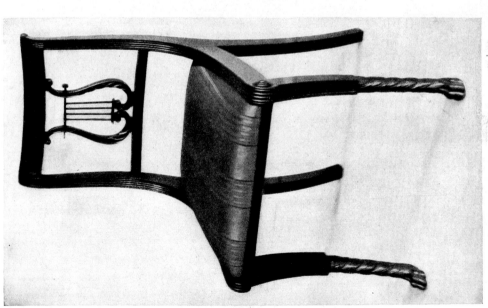

2399. Duncan Phyfe, Lyre Back, Animal Feet, Sweeping Reeded Back Rail Coming to the Front. Above the Foot the Leg Is Carved with a Hairy Shank. 1800–20. Louis G. Myers.

2400. (Right.) Cross-Legged Duncan Phyfe, Animal Feet. Rosette at Intersection of Curve and Single Stretcher Running to the Middle of Back Stretcher and Forming a T. Half-Moon Intersecting Back. Reeded Throughout. 1800–20. Mrs. Harry Horton Benkard.

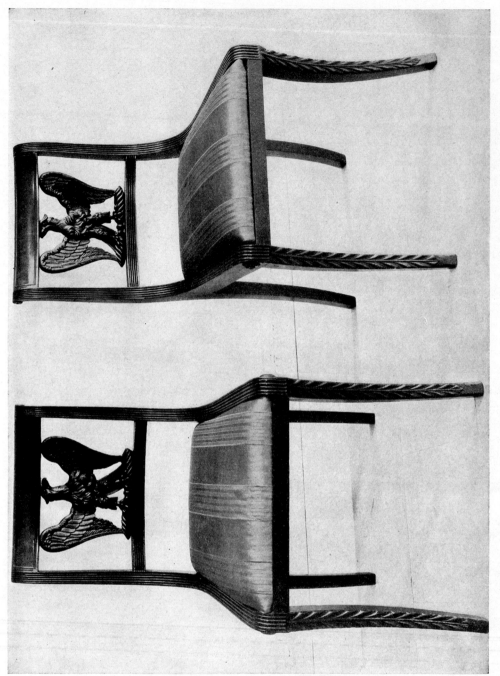

2401–02. A Pair of Phyfe Chairs with Eagle Backs, Carved So that the Eagles Face Each Other. 1800–20. Harry Wilmerding Payne.

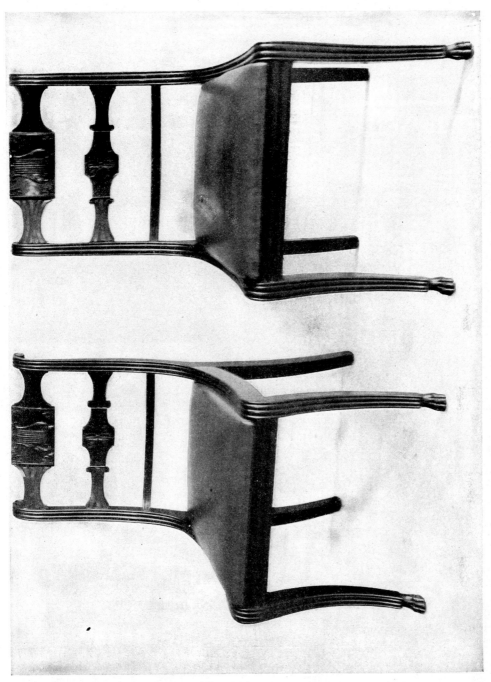

2403–04. Animal Feet Below a Sweeping Line of Leg, Seat Rail and Back. Reeded Throughout. Top Rail with a Carved Lyre; Bottom Rail with Foliage Rosette. 1800–20. Metropolitan Museum.

2405. SHERATON OR ADAM. EASTERN MASSACHUSETTS. PAINTED DECORATION. NEW CANE.
33 x 21 x 18½. 1800–20. CLIFFORD S. DRAKE, NORTH HAMPTON.

2406. (Right.) A VERY SIMILAR CHAIR WITH VARIATIONS IN THE ARM POST AND THE FEET, AND THE
DECORATION. ONE OF SIX BOUGHT IN SPAIN BY THE FIRST UNITED STATES MINISTER. OWNED BY
GEORGE GIBBONS, GRANDFATHER OF PRESENT MRS. J. S. ROOSEVELT.

2407. EMPIRE TYPE. BACK SHAPED AND CARVED. 1820–30. CHARLES P. COOLEY.
2408. (Right.) THE DETAIL OF LYRE BACK FROM NO. 2399.

2409–10. AMERICAN EMPIRE. SHARPLY ROLLED BACKS. c. 1800. EDITH RAND, NEW YORK.

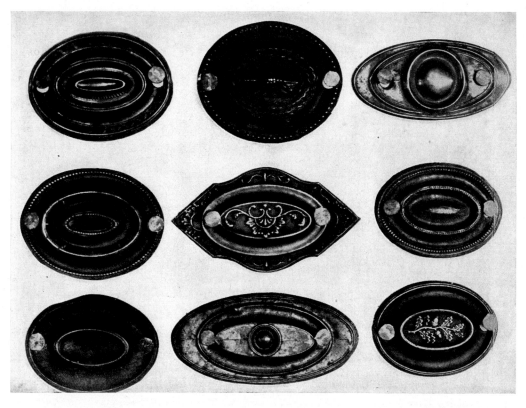

2411–19. EMPIRE HANDLE PLATES FROM THE COLLECTION OF FRANK A. ROBART.

2420–21. LATE SHERATON, IN WHITE AND GOLD. QUIVER, BOW AND ARROW. 1820. FRANK A. ROBART.

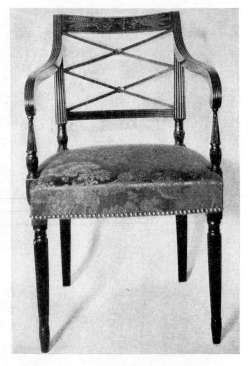

2422. ROUND-FRONT SEAT, CARVED BACK RAIL. 1800–20. MRS. HARRY HORTON BENKARD.

2423. (Right.) LATE SHERATON. MAHOGANY. DUNCAN PHYFE MODE. CARVING ON ARM, BACK STILES AND TOP RAIL. NEW ENGLAND, PROBABLY CONNECTICUT. c. 1800. H. W. ERVING.

2424–25. Side and Arm in Late Sheraton. Graceful Lines, Diamond Lattice Back. 1800–20. Frank A. Robart.

2426. Cane Seat and Cane Back Panel, Spiraled Rail and Sections of Post, with Same Effect without Spiral on the Front Seat Rail. 1800–20. Pennsylvania Museum, Phila.

2427. Late Empire with Amusing Cabriole Legs, Rather Overdone. Lyre Back. 1800–20. Samuel Wineck, Hartford.

2428-29. ARM AND SIDE, LATE SHERATON. ENGLISH. LYRE BACK. 1800-20. I. SACK.

2430-31. A PAIR OF HITCHCOCK CHAIRS WITH UNUSUAL DECORATION. CORNUCOPIA BACKS. NOTE THAT A MARK OF THIS STYLE IS THE SLIGHTLY BENT LEG IN FRONT. IRVING P. LYON, M.D., BUFFALO, N. Y.

2432-33. Arm and Side, Empire. Boldly Curved Arm, Back Carved with Rosettes and Foliage. 1810-30. Morris Berry.

2434. Late Empire, Cabriole Leg, Carved Back and Knee. 1820-40. W. A. Hitchcock.

2435. (Right.) Curly Maple, from Family of Gen. Henry Burbeck, New London. In 1848, at 95 Years, He Was the Oldest Living Revolutionary General. 1810-30. James Davidson.

2436–37. ARM AND SIDE, ANTHEMION BACK, TOPPED BY A SHELL. 1810–30. MORRIS SCHWARTZ, NEW YORK CITY.

2438–39. FROM PALMER COLLECTION. THE FORMER CHAIR IS GRACEFULLY CARVED, AND SPIRALED, AND IS THE EARLIER. 1810–30.

2440. Mahogany, Cane Seat. From Virginia. Reeded Throughout, except the Fluted Back. 1810–20. Robert T. Smith, Hartford.

2441. (Right.) American Late Sheraton, Mahogany and Satinwood. 1810–25. Metropolitan Museum.

2442–43. Set of Late Sheraton, from Middletown, Connecticut. Curly Maple. 34½ x 21 x 15. 12 Chairs. By Cabinetmaker Named Bull. His Work Includes Carving, Turning, Bending, and Fretwork. Before 1821. William B. Goodwin, Hartford.

2444. PAINTED LATE SHERATON. HOLLOWED BACK. INTRICATE LATTICE WORK. SEAT ONLY
14 INCHES FROM FLOOR. PAINTED DECORATION. $30\frac{1}{2}$ x $19\frac{1}{2}$ x 16. 1815–25. CLIFFORD S. DRAKE.
2445. (Right.) DECORATED LATE SHERATON OR EARLY HITCHCOCK. MAPLE. 1820. JAMES DAVIDSON.

2446. LATE SHERATON. TAPERED SQUARE ARM POSTS. 1810–20. RUDOLPH P. PAULY.
2447. (Right.) LATE SHERATON, FEET LIKE THE HITCHCOCK. BALL-AND-SLAT BACK AND STRETCHER.

2448-49. Painted Maple Chairs. Plymouth County, Massachusetts. 35 x 18¼ x 15¼.
1810-30. S. Prescott Fay.

2450-51. The Former a Plain Hitchcock, the Latter Decorated with an Eagle Standing on
a Globe. 1830-45. Flayderman & Kaufman.

2452. LATE EMPIRE, CARVED EAGLE BACK. 1820–30. THE UNSUPPORTED LEGS OF THE LATE EMPIRE ARE AN OBJECTIONABLE FEATURE. SAMUEL WINECK.

2453. (Right.) A VERY HIGH CHAIR, FORMERLY OWNED BY NATHANAEL BROOKHOUSE MANSFIELD, OF SALEM, NOW OWNED BY HIS GRANDDAUGHTER, MRS. ALEC THAYER. 1830–40.

2454–55. SHERATON WINDSORS. 1810–20. DECORATED. ROBERT T. SMITH.

2456–57. SHERATON WINDSOR AND EARLY HITCHCOCK. 1820–30. J. J. SULLIVAN, WOODBURY, CONNECTICUT.

2458–59. LATE SHERATON. 33 x 17½ x 16. PAINTED DECORATION. NEW YORK ORIGIN. MRS. FRANCIS P. GARVAN.

2460–61. Late Sheraton. Painted. Reeded Legs. 1820. Flayderman & Kaufman.

2462–63. Stenciled, Late Sheraton. Early 19th Century, Frank A. Robart.

2464. Late Turned Sheraton, Decorated in White and Gold. Early 19th Century.
2465. (Right.) Painted Sheraton. Turned. Rush Seat. Early 19th Century. Essex Institute.

2466. Late Arrow Back, Windsor Rocker. The Last Style before the Boston Rocker.
Early 19th Century. Pynchon Hall, Connecticut Valley Historical Society, Springfield.
2467. (Right.) The Boston Rocker, with the Famous Roll Seat and Arm. The Most Popular
Chair Ever Made, the Type Which People Use, Antiquarians Despise, and Novices Seek.
Same Owner.

2468. We Class Children's Chairs by Themselves, Going through All the Periods. Above Is the Cotton Mather High Chair. 1640–60. It Is Perhaps the Best Example of the So-Called Brewster Type, in Existence. Worcester Antiquarian Society.

The author recently heard of another just like it, burned up the road for sixty miles to reach it, offering a dealer a sum reaching into four figures, and arrived just after the owner had sawed it up for kindling wood.

2469. A TRUE CARVER CHILD'S CHAIR, WITH THREE VERTICAL AND THREE HORIZONTAL SPINDLES IN THE BACK. THE FLATTENING OF THE POSTS IS CAUSED BY THE CHAIR BEING DRAGGED ABOUT BY CHILDREN. 17TH CENTURY. WADSWORTH ATHENEUM.

2470. (Right.) A PILGRIM SLAT-BACK BABY CHAIR. HICKORY. 17TH CENTURY. BERYL DE MOTT, MILLINGTON, NEW JERSEY.

2471-73. TWO 17TH CENTURY CHILDREN'S CHAIRS, VARIANTS OF THE CARVER, AND AN EARLY 18TH CENTURY CRICKET. GEORGE McKEARIN, NEW YORK CITY.

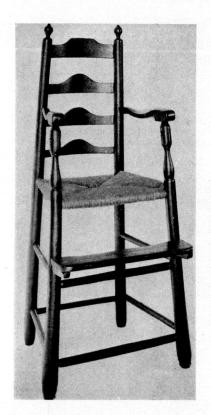

2474-75. Pennsylvania and New England High Chairs. The Former Owned by Chauncey C. Nash. The Latter Formerly Owned by the Author. 1720-50.

2476-77. A Rush Stool and Baby Corner Chair. Formerly in Ives Collection. 1700-30.

2478–79. A Dutch and an Oxbow Serpentine Child's Chair. The Former 1730. The Latter 1720. Formerly in Ives Collection.

2480–81. The Former a Slat Back with Turned Arms Projecting over the Post. The Latter a Pennsylvania Arched Slat Back. 1720–40.

2482–83. Top Rail of the Former Was Like the Lower Rails. Early 18th Century. Collection of J. Stogdell Stokes.

2484–85. The Former Owned by Chauncey C. Nash. The Latter by the Author. 1710–40.

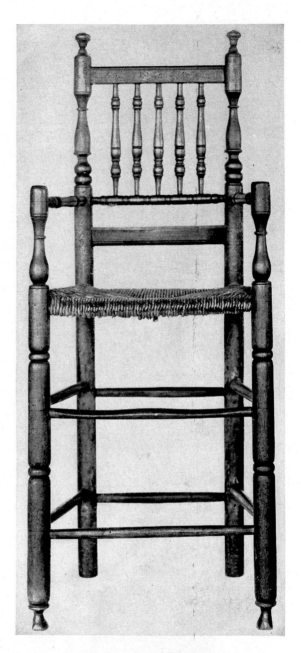

2486. Reeded Banister, Heart and Crown with an Intermediate Sausage Spindle. 1710-30. Portion of the Top Rail Missing. George Dudley Seymour.

2487. (Right.) A High Chair with Odd Spindles in the Back Which Do Not Harmonize. The Author Does Not Understand It. Formerly in Ives Collection.

Practically all the types of every period up to the latest are found in children's chairs. It seems to be only in the 19th century, that the children are neglected in this respect. There is nothing more appealing than a child's chair, and nothing that can give more delight to a child.

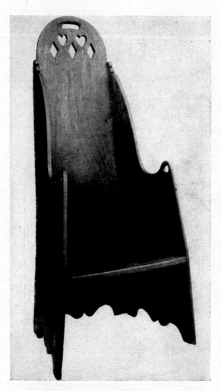

2488. A Child's Chair Decorated with Cutouts of Hearts and Diamonds. 18th Century. T. T. Wetmore.

2489. (Right.) A Reversed Back, Baby Carver, 18th Century. Was B. A. Behrend's.

2490. Child's Wing Chair Extended at Back To Render It More Stable. 18th Century. Wadsworth Atheneum.

2491. (Right.) Child's Chair, with Original Rockers. Finger Holes at Back. 18th Century. Flayderman & Kaufman.

2492–94. Children's Chairs. 18th Century. Wadsworth Atheneum. Author's Collection.

It was such an easy matter to have saved these chairs! But most have been destroyed. There is room in most attics for a relic. The reason so many chairs are cut down, of all sorts, is that a short person occurs about every third generation. The right and the left chairs above are cut down.

2495–97. A Wing Chair, a Slat Back, and a Stool. All 18th Century. Wadsworth Atheneum.

2498. Three-Slat Back, with Sausage Rungs, and Original Foot Rest. 1700–10. Wadsworth Atheneum.
2499. (Right.) Banister Back, Child's High Chair. 1720–30. Formerly the Author's.

2500–2501. Washington Brasses, End of 18th Century.

2502–04. Baby High Chairs, Two with Rolled and One with Turned Arm. Amusing Rake to the Middle Specimen. Early 18th Century. Wallace Nutting.

2505–06. A Turned Arm and a Mushroom Arm. 18th Century Baby Chairs. Rockers Not Original. Charles P. Cooley.

2507. The Earliest Type of Windsor Chair, with a Queen Anne Stretcher. Amusing Straddle. 1720. Formerly the Author's.

2508. (Right.) A High Chair with Front Spindle Suggesting the Brewster. 17th or 18th Century.

2509–10. Stamped Brasses. 1700–10. Collection of F. A. Robart.

2511. A HEART-BACK WING CHAIR, POSSIBLY FOR TWINS. 18TH CENTURY.

2512–13. (Right.) HIGH BEADED AND HOLLOWED TURNED STOOL. 18TH CENTURY. J. STOGDELL STOKES. CHILD'S ARM WINDSOR WITHOUT STRETCHERS. CUPID'S BOW TOP RAIL. TENONED ARM. ONLY THREE BACK SPINDLES. PERHAPS UNIQUE. c. 1800. J. STOGDELL STOKES.

2514–15. CHILD'S WINDSORS, A COMB BACK, AND A SIDE CHAIR WITH THE REMARKABLE NUMBER OF SEVEN SPINDLES FOR SO SMALL A PIECE. 1780–90. MRS. FRANCIS P. GARVAN.

2516. Baby's Bow Back High Chair. Meritorious Turning. Arthur Leslie Green, Newport.
2517. (Right.) Excellently Turned. The Bow Is Mortised into the Arm with a Sloping Elongation.
Both Date c. 1770. Formerly the Author's.

2518-19. Child's Love Seat and Chair. Very Appealing. 1760-80. J. Stogdell Stokes.

Windsor chairs were as a rule made with hickory spindles, and bent work. Seats were ordinarily of pine, but beyond New England they are often found of other woods. The legs were maple or birch as well as the large front spindles. They were probably first made in Philadelphia, as early as 1720, their Queen Anne stretchers indicating the period. For detailed information, too full even for this work, reference is made to the author's handbook on them.

2520. A Sheraton Back Child's Side Chair. Perhaps Unique. Late 18th Century.
2521. (Right.) A Comb Back Child's Chair, Rockers, of Course, Never Original. Second Half 18th Century. Both, J. Stogdell Stokes.

2522–23. A Bow-Back Arm, Late Turnings. A Low Baby's Chair, Bow Back. Feet Cut Off. Fourth Quarter 18th Century. Herbert G. Newton, Holyoke, Massachusetts.

2524–25. Late Baby's High Chairs. Both with Sheraton Influence, and Outside Stretchers. Probably Early 19th C. Formerly the Author's.

2526. A Baby Chair with Perfect Turning. Note the Strong Bulbous Base Legs, and Stretchers. Single Piece Bow and Arm. 1750–70. J. Stogdell Stokes.

2527. (Right.) A Late Comb Back. 1800. Formerly in the Stiles Collection, York.

2528. A Fine Comb Back. 1750–60.
Mrs. Morgan G. Bulkeley.

2529. A Side Bow Back. 1770.
The Author's.

2530. A Good Pennsylvania Baby High Chair, but Not Equal to No. 2507.
Formerly the Author's.

2531. (Right.) A Late Sheraton Bamboo. 1800–10. Arthur Leslie Green.

2532. A Good Baby Comb Back, Formerly in the Collection of Samuel Stevens,
North Andover. 1770–80.

2533. (Right.) A Tenoned Arm, Bow Back High Chair with Original Foot Rest. Moderate
Merit. Late 18th Century.

2534-37. LATE CHILD'S CHAIRS. FORMERLY THE AUTHOR'S. ROCKERS NOT
ORIGINAL. THE OTHERS ALL SHOW SHERATON INFLUENCE. EARLY 19TH CENTURY.

BEST EARLY SIDE CHAIR

BEST LARGE ARM CHAIR

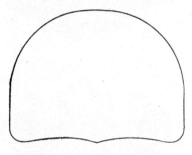

GOOD SETTEE SHAPE
PENNSYLVANIA ARM CHAIR

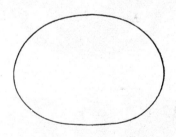

ELLIPTICAL SEAT
ARM CHAIR

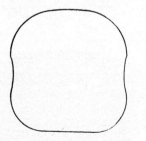

DEGRADED SIDE CHAIR

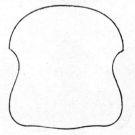

GOOD LATE SIDE CHAIR

2538-43. OUTLINES OF CHAIR SEATS FROM THE BEST TO THE WORST WINDSOR TYPE.

2544. TWIN HIGH CHAIR, PROBABLY UNIQUE. INTEREST PURELY SENTIMENTAL. 1800–10.
2545. (Right.) REMARKABLE NUMBER OF SPINDLES BUT NO EARS. STILES COLLECTION.

2546–51. BRASSES, ALL BUT ONE OF WHICH BELONG TO THE CHIPPENDALE ERA OR EARLIER. ALL
THE PATTERNS ARE UNUSUAL. A. H. EATON, COLLINSVILLE, CONNECTICUT.

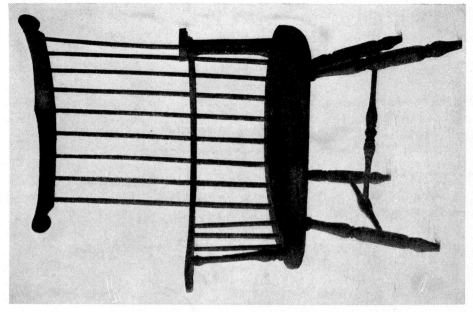

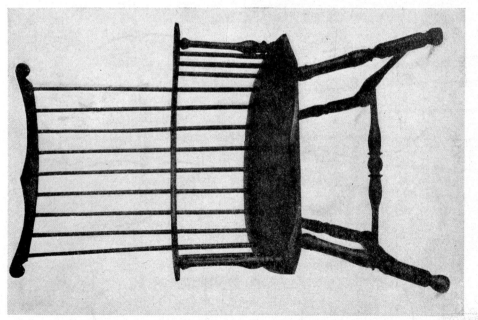

2552–53. Great Windsors, Pennsylvania Type, Shown by the Ball Feet. Queen Anne Stretchers. 1725–60. The Former Arthur Leslie Green. The Latter Formerly the Author's.

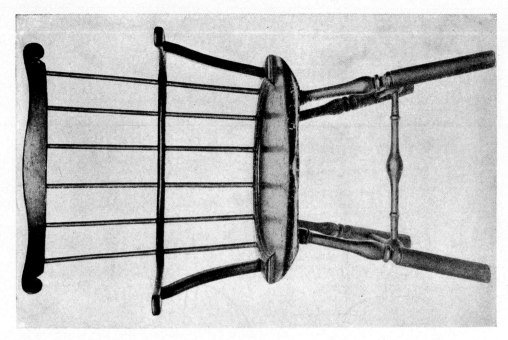

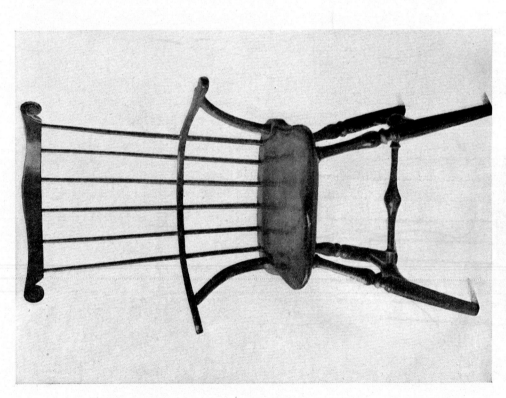

2554. An Odd, Possibly Canadian Type. More Likely American. It Suggests the Goldsmith Windsor. 1770–90.
Mrs. Annie B. Hunter, Freehold, New Jersey.

2555. (Right.) A Somewhat Similar Chair, with Curved Arm Supports.

2556. A Very Handsome Windsor with Well-Carved Arms, and Nine
Back Spindles. Pennsylvania Type. Francis Mireau.

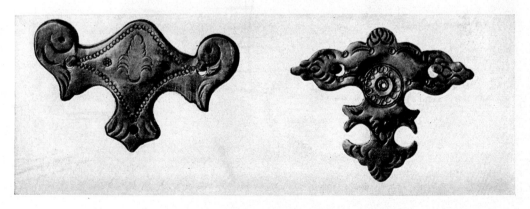

2557-58. Stamped. 1700. Frank A. Robart.

2560. Highest Example of Early Braced Bow Back. Once the Author's.

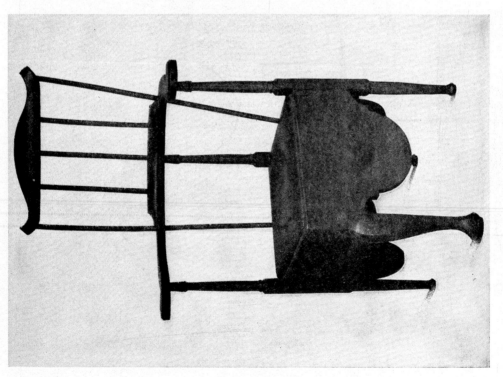

2559. Corner Chair, Comb-Back Motive. 1720. Top Shows Windsor Origins. Met. Mus.

2561–62. The Former a Fine Type of Three-Back Waved Comb. Wm. B. Montague. The Latter Very High Back, Bent Arm.
1760. J. Stogdell Stokes.

2563. An Eleven-Spindle Comb Back. 1760–80. Formerly in
Stiles Collection.

2564–65. Stamped Brasses. 1700–10. Frank A. Robart.

2566. Extra Stretcher in Back. Arm Curved in Strong Forward Sweep. Date Difficult To Fix. This Arm Is Found in Pennsylvania. Arthur Leslie Green, Newport.

2567. (Right.) Early Philadelphia Type, Low Back with Wide Splice. Deeply Shaped Seat. 1740–50. Wayside Inn.

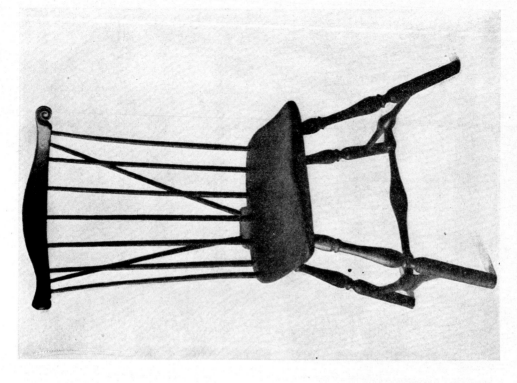

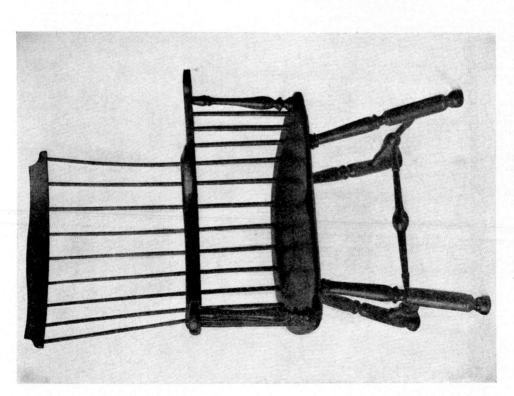

2568. Pennsylvania Comb Back, with Cropped Ears. A Good Shape. 1740–60. Formerly the Author's.
2569. (Right.) Built without Turned Side Posts. A Curious Variant. Late 18th Century. Was the Late J. B. Kerfoot's, Freehold, New Jersey.

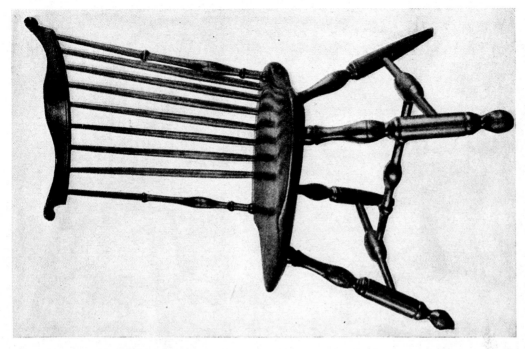

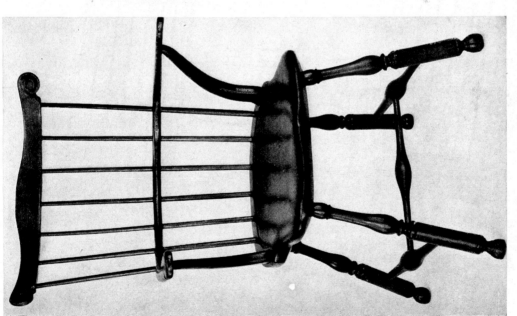

2570. Pennsylvania Comb Back, Moderate Size, Forward Swept Arm Support. Mid 18th Century. J. Stogdell Stokes.

2571. (Right.) Unusual Side Chair in Pennsylvania Turning. The Side Chairs in This Type Are More Rare Than the Arm. Mid 18th Century. Formerly the Author's.

2572–73. A Page of J. Stogdell Stokes' Windsors. These Two Have the One-Piece Bow and Arm. The Former Is the Quainter, and the Latter Has the Better Lines, and Very Excellent Base Turnings, Both in the Feet and the Front Arm Spindle. This Type Is Found in New England and the Delaware Valley. Latter Half 18th Century.

2574–75. The Former a Beautifully Turned Pennsylvania Pattern; the Latter with Unique Side Posts on the Comb. 1740–80.

2576–77. Both, J. Stogdell Stokes. The Former the Highest Class Turning in the Fan-Back Chair; the Latter a Less Bold Turning, but with Braced Back and Plain Comb. 1760–80.

2578. Unique, Fore and Aft Stretcher, and Cupid's-Bow. 1760–80. J. Stogdell Stokes.

2579. (Right.) The Back Stiles Suggest the Dutch Day Bed Pattern. Found in Southern Massachusetts. 31 x 19 x 16. Maple and Oak. Mary M. Sampson.

2580. A Bent Arm with Carved Knuckle, without the Application of the Usual Thickened End. Pennsylvania Turning. 1740–70. J. Stogdell Stokes.

2581. (Right.) A Sport. The Humorous Low Comb Attached to a Secondary Back Applied to a Bent Back. Finger Carving. 1760–80. J. Stogdell Stokes.

2582–83. The Former with Suggestions of the Bamboo Turning. A High Back, and Bent Carved Arm. The Latter a Sawed and Spliced Back, the Arm Ramped Outward. Dates Respectively About 1790 and 1770. J. Stogdell Stokes.

2584-85. WELL TURNED, BOTH IN FRONT ARM SPINDLES AND LEGS AND STRETCHERS. LATTER
HALF 18TH CENTURY. FOSTER DISINGER, BINGHAMTON.

This type of chair has always been popular because it is very light. Great difficulty was experienced by breaking of the arm at the turn, so that those that are whole are much sought for.

2586. A WELL-PROPORTIONED, GRACEFUL COMB BACK. PENNSYLVANIA. 1740-60. FORMERLY STILES COL.

2587. (Right.) SIMILAR TO THE PRECEDING, BUT WITH BETTER STRETCHERS. SAME OWNER.

2588. A J. Stogdell Stokes' Page. Pennsylvania Chair with Bent Arm Support. Light Knuckle Arms.
2589. (Right.) The First of an Interesting Class, Which the Author Has Named Tenoned Arm. The Object of This Construction Was To Do Away with the Arm Rail behind the Back. The Chair Is Handsome, but the Back Post Requires To Be a Good Size. Strong Outward Ramp.

2590–91. Good Comb Backs, the Former Perhaps the More Graceful and Conventional. Perhaps Lost an Inch of Its Feet. The Second Has an Extraordinarily High Comb, and the Amazing Number of Eleven Spindles. Extremely Rare. Date for All 1750–80.

2592. An Eleven-Spindle Back, with No Less than Six Short Spindles on Each Side. The Comb, However, Is a Disappointment, Possibly It Was Intended to Be Finished.

2593. (Right.) A Comb Back That Is an Anomaly, with an Extra but Good Stretcher in Front.

2594. A New Jersey Specimen with Unique Stretcher Arrangement, and Three Legs. Evidently the Comb Was Not Long Enough for the Spindles.

2595. (Right.) Comb Like Back Splice on a Low Back, Spindles Indicate Late 18th Century. Chair Entirely Walnut. All This Page, J. Stogdell Stokes.

2596. A Very Light, Graceful Chair with Dainty Turnings. It Is Probable that Such Chairs Were Not Attempted at First. From Cape Cod. 45 x 23 x 16. Rudolph P. Pauly.

2597. (Right.) A Comb Back with Up-Tilted Ears, and Arm Rail. J. Stogdell Stokes.

2598. Somewhat Heavy Turnings, Perhaps Made Away from Centers. A Very Low Back.

2599. (Right.) Lofty Bow, with a Concave Turn on the Lower Part, Carved Knuckles. Both 1750. J. Stogdell Stokes.

2600–01. Four Chairs of Mr. Stokes. They Are All Fan Backs. The Term Applies to the Side Chairs with Combs. The First Is Well Turned with a Specially Good Back Post, and Plain Ears. The Second Is in the Bamboo Turning, Cross Stretcher, One Running through Another.

2602. A Hollow Seat with Crude Turnings. The Extraordinary Back Is Captivating from Its Odd Design. We Might Call This a Shovel Seat. The Bob Tail or Extension Is One Piece with the Rest of the Seat, as Always in Side Chairs.

2603. (Right.) A Good Braced Fan Back. All, Except the Bamboo, 1750–80.

2605. A Cutaway Arm, with Gouge Turning. 1770–90. Wayside Inn.

2604. A Tenoned-Arm Bow Back. Rare. 1760. C. C. Littlefield.

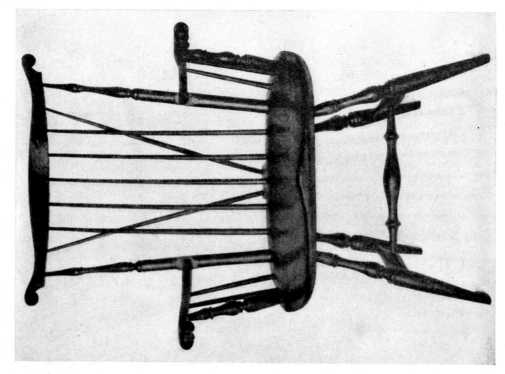

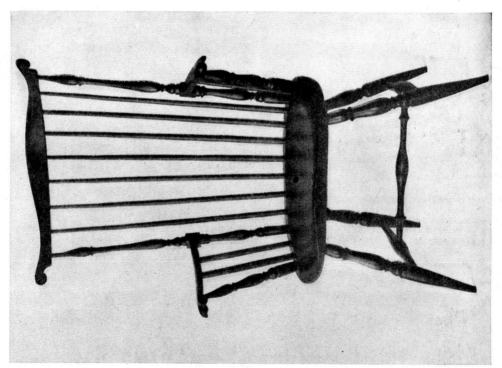

2606-07. CHAIRS FORMERLY THE AUTHOR'S, WITH TENONED ARM, THE SECOND WITH A BRACE. VERY GOOD. 1760-90.

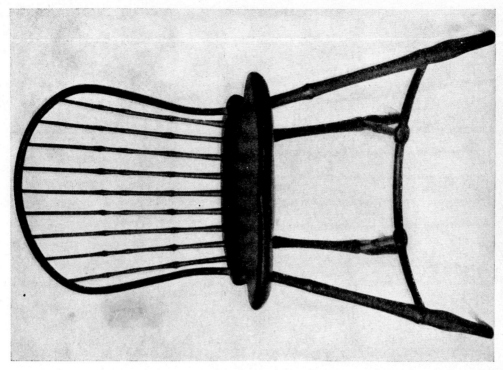

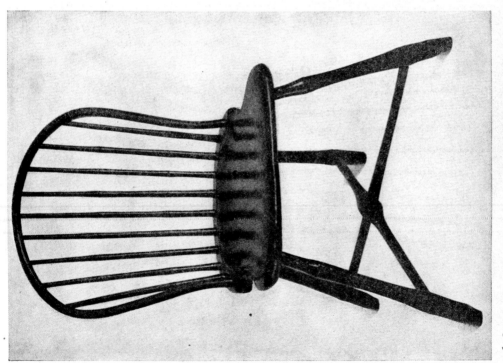

2608-09. THE FORMER WITH CROSS STRETCHERS, THE LATTER WITH BENT OR SPOKE STRETCHER. THE LATTER IS THE BEST CHAIR OF THE KIND THE AUTHOR HAS SEEN. LATE 18TH CENTURY. J. STOGDELL STOKES.

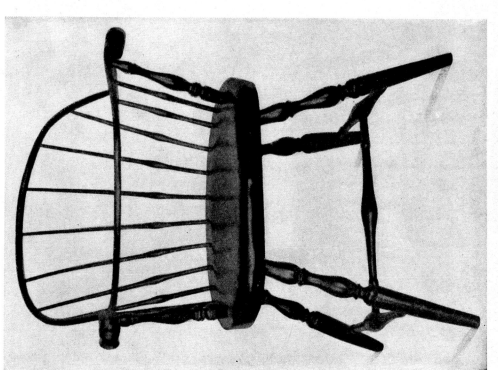

2610. The Commonest Shape in Bow Backs. Seat Shallow. Carved Arms Better than Usual. The Bulb in the Spindles Shows That in Early Times the Spindle Was Whittled, and It Was Natural To Leave This Section Larger. 1770–90.

2611. (Right.) Entering upon the Much-Sought Writing Armchair. Two Horns on the Seat. A Drawer for Stationery. Bamboo Turnings Below, and on Large Spindles. Formerly the Author's.

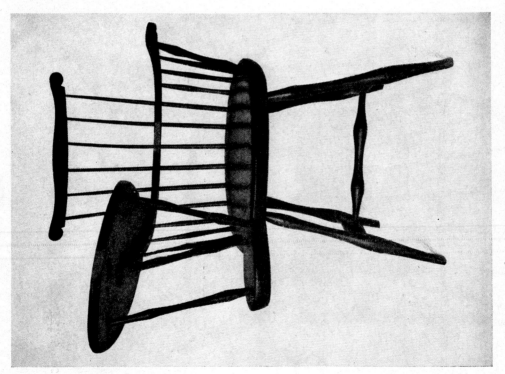

2612. A Writing Arm without a Drawer, Bamboo Turnings. It Shows the Construction Very Well.

2613. (Right.) A Fine Writing Arm. Fat Turnings of the Vase Type. Table Slanting for Convenience. Comb Set to One Side for the Same Purpose. Formerly the Author's.

2614. A Light Writing Arm, with Two Drawers. Not the Best Style, because the Bent Arm Does Not Allow the Table Top to Be Met by the Splice of a Sawed Arm.

2615. (Right.) A Writing Arm, with a Left Leg Larger than the Others. Comb Too Short, Probably Not of Set Purpose. Both Formerly the Author's.

2616–17. Two Views of a Rare and Important Windsor, Tenoned Arm, with a Comb Such as Is Used on a Spliced Sawed Arm. While Not Graceful, It Indicates an Evolution. 1740–60. J. Stogdell Stokes.

2618–19. Heavy Writing Arm with a Bow Back instead of the Usual Comb, Good Drawers, Two Horns. A Remarkable Bracket Toggle Joint Lamp Is Attached to the Arm.

2620. A Fine Writing Arm Showing Distinctly the Shape of the Two Tongues. Extraordinarily High Comb. Found in Connecticut. 48 x 47 x 32. Rudolph P. Pauly.

2621. (Right.) A Writing Arm, Perhaps Unique Since It Is Attached to What Would Otherwise Have Been a Side Chair. Fuessenich Collection.

2622. A Low-Back Writing Arm, with No Less than Three Drawers. Date of All 1760-80. J. Stogdell Stokes.

2623. A Light Bamboo-Turned Writing Chair, with a Good Carved Arm. J. Stogdell Stokes.

2624. (Right.) A New England Writing Arm with an Abbreviated and Scrolled Comb. Hickory and Pine, as Are Most Windsors. Mrs. Francis P. Garvan.

2625. A Light Writing Arm. The Arm Is an Adaptation, Swiveling by a Detachable Thumb Nut over the Ordinary Arm. J. Stogdell Stokes.

2626. (Right.) A Broad-Based Writing Arm, with Candle Slide. Bow Back, One-Piece Arm and Bow. Shallow Drawer under the Seat. W. A. Hitchcock, Farmington.

2627. A WELL-TURNED LOW-BACK, WRITING ARM, WITH SHARP TURNS AT THE BACK OF THE SEAT. MRS. FRANCIS P. GARVAN.

2628. (Right.) A WRITING ARM, WITH CARVED KNUCKLE, AND THREE DRAWERS. THE TWO DRAWERS UNDER THE ARM MOVE IN DIFFERENT DIRECTIONS. MORRIS SCHWARTZ, NEW YORK. DATE OF THE TWO 1760–80.

2629. A WRITING ARM IN THE LATE SHERATON STYLE. 1800. FORMERLY IN STILES COLLECTION.

2630–31. (Right.) BEAUTIFULLY TURNED SPECIMEN, WITH AN EARLY BRASS CANDLESTICK ON THE SLIDE, PULLED OUT ESPECIALLY TO HOLD IT. NOTICE THE SIDEWISE CONSTRUCTION OF THE COMB, AS THE BACK OF A PERSON WOULD SWING IN ITS DIRECTION. JOHN H. BUCK, HARTFORD, CONNECTICUT.

2632. A Small Drawer, Perhaps Intended for Smoker's Material. The Arm Perhaps Large Enough To Hold Drinking Glass. Small Three-Spindle Comb. Former Stiles Collection.

2633. (Right.) A Bow-Back Side Chair with Ears. A Very Odd Affair, but not Unique.

2634. A Fan Back, with an Even Dozen Spindles, Including the Turned Posts. Sanderson Col.

2635. (Right.) A Chair with Canadian Suggestions and Three Backs. The Author Has Not Examined It. A Third Back Would Bear Examination, but the Spindles Run Through.

2636-37. The Former, a Bow Back, Unusually Drawn in at the Bottom of the Bow, and
with a Straddling Brace. The Latter, with a Quick Change in the Turning of the Legs.

2638. A Fan Back with Small Ears. This Ear Is Occasional in Pennsylvania.

2639. (Right.) A Pennsylvania, with a Seat Rather Wide for the Depth, Lacking a Side
Ramp. Blunt Arrow Turnings, Serpentine Back. Small Carved Ears. Only Five Spindles.
This Page All 1750-80. J. Stogdell Stokes.

2640–41. The First with an Amusingly High Stretcher. Not a Large Chair. The Second with Its Seat Shaped to the Extreme Saddle Contour. Frank A. Robart.

2642. A Prim High Back. Thick Arm. Legs Raked Less than Usual. 1770–90. J. Stogdell Stokes.

2643. (Right.) Beautifully Turned, Including the Front Spindle. Well-Shaped Bow. Necking to Small Dimensions, and Enlarging Like a Mortise. 1760–70. Foster Disinger.

2644-45. All on This Page, J. Stogdell Stokes. About 1770. The First Finely Turned with a Hollow Taper. Often Called the Rhode Island Pattern. The Second, Carved Ear, with Usual Block To Assist in Forming It.

2646. A Peculiar Upward Sweep to the Arm. It Was Difficult Enough To Make a Square Turn, and This Special Effort Seems Superfluous.

2647. (Right.) Extremely Rare. Comb Formed by Running through a Bow. A Prim Back.

2648. A STOKES PAGE. VERY GOOD TURNINGS. A SLIGHT WIDENING ON THE FRONT OF THE ARM.
1760–70.

2649. (Right.) A BOW WITH SHARP TURNS AT THE CORNERS. THIS CHAIR PROVES THE WIDESPREAD NATURE OF THE CHAIR INDUSTRY. OTHERWISE WE COULD NOT HAVE SO MANY PATTERNS.

2650. A CUPID'S-BOW FAN BACK. FEET SOMEWHAT CUT OFF, HOLLOW TAPER TURNED. 1770–90.

2651. (Right.) A VERY LOW FAN BACK. IN CASE CARVING IS TO BE OMITTED THIS IS GOOD.

2652. A Stokes Page. A Low Back. Well-Turned Stretcher, Feet Missing. Pennsylvania. Probably Before 1750.

2653. (Right.) An Extremely Low Comb. Carving on Arm Done without Adding Block. 1770-90.

2654. Well Turned. Arm Tenoned into the Bow. Rare. 1760-80.

2655. (Right.) Cutaway Arm. Supposed To Have Made the Back Easier. At the Same Time the Maker Avoided the Necessity of Bending. Note the Deep Cutting Away of the Seat.

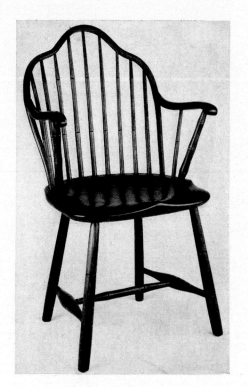

2656. A Serpentine Arm, with a Tenoned Bow. Bamboo Style. c. 1800.

2657. (Right.) Very High Stretchers. Purpose Unknown. Late 18th Century.

2658. The Bow Was Started as if To Sweep Around to the Arm Rail. An Amusing, but Not Elegant Example.

2659. (Right.) Sheraton Type. Whenever the Rungs Are on the Outside, We Have Lost Real Windsor Character. All on This Page J. Stogdell Stokes.

2660. Sheraton Back with Secondary Comb, the Spindles of Which Are Bent. Unusual. Late.
2661. (Right.) While the Rockers Here Are Believed by the Writer To Be Subsequent to the Making of the Chair, He May Not Be Right. Both Chairs c. 1800. J. Stogdell Stokes.

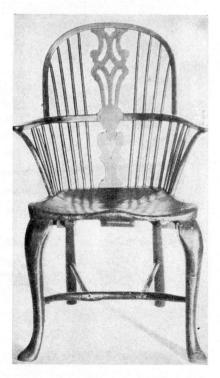

2662. A One-Piece Bow and Arm, with Rolled Knuckle, Bob-Tail Back, Braced. J. Stogdell Stokes.
2663. (Right.) An English Type, with a Pierced Splat, Cabriole Legs, and Spoke Stretchers. This Style Also Found in Canada. Mrs. Alexander Armstrong, Baltimore.

2664–65. New England Comb Backs, One with Well-Shaped Seat, One with a Rounded Seat. The Former, Metropolitan Museum. The Latter, Formerly the Author's.

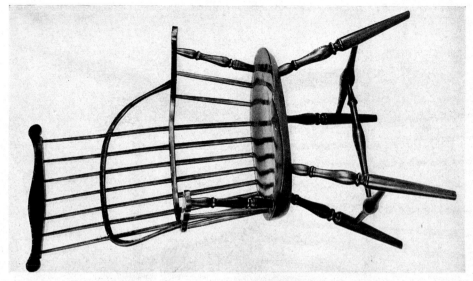

2666. Rare, Three Back. Fine, Boldly Carved Arm. Well Turned. Apologies to the Owner, Whose Name Has Been Lost.

2667. (Right.) Seven Spindles Running through the Three Backs, All without Bending. J. Stogdell Stokes.

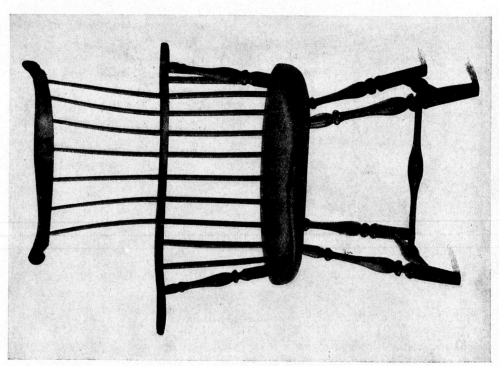

2668–69. COMB BACKS, ONE WITH CARVED ARM, THE OTHER WITHOUT. SEAT SHALLOW. ONE HAS FLARED SPINDLES IN COMB, WHEREAS THE OTHER HAS STRAIGHT SPINDLES. 1760–80. FORMERLY THE AUTHOR'S.

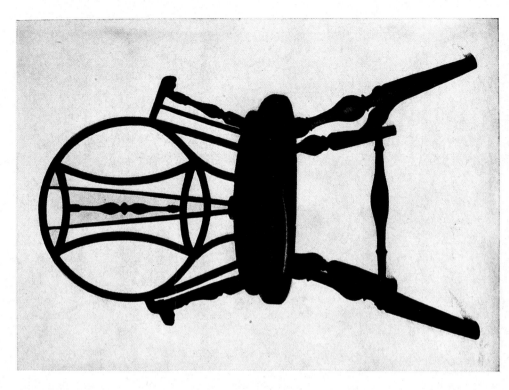

2670. SHOWN AS AN EXAMPLE OF THE GRACELESS ARM, AND BOW AND LEG OF THE ENGLISH WINDSOR. ALL OF THESE MEMBERS LACK CHARACTER. THE SPLAT WAS GOOD IN STYLE, BUT NOT COMFORTABLE. FORMERLY THE AUTHOR'S.

2671. (Right.) A CHAIR WITH A ROUND BACK, FINE TURNING, BUT WITH OTHER ELEMENTS WHICH PUT IT IN A CLASS BY ITSELF. A TENONED ARM. WILLIAM F. HUBBARD, HARTFORD.

2672. A Good Bow Back, with Nine Spindles, the Bulbs of Which Are Long and Obviously Whittled. 1760–70. J. Stogdell Stokes.

2673. (Right.) A Late Turning. Interesting from the Cross Stretcher. 1790–1800.

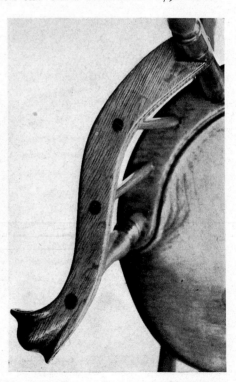

2674. Rockers Not Original. Three Backs with Unusual Comb. Sanderson Collection.

2675. (Right.) Shows the Shape of a Good Arm, and the Method of the Carving on a Tenoned Chair. Henry A. Hoffman, Barrington, Rhode Island.

2676. A Tenoned Arm with a Little Turning in the Middle of the Back, Just Where It
Ought Not To Be for Comfort. Perhaps It Might Have Been a Watchman's Chair.
1750–70. Arthur Leslie Green, Newport.

2677. (Right.) A Tenoned Arm with Rockers Which Are Not Original, and Five Spindles
instead of Seven, as in the Previous Example. Formerly the Author's.

2678. Small Ears, Odd Turnings, Braced Back.

2679. (Right.) Bold Turnings, Fan Back Braced. Good Example. Both Formerly the Author's.

2680. A, B. Mahogany, Corner Chairs. The Second Is Most Rare, Having Square Enlarged Feet. The First Has a Carved Raised Edge and Drake Feet. Thorpe's Antique Shop, Plainfield, N. J.

2681. A, B. Maple Chairs of the Walnut Period, Molded Backs. The Side Chair Had Spanish Feet Which Are Partially Worn Away. Upholstery New. 1700–10. Benjamin A. Jackson, Wickford, Rhode Island.

2682. A Straighter and Stiffer Back than Usual. Ears Not Carved. It Has Been Suggested that the Ear Was for the Purpose of Hanging a Betty Lamp, While One Read.

2683. (Right.) A Very Rare Chair. Spindles Run through. Wayside Inn.

2684. A Late Chair with Sheraton Influence in the Back. Some Have Called These Openings Dovecotes. Now or Formerly, Wayside Inn.

2685. (Right.) A Boldly Turned Rhode Island Type, with Nine Spindles in the Fan Back. Formerly the Author's.

2686. An Unusual, but Good Turning, Perhaps Rhode Island. The Spiral of the Ear Is a Wide, Hollowed Shape. Formerly the Author's.

2687. (Right.) Attractive Small Bow Back without Carving. It Has Grace and Good Taste. Good Flare of Spindles, but Should Have Had One More on Each Side.

2688. A Large Nine-Spindle Comb Back, with a Waved Stretcher. Not Over-Graceful.

2689. (Right.) Seven Spindles in the Comb, but without Very Much Style. Good Small Carved Arm. Formerly the Author's.

2690. A Light, Small Comb Back with Graceful Comb. Arthur Leslie Green, Newport.

2691. (Right.) A Very Perfect Type for a Light Side Chair with a Fan. A Good Taper of the Legs, and Fine Harmony between Them and the Back Stiles. Mrs. M. E. Welles, Hartford.

2692. A Fine Example of a Bamboo-Turned Armchair. It Is Graceful in All Respects. The Author Challenges, However, the Tenoning of an Arm into so Small a Space.

2693. (Right.) Heavy Carved Arm. Pennsylvania. Both Were Author's.

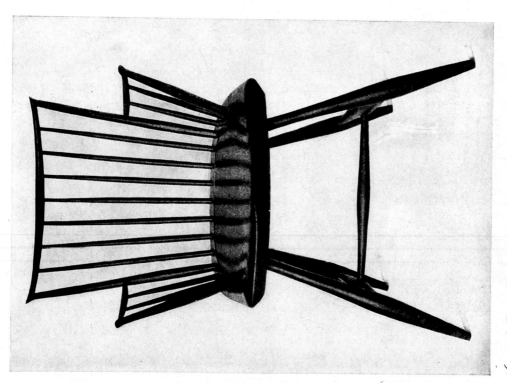

2694. A Duck-Bill Windsor, Which Has Its Name from the Pointed Meeting of the Vertical and Horizontal Members of the Arm. Of Course, the Turnings Are Late, and the Seat Has Not Much Shaping, but the Effect Is Good. William F. Hubbard, Hartford.
2695. (Right.) Sheraton Square-Back Arm. The Seat Is Not Cut Away to a Feather Edge as in Best Examples. The Back Post Is Enlarged Sufficiently To Take a Tenon. All Bamboo Turning. Both These Chairs About 1800.

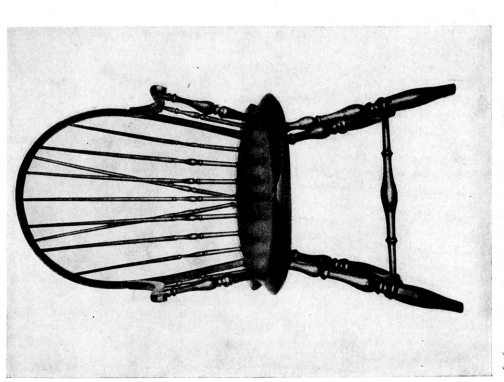

2696. A Mahogany Arm, Rhode Island Chair. An Inch Gone from Feet. Turned Spindles. In Early Chairs Spindles Could Not Be Turned, as the Back Rest Had Not Been Invented for the Lathe. Moderate Size.

2697. (Right.) A Well-Turned Bow Back with Brace. When Back Is Braced, the Number of Spindles Is Usually Seven.

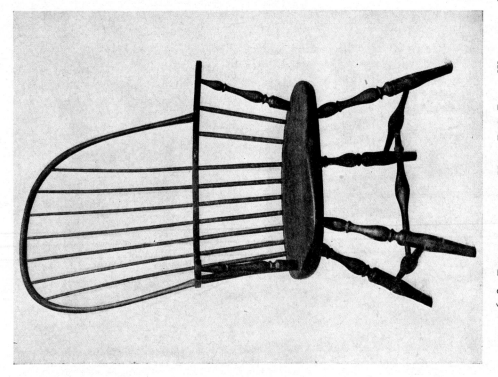

2698. Extraordinarily High Bow Back, Which the Author Has Called a Spinster Chair. Metropolitan Museum.
2699. (Right.) Conventional Bow Back, Which Has a Shallow Seat, Not More than 12 or 13 Inches. Both Formerly the Author's.

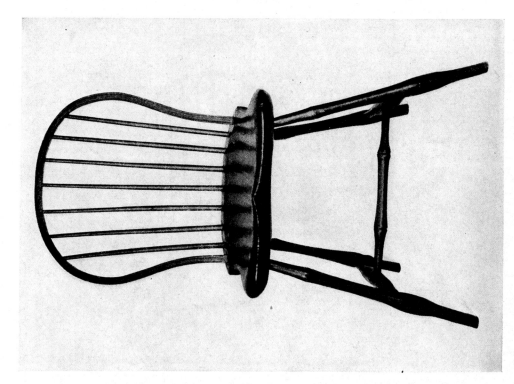

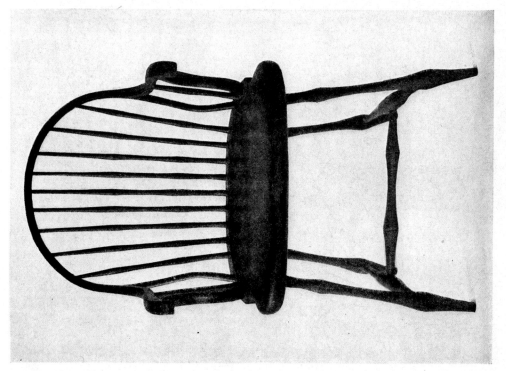

2700. Bamboo, with Ogee Arm Supports. Odd Quick Bent in the Bow.

2701. (Right.) Well-Shaped Seat, Bamboo Turning Below, Plain Above. A Well-Shaped Bow, Bamboo Type. Both Formerly the Author's.

2702–03. ROCKERS ORIGINAL IN NEITHER. THE FIRST HAS THE ARROW
SPINDLES, AND THE PIGEONHOLE BACK. THE SECOND HAS FINE LINES
ABOVE, EXCEPT FOR THE TURNINGS. BOTH FORMERLY THE AUTHOR'S.

2704–05. SHERATON WINDSORS, OF GRACEFUL TYPE WITH BAMBOO TURNINGS EXCEPT FOR THE
OUTER FRAME OF THE BACK. MR. MIREAU, DOYLESTOWN TAVERN, PENNSYLVANIA.

2706. Joint Stool with Drawer, Very Rare. Feet Lost. 1680–1700. Wadsworth Atheneum.

2707. Joint Stool with Vertical Legs. Perhaps American. 1670–90. Wadsworth Atheneum.
2708. (Right.) Stool Raking in All Directions, Feet Lost. Turnings Fine. 1690. Fuessenich Col.

2709. Rare or Unique, American Stool. Feet Lost. Long Enough for Two People. Very Early Turnings. 1660–80. Mary M. Sampson.

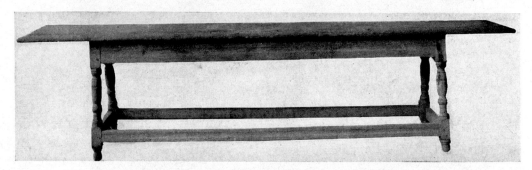

2710. A Long Form. In America the Term Is Bench. 20 x 81 x 11½. The Wide Overhang Would Seem To Have Invited Disaster. Very Rare. 1680–1700. Rhode Island School of Design.

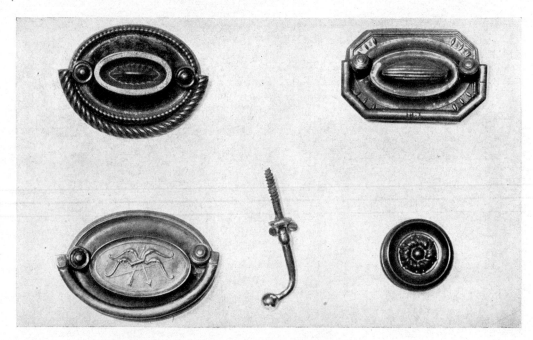

2711–15. Sheraton and Empire Handles. No. 2712 Is an Ear of Corn; No. 2713 Consists of Two Bows and Two Arrows; No. 2714 Is a Brass Hook of the Same Period; No. 2715 Was in Use About 1810.

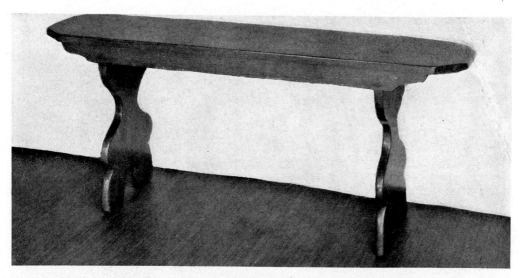

2716. TRESTLE STOOL, MORTISED THROUGH THE TOP AND SIDE RAILS. LATE 17TH OR EARLY 18TH CENTURY. HOWARD REIFSNYDER.

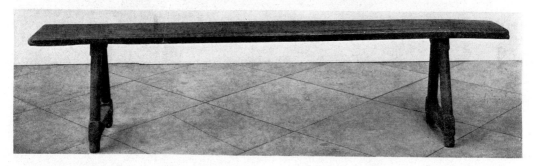

2717. PEAR WOOD BENCH, WITH TURNED, RAKED LEGS, AND FRAMED STRETCHERS. LATE 17TH OR EARLY 18TH CENTURY. J. STOGDELL STOKES.

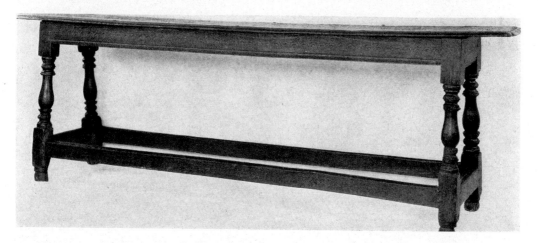

2718. BENCH WITH STAMPED DESIGN ON THE BEADED RAIL. A SIMILAR STAMP IS FOUND ON SOME LEATHER CHAIRS. THE BEST LONG FORM DISCOVERED IN THIS COUNTRY. 1680–1700. J. STOGDELL STOKES.

2719. JOINT STOOL FOUND NEAR GUILFORD, WITH TURNINGS PRECISELY LIKE A WAINSCOT CHAIR
IN THE SAME TOWN. HEIGHT 14 INCHES. LEGS VERTICAL. PERHAPS UNIQUE.
WADSWORTH ATHENEUM.

2720–21. JOINT STOOLS, THE FORMER LIGHTLY, AND THE LATTER HEAVILY TURNED. AND WITH
SLIGHT CARVING. BOTH HAVE LOST FEET. THE SECOND EXAMPLE IS MORE GENERALLY SEEN
IN ENGLAND. 1660–1690. DWIGHT BLANEY.

2722. Neatly Turned Stool, Legs Raking One Way Only. Most Stools Like This Have the So-Called Stone Mold on the Bottom of the Frame. 1680–1700. J. Stogdell Stokes.
2723. (Right.) Stool with Odd Turnings, a Ring Balanced by Two Balls, with a Small Fillet Above. Rare. Maple. 1680–1700. Henry A. Hoffman, Barrington, Rhode Island.

2724. Well-Turned High Stretcher Stool. Double Pinned at Each Mortise. 1680–1700.
2725. (Right.) Joint Stool, Legs Raking One Way, as Usual. 1680–1700. Fuessenich Collection.

2726. Feet Lost, Strong Rake One Way. Formerly Miss C. M. Traver's, New York.
2727. (Right.) Heavy Early Turning. Top Not Original. 1670–90 for Both.

2728. Maple Stool, Original Top, with Oak Pins. Feet
Lost. 1680–90. Wadsworth Atheneum.

2729. QUAINT, IN ORIGINAL CONDITION. AN ARTICLE LIKE THIS WOULD HAVE BEEN SCORNED TWENTY YEARS AGO. NOW IT HAS LARGE VALUE. C. 1680. FUESSENICH COLLECTION.

2730. (Right.) WALNUT "SQUARE" TURNING, SCROLLED SKIRT ALL AROUND. BUILT LIKE, AND DOUBTLESS TO MATCH, A TABLE. C. 1700. J. STOGDELL STOKES.

2731. GATE-LEG TURNING. OVAL TOP. COULD BE COUNTED A SMALL TABLE. 1690–1710. FUESSENICH COLLECTION.

2732. (Right.) HIGH STOOL, MOLDED, AS OFTEN, ON THE FRAME AND ON THE STRETCHER. CHAMFERED CORNERS. C. 1700. FLAYDERMAN & KAUFMAN.

2733. ALL TURNED STOOL, WELL-WORN STRETCHERS. 1700–1720. HORATIO H. ARMSTRONG, HARTFORD.

2734. (Right.) 17TH CENTURY TURNINGS. WADSWORTH ATHENEUM, HARTFORD.

The American stool is ordinarily in maple. If in oak, it needs careful second inspection, before determining its American character.

2735. A PERFECT LITTLE MAPLE STOOL, RAKING IN ALL DIRECTIONS. FOUND IN MAINE. SIZE OF FRAME AT THE STRETCHERS, 13½ x 16½. 1680–1700. WADSWORTH ATHENEUM.

Stools were usually from 20 to 22 inches high, even when worn down somewhat. For such the term stool-table, is good.

2736-37. Pair of Unique Cross-Stretcher Stools. Newburyport. Basswood. Turning Like That of Chairs of Late 17th Century. Covers Are Old, but Later. Wadsworth Atheneum.

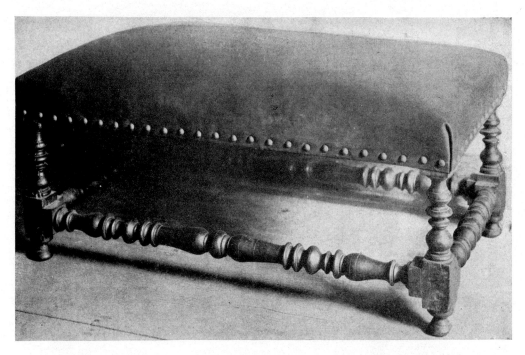

2738. Long, Well-Turned Stool. 1680–1700. Chauncey C. Nash.

2739. High-Stretcher Squab Stool. Designed, of Course, for a Cushion. Note the Stretchers on One Side Only, Leaving the Other Side Free To Draw in the Feet. About the Height of a Chair. 1680–1700. Was Brooks Reed's.

2740. Attractive Stool with Ogee Scrolls on Skirt. Repeated on Stretchers. Small Drawer. 1690–1710. J. Stogdell Stokes.

2741. (Right.) Unusual Turning. Probably Pennsylvanian, About 1690. J. Stogdell Stokes.

2742. Purely English, Bulbous Turned Stool, with Flemish
Scrolled Stretchers. Late 17th Century. I. Sack.

2743-44. Owned by Benjamin A. Jackson, Wickford, Rhode Island. Left: Queen Anne
Type, Very Rare in America. Walnut. Right: Cherry with Middle and High Stretchers.
Dates Respectively 1730 and 1690.

2745-46. Mahogany. Left: Chippendale, Fluted, with Brackets. Very Rare. 17 x 20 x 19.
Right: Queen Anne, Carved Knee. 18 x 22 x 17, Heights Being Given First. 1760 and 1750
Respectively. Edward Bringhurst, Wilmington.

2747. QUEEN ANNE STOOL WITH GOOD LINES, PRESUMABLY IN WALNUT.
1730–50. HOWARD REIFSNYDER.

In the early times stools were quite general and chairs were rare. As the 18th
century wore on, this condition was reversed. A chair was no longer a seat of
special honor. The progress of the position of women can almost be measured by
this change. In the 17th century, except in high society, there was often only
one chair, that for the head of the house. It is partly for this reason that the
Queen Anne, and especially the Chippendale stools are rare. Foot stools of an
ordinary character have always, of course, been in use.

2748. A RICH CHIPPENDALE STOOL WITH CARVED KNEE, AND BALL-AND-CLAW FOOT. THESE
LEGS ARE FOUND SOMETIMES AS HIGH AS THOSE OF A CHAIR. ENGLISH. 1760. I. SACK.

2749. A Swivel Stool of Very Odd Turning, and a Shaped Seat. 18th Century. Perhaps Unique. J. Stogdell Stokes.

2750. (Right.) A Windsor Stool. Rare. Latter Half 18th Century. J. Stogdell Stokes.

2751-53. Three Windsor Stools, All Good, and Rare. Present Owners Unknown. 18th Century.

2754. Hitchcock, Eight-Leg Bench, Rush Seat. 1840. Rudolph P. Pauly, Boston.

2755. AN EMPIRE STOOL, FOLLOWING THE LINES OF THE MOST ANCIENT EGYPTIAN DESIGN. IN THE MODE OF DUNCAN PHYFE. ROSETTES AT INTERSECTIONS OF CROSS STRETCHERS. 1800–20. JOE KINDIG, JR., YORK.

2756. TURNED STOOL, PERHAPS IN THE 1800'S. STRAIGHT ON ONE SIDE AND ROUNDED ON THE OTHER, AS IF TO PLACE AGAINST THE WALL. ALBERT C. BOWMAN, SPRINGFIELD, VERMONT.

2757. A Stump Frame Glass, 17th Century. Initials M. B. Date 1660. Rose, Iris, and Other Floral Forms. Original Beveled Glass. Earliest Type Known. Probably Foreign. L. G. Myers.

2758. A Strongly Featured Burl Bowl. Very Large. Wadsworth Atheneum.

2759. GLASS, SAID TO HAVE BELONGED TO PEREGRINE WHITE. HE WAS BORN
ON THE "MAYFLOWER" AND PROBABLY DID NOT BRING HIS GLASS WITH HIM.
HE LIVED INTO THE 18TH CENTURY.

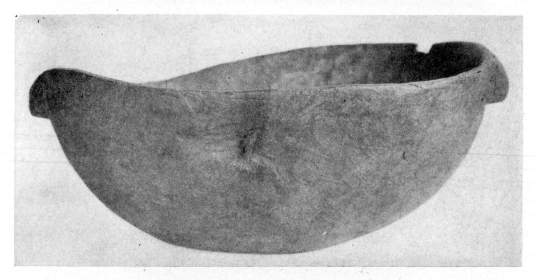

2760. HANDMADE BOWL. COCKED HAT SHAPE. BURL. ALBERT C. BATES, HARTFORD.

2761. Glass, Which Had Decorative Crest, Now Lost. Original Plate. Shape of Frame Is Convex, and Not To Be Confused with the Victorian Type. 27¾ x 21¼ Outside. Walnut Veneer on Pine, as Usual. Wadsworth Atheneum.

2762. (Right.) A Different Contour in the Border. Decorative Surface. Frame 4 Inches Wide. This Alone Is Indication of Great Age. Inlay in Satin and Tulipwood. Dates of Both, 1690–1700. Francis Hill Bigelow.

2763. Glass Now Cleaned of Quicksilver, and Having the Howe Coat-of-Arms. They Were the Keepers of the Wayside Inn. 1690–1700.

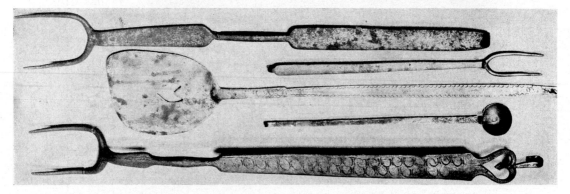

2764–65. Culinary Forks with Hooks. 2766. A Flapjack Shovel with a Heart Cutout and Decorated Handle. 2767. A Copper Spoon Riveted to an Iron Handle. 2768. A Rare and Fine Gift Fork with Handle Decoration Terminating with a Heart and Ending with a Hook. All Pennsylvania. Wadsworth Atheneum.

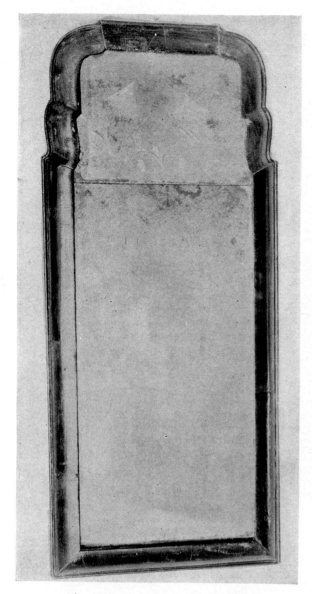

2769. TWO-PART GLASS, 37 INCHES HIGH. C. 1710. MOST EARLY FINE GLASSES WERE BEVELED AND, IF LARGE, WERE IN TWO PARTS. FRANCIS HILL BIGELOW.

2770. (Right.) UPPER SECTION SHOWS SHIP IN FULL SAIL. THE PAINTING IS ON WOOD, A BACKGROUND FREQUENTLY USED BY GREAT PAINTERS. C. 1710. CHAUNCEY C. NASH.

2771-74. TWO BOWLS, A SAUCER AND A SALT, ALL IN BURL. THE USE OF THIS MATERIAL WAS TO PREVENT CHECKING. WHILE WALNUT IS FREQUENT, ASH, MAPLE, AND OAK ARE FOUND. JOSEPH SKINNER, HOLYOKE.

2775. A Scrolled Top in Position, Glass 15½ x 18¼. Walnut on Pine. 1700–20. Francis Hill Bigelow.
2776. (Right.) Glass with Japanese Design. Upper Glass Cut in a Foliage Pattern. 1710–20. L. G. Myers.

2777–80. A Medium and Small Bowl. Toddy Stick for Crushing Sugar. A Mortar and
Pestle. All in Burl.

2781. GLASS OF GREAT HEIGHT IN WALNUT VENEER. QUEEN ANNE TYPE. ESTATE OF HARRY W. WEEKS, FRAMINGHAM.

2782. (Right.) QUEEN ANNE GLASS, TWO PART. 20 x 61. RICHLY DECORATED. JOHN H. BUCK, HARTFORD.

2783. Rich Veneer, with Shell in Crest. Cut-Glass Foliage Ornaments. 1710–20. I. Sack.

2784. Walnut, Queen Anne, Two Part. Open Fretwork at Top, and Band around the Glass Gilded. 24 x 58. 1720–30. Joe Kindig, Jr.

2785–86. Carved, Gilded Eagles.

2787-89. Rich Lacquered Mirrors, a Center and Two Sides. Done in Hunting Scenes. The Side Mirrors Have Sconces. Early 18th Century. Flayderman & Kaufman.

2790-93. Beginning of the 18th Century. Drops and Escutcheons. Frank A. Robart.

2794. Queen Anne, Fully Carved. Rosettes, Shell, and Cartouche. Two Plain Surfaces on the Lower Part of the Frame, Look as if They Were Intended for Sconces. 1730. Mrs. Francis P. Garvan.

2795. (Right.) Fully Carved. Scrolled Top Glass. Shells on Central Ornament and Lower Portion of Frame. 1730–60. 34 x 86. Found in Newport. Flayderman & Kaufman.

2796–97. An Open and a Solid Chippendale Brass. 1760–75. Frank A. Robart.

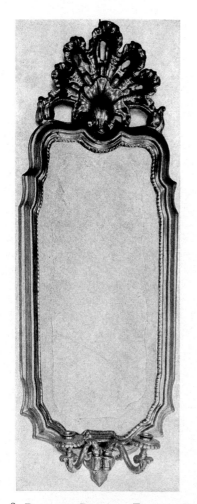 

2798. Probably Dutch or French. Fine Double Shell. Carved Sconces. 12¼ x 34. 1770. H. W. Erving.
2799. (Right.) A Carved, Three-Feather Glass. 1750–70. Estate of H. W. Weeks.

2800–01. Walnut with Applied Gilded Ornaments. 10¼ x 10½. 1730–50. Flayderman & Kaufman.

2802. A Double Sconce of Quill Work. When Lighted up These Sconce Backgrounds Gave a Very Brilliant Effect. 1710–20. Francis Hill Bigelow.

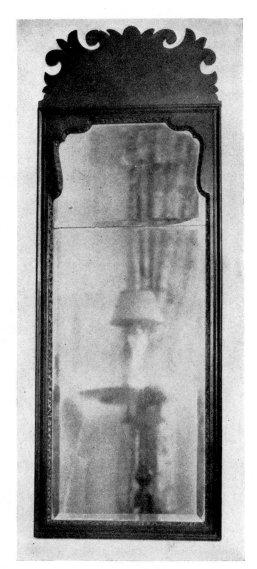

2803. WALNUT, TWO PART. UPPER GLASS CUT. 1710–30. KATRINA KIPPER.
2804. (Right.) UNUSUAL SCROLL. THE TWO-PART GLASSES ARE JOINED ON THE BEVEL, AND THE UPPER
GLASS SETS IN A RABBET A LITTLE DEEPER THAN THE LOWER. 1720–30. SANDERSON COLLECTION.

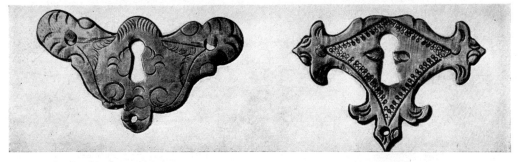

2805–06. HANDSOME STAMPED BRASSES. 1700–20. MUCH MISCONCEPTION EXISTS ABOUT THESE.
THEY WERE NEITHER ENGRAVED, CHASED, NOR ETCHED. THEY WERE SIMPLY STAMPED, WITH A
VARIETY OF TOOLS TO GIVE THESE SHAPES. OF COURSE, THE STAMPING WAS DONE IN SECTIONS
WITH SMALL TOOLS. FRANK A. ROBART.

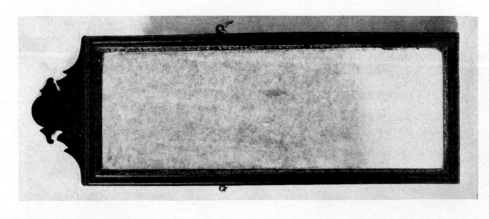

2807. Walnut, Unusual and Attractive. Swampscott. 15 x 36. 1710–30. Flayderman & Kaufman.
2808. (Middle.) One of a Pair of Sconce Glasses. Pencil and Pearl Ornament. Mid 18th Century. Fuessenich Collection.
2809. (Right.) Design the Same Period as the Preceding. Katrina Kipper, Accord, Massachusetts.

2810. Walnut. Unusual Carved Eagle. 13 x 27½. 1710-30.
2811. (Middle.) With This Mold These Glasses Are Regarded as Much Later in Date. 1785-95. The Author's.
2812. (Right.) Interesting Carving and Decoration. This and No. 2810. Flayderman & Kaufman.

2813–14. Quill Work Sconces. Walnut. Flowers Principally Carnations and Roses, Perhaps Mixed with Mica. Each Petal Edged with Silver Wire. Colors Are Red, Blue, Purple, and White. Made by Ruth Read, Daughter of the Honorable John Read, Distinguished Lawyer in Boston, 1722–49. Brackets Made by Knight Leverett of Boston (1703–53). Engraved R. R. 1720. Supposed To Be Unique. The Purpose of Sconces in Front of Such Glasses, Was To Give a Brilliant Effect of Lighting. Francis Hill Bigelow.

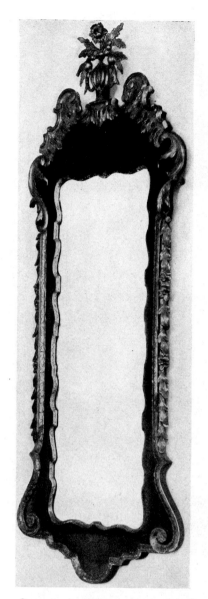

2815. Large Elegant Glass. Fine Central Ornament. 1740–60. I. Sack, Palmer Col.
2816. (Right.) Mahogany on Pine. 26 x 56. Transition Georgian-Chippendale. Early Use of Mahogany. 1750. William B. Goodwin.

2817–18. Fine Brasses. British Lion with Flag, and Intertwined Dolphins. 1790. Rudolph P. Pauly.

2819. Sconce Glass, with Jointed Sconce Brackets. Walnut. 1785–95. J. Stogdell Stokes.
2820. (Right.) Glass with One Carved Applied Piece. Others at Top Missing. 1710–30.

2821–22. Brasses of 1790–1805. The Rose Pattern and the Dove of Peace.
Rudolph P. Pauly.

2823. Shaped Upper Glass, Cut with Pot of Flowers and Stars. 17 x 35. Portsmouth, New Hampshire. 1710–20.

2824. (Right.) Decorated Frame, Upper Glass Shaped and Cut. Pine Black and Gold Lacquer. 17½ x 43. Ipswich. 1710–20. Both Glasses Flayderman & Kaufman.

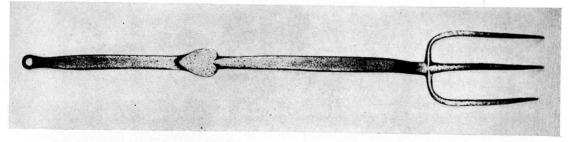

2825. A Gift Fork, More Properly Called Tormentor, with a Heart Motive. 18th Century. Pennsylvania.

2826. Petit Point Needlework. 17th Century. Frame Like a Looking-Glass. Rich Coloring, Quaint Drawing, Faithful Costume. Frame Pine with Wide Gold Line. To Show Cloud Effect Top Is Made with Double Arch. H. W. Erving.

2827-31. Wooden Spoons, Some Decorative. Rare. Bowl with Decorated Edge. Probably 18th Century. Albert C. Bates.

2832. Glass with Inlaid Medallions. Satinwood with Walnut Outside Edge. A Three-Inch Mold. Inlaid with Thuya and Tulipwood. 13½ x 16¾. 1710-20. Francis Hill Bigelow.

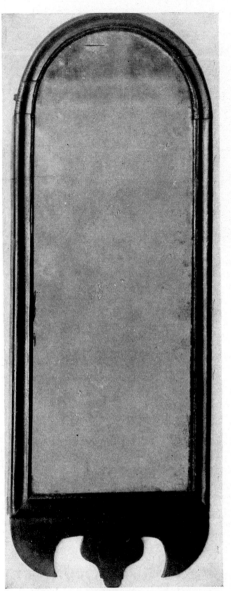 

2833. A Sconce Glass, Probably One of Two. Unusual Top. The Mold Should Be Compared with That on Walnut Chairs. 7½ x 20¼. 1710–30. Francis Hill Bigelow.

2834. (Right.) Stained Maple Frame, Ornamented with a Boss. Narrow Portion of the Frame 1⅛ Inches Wide. Glass 11¼ x 17. Francis Hill Bigelow.

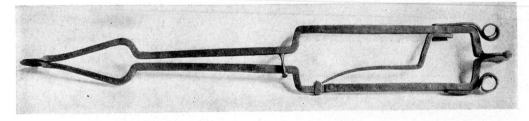

2835. Rare 18th Century Pipe Tongs. As They Open by Squeezing, the Use Must Have Required Some Dexterity. Mrs. DeWitt Howe.

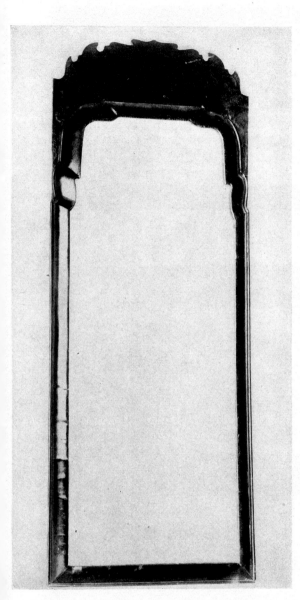

2836. Cresting is Part of Frame. Inlaid Design in Tulipwood. Two Glasses Originally. 1710–20.
2837. (Right.) Walnut, with Convex Mold. Top in Style Often Seen Abroad. Glass 11⅞ x 13⅞. 1710–30. Bigelow Col.

2838–39. Burl Bowls, the Second with Handle, Often Called Indian Head. Samuel Wineck.

2840. HANDSOMELY LACQUERED. 1700–20.
KATRINA KIPPER.

2841. (Middle.) VERY EARLY. PINE. ORIGINAL
GLASS. 8 x 13½. PAINTED. H. H. ARMSTRONG.

2842. (Right.) WALNUT. UNUSUAL TOP. 20 x 54½.
1720–40. FLAYDERMAN & KAUFMAN.

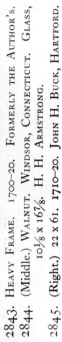

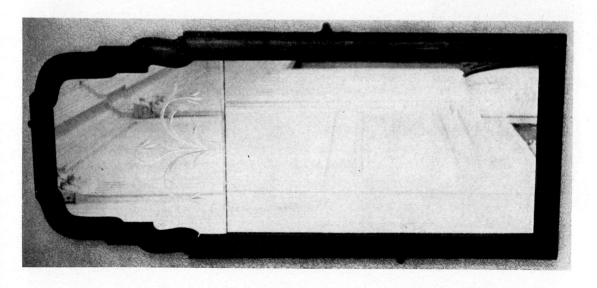

2843. HEAVY FRAME. 1700–20. FORMERLY THE AUTHOR'S.
2844. (Middle.) WALNUT. WINDSOR, CONNECTICUT. GLASS,
10⅛ x 16⅞. H. H. ARMSTRONG.
2845. (Right.) 22 x 61. 1710–20. JOHN H. BUCK, HARTFORD.

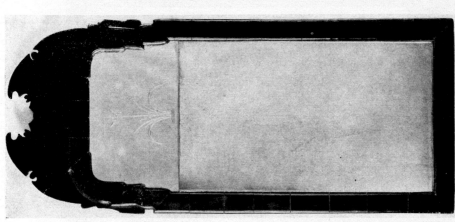

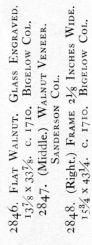

2846. Flat Walnut. Glass Engraved. 13⅞ x 33⅞. c. 1710. Bigelow Col.
2847. (Middle.) Walnut Veneer. Sanderson Col.
2848. (Right.) Frame 2⅛ Inches Wide. 15¾ x 43¼. c. 1710. Bigelow Col.

2849 and 2851. (At Each Side.) Walnut.
1710-30. Flayderman & Kaufman.
2850. Rare or Unique. Engraved Glass at
the Top in an Irregular Form. Walnut.
H. H. Armstrong, Hartford.

2852-53. Carved, Applied Decoration. Early 18th Century. Left: Katrina Kipper.

2854-58. Burl Plates or Trenchers, and Large Shallow Bowl. The Knives Are Cutters for Fine Basket Work. Indian Original. Albert C. Bates.

2859–60. Cape Cod. Bright-Hued. 21½ x 9½. Right: Connecticut. Crown Attached by Pegs. Painted. 14 x 8¾. 18th C. Wm. B. Goodwin.

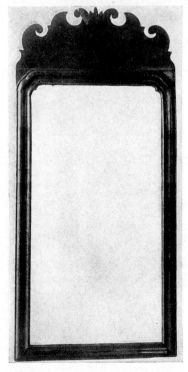

2861–62. Walnut Sconce. Rhode Island. 9 x 24. Early 18th Century. Flayderman & Kaufman.
2863. (Right.) Queen Anne. Indented Corners. Katrina Kipper. 1710–30.

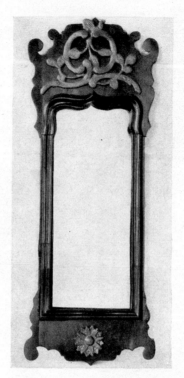

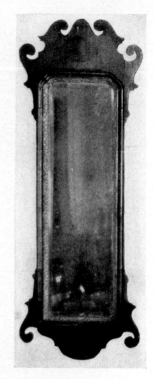

2864. GOOD SMALL SCONCE.
KATRINA KIPPER.

2865. APPLIED CARVING.
FLAYDERMAN & KAUFMAN.

2866. EARLY CHIPPEN-
DALE.

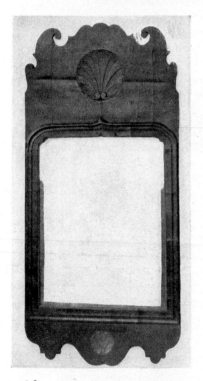

2867. INCISED CARVED SHELLS.
WALNUT.

2868. TWO PART, ENGRAVED.

2869. CARVED SHELL.

ALL EARLY 18TH CENTURY. CENTER: KATRINA KIPPER. OTHERS: FLAYDERMAN & KAUFMAN.

2870-71. ATTRACTIVE SCROLLS. APPLIED GILT CARVING. 18TH CENTURY. KATRINA KIPPER.

2872. SAME OWNER AS ABOVE.
ALL WALNUT.

2873. CURLY MAPLE, CHIPPENDALE.
CHARLES P. COOLEY.

2874. A Small Glass in Pine Frame, Fully Carved.
18th Century. Mark LaFontaine, Springfield, Vermont.

 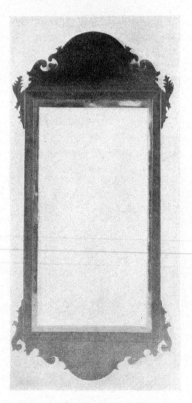

2875. Convex Frame. c. 1700. 15 x 26. Walnut. John H. Buck, Hartford.
2876. (Right.) Sawed Scroll. 1760-75. Katrina Kipper.

2879. Fully Decorated, with Double Shells and Scrolls. Early 18th Century. Shaped Glass. Bigelow Collection.

2878. A French Type, About 1750. Katrina Kipper.

2877. Inlaid Sconce Frame. Unusual Shape. Owner's Name Lost. Apparently Something at Top Lost.

2882. A Flower Basket Set in Scrolls Such as Are Found on the Cape. Probably of Foreign Origin. A Carved Pheasant Sits on Topmost Scroll. John H. Buck.

2881. Scrolled in the Form of Pigeons. Walnut. Flayderman & Kaufman.

2880. Walnut, Attractive Scroll. A Gilded Dove on an Applied Scroll. 1710–30. John H. Buck.

2883. French. Glasses Are International, the Greater Part of Those Found in This Country of Foreign Origin. Probably Made in the Provinces. James Davidson.

2884. (Right.) Engraved and Etched. Pine, Painted Green, with a Landscape in the Panel at the Top. 12½ x 20½. From Portsmouth, Date Uncertain. Flayderman & Kaufman.

2885. Sconce Glass, Pine. 15 x 28. Queen Anne Period. Flayderman & Kaufman.

2886. (Right.) Interesting Dated Glass, with Fighting Cocks, Facing Each Other, Quaint Designs and Initials. Anything of This Sort Is Important. John H. Buck, Hartford.

2887. Detail of a Glass Door Frame. Rhode Island School of Design.

2888. Sconce Reflector, Made in Shape of Queen Anne Glass Top. Pine, Shaped, Gilded, and Beveled. Newburyport. 22¼ x 27½. Flayderman & Kaufman.

2889. (Right.) Glass To Reflect a Sconce. Like Top of Queen Anne Looking-Glass. 1710–30. Mrs. Francis P. Garvan.

2890. Small Painted Queen Anne Glass. 1710–20. W. F. Hubbard, Hartford.

2891. (Right.) Pine, Gilded. 10 x 15. Near West Point, New York. Queen Anne Period. Flayderman & Kaufman.

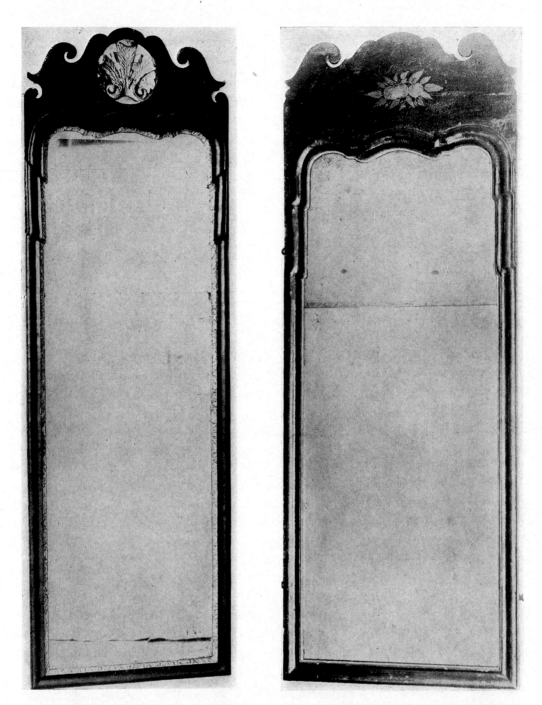

2892–93. LEFT-HAND WALNUT, RIGHT-HAND MOLDED PINE. THEIR DATE IS ABOUT 1720–40.
GLASS IN FORMER, 14¾ x 48¾. GLASS IN LATTER, 16 x 40. THIS FRAME IS GRAINED IN IMITATION
OF ROSEWOOD. IT IS GILT INSIDE. THE STENCILING IN GILT WAS PROBABLY 19TH CENTURY WORK.
BIGELOW COLLECTION.

As to looking-glasses in general it is sometimes difficult to determine whether they are English or American.
The styles also were much the same. It would be impossible, however, to secure a fine and elegant collection
of American looking-glasses covering the various periods. In the notations made, it has been thought best
not to be too specific regarding origins, partly owing to the difficulty of making an authoritative statement.

2894. FOREIGN. SOMEWHAT OF BILBAO TYPE. KATRINA KIPPER.
2895. (Right.) SCROLLS TERMINATE WITH DROOPING FOLIAGE. 1740–50. HELEN T. COOKE.

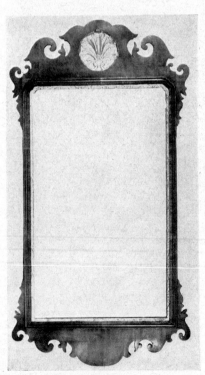

2896. QUEEN ANNE PERIOD, FULLY CARVED. FOUR ROSETTES ON THREE-FEATHER CREST.
1730–60. WE USE THE TERM QUEEN ANNE FOR A STYLE OFTEN AFTER HER DATE.

2897. (Right.) A CHIPPENDALE SCROLL. PERHAPS 1740.

2898. Width of Mold on Side 1¼ Inches. Edges Outside Gilt. Burl Walnut. Glass 21 x 33½. 1720–40.
2899. (Middle.) Walnut, 13½ x 21½. Frame Only One Inch Wide. Gilt Inside and Out. 1730–50. Francis Hill Bigelow.
2900. (Right.) Walnut. 21 x 32¾. Frame 1¼ Inches Wide. Boxwood Edges Inside and Out. 1730–50.

2901. Beautiful Marquetry. 1700–20. Bigelow Collection. 44 x 29¾. Coffin Family in 1732.

2902. (Right.) Glass Painted as Tortoise Shell. The Portion That Has Been Repaired Readily Shows. Very Rare. 1660–1685. Bigelow Collection.

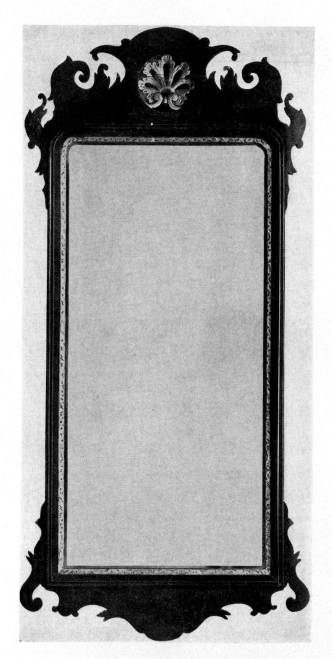

2903. LATE QUEEN ANNE. 1740–60. BIGELOW COLLECTION.

2904. (Right.) BOUGHT BY CAPTAIN WORMSTED IN BILBAO AND BROUGHT TO MARBLEHEAD. THE CROWN, ARROWS, QUIVER, AND THE CENTRAL ACANTHUS LEAVES WERE ALL SYMBOLS OF THE PERIOD. BLACK FRAME, WITH LINE OF GILT BEADING INSIDE; ROSETTES ON CORNERS; DECORATIONS IN CARVED WOOD. 27 x 61. DARK GROUND TO EMPHASIZE DESIGN.

Bilbao was the meeting place of trade. Thence these designs went everywhere; and also they were brought to Bilbao. Thus looking-glasses of all forms were brought by captains returning from Italy, Spain, England, Holland, and China.

2906. WILLIAM AND MARY, 1690–1700.
BIGELOW COLLECTION.

2905. ITALIAN, SAID TO DATE FROM THE 17TH
CENTURY. BIGELOW COLLECTION.

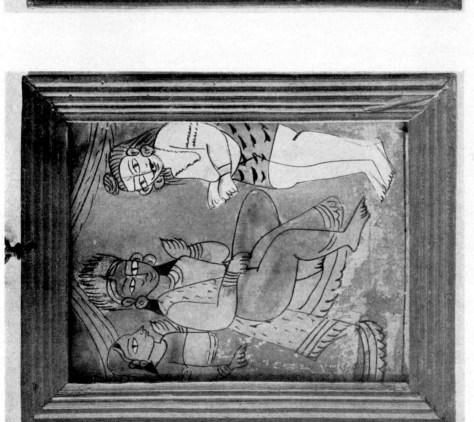

2907. CAPTAIN SMITH AND POCAHONTAS. H. W. ERVING. 2908. REVERSE OF SAME.

17th Century glass, 7 x 9 inside, with frame made double and a picture on glass in the back. Powhatan sits in judgment on John Smith, known by his white color, mustache, and bound hands, while Pocahontas in the rear intercedes for the captive. Frame reeded on one side, broad flutes on the other. It is no wonder that John Rolfe fell in love with such a maiden. Their home near Williamstown, Virginia, as the author is writing, has been bought for preservation.

2909. MARQUETRY GLASS. ENGLISH. PIERCED FRET. C. 1700. I. SACK.

Olive ebony and walnut were the materials of the earliest frames. It is likely that
all or almost all of the marquetry frames, and the richer frames in general, were imported. Foliage, flowers and grotesque animals supplied the subjects. The crown
of this frame shows two monsters with bodies of oxen and fanciful heads. Only in
homes of wealth could such glasses be found. At first glasses nearly square as here
were used, because the methods of making plate were expensive.

2910. Queen Anne, Carved on Wood and Gilded. Shell, Feather, and Leaf Motive. Bird Head Carved below the Top. 1710–40. Bigelow Collection.

2911. (Right.) Georgian. Crane on Branch. The Applied Carving on the Top Scroll Was Obviously Copied for the Finest Highboy Tops. The Little Crest Feather at the Extreme Top Is a Touch of Beauty Often Omitted. Most Glasses of This Shape in the Top and with the Bird Go under the Name Georgian, Chippendale, or Martha Washington. 1740–60. Bigelow Collection.

The very earliest frame was convex and broad, even up to four inches, and the glass was almost square. In the next period, about 1700, we get the William and Mary shortly followed by the Queen Anne, with a frame like No. 2910 above, often in walnut, but sometimes gilded, as shown. Then come the frames such as that shown in No. 2914. Then the frame above on the right; then follow at about the same time frames like that on the right, but without any applied decoration, as, for instance, No. 2948, and frames like No. 2915. After that we come to the Hepplewhite, with or without filigree, and the Sheraton or early Empire.

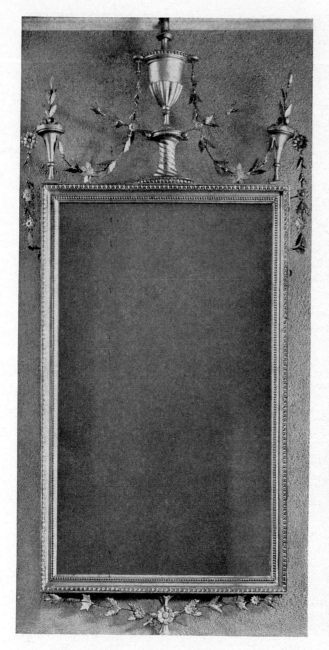

2912. HEPPLEWHITE. 1780–90. BIGELOW COLLECTION.   2913. FILIGREE GLASS. HEPPLEWHITE. 1780–90.
ALL ORIGINAL. BIGELOW COLLECTION.

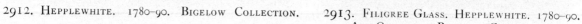

2916–17. (Opposite.) BATTERSEA KNOBS. 18TH CENTURY. CONTINUOUS SINGLE LANDSCAPE.
TRANSFER PATTERN. HAND COLORED. UPTURNED FLANGE BEZEL. DIAMETER 3¾ INCHES. HAND
TOOLED. CHRISTINE J. STEELE.

2914. GEORGIAN, CARVED ON WOOD. GOLD LEAF AND MAHOGANY. 30 x 76. c. 1760. JOHN H. BUCK.
2915. (Right.) OPENWORK, CARVED, CHIPPENDALE. GOLD. WEBB HOUSE, WETHERSFIELD, COLONIAL DAMES.

2918. AMERICAN. 1770. MRS. FRANCIS P. GARVAN.   2919. (Right.) GEORGIAN, MAHOGANY. 1750.

2920–21. BATTERSEA. HAND-TINTED ENGRAVINGS UNDER GLASS. 1790–1810. CHRISTINE J. STEELE.

2922. Richly Carved with Unusual Finial. Georgian. 1740–70. Howard Reifsnyder, Philadelphia.
2923. (Right.) Georgian. Mahogany and Gold. 1740–70. I. Sack.

2924–25. "Sacred To Friendship." Knobs for Glasses. 1790–1810. J. Grossman.

2926. SHELL AND SCROLL, WOOD CARVED AND GILDED. 1740–70. FLAYDERMAN & KAUFMAN.
2927. (Right.) UNUSUAL DESIGN. CROSS BANDING, APPLIED BEADS AND SIDE SCROLLS. BROOKS REED.

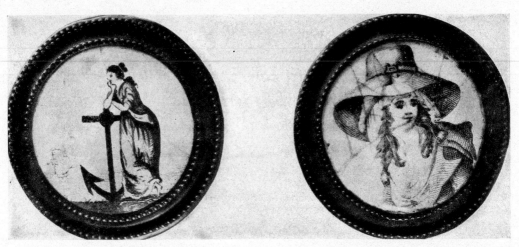

2928–29. BATTERSEA. THE FRENCH REVOLUTION; "HOPE." CHRISTINE J. STEELE.

2930. Open Scroll. Queen Anne. 1740–60. Applied Ornament. I. Sack.

2931. (Right.) Pheasant Carved in Circle. Applied Carved Wood Decoration. 1740–60. H. C. Valentine & Company.

2932–35. The Lady May Be a Portrait. At Any Rate, It Shows the Costume of the Times, and the Same May Be Said of the Gentleman. The Third Figure in the Style of an Early Engraving. The Last, an Urn. 1790–1820.

2936. APPLIED CARVED DECORATION. ON INSIDE THE GILT IS ON THE GLASS. 1740–70. MALCOLM A. NORTON.
2937. (Right.) GEORGIAN, WITH A SPRAY PENDING FROM THE ROSETTE. THE APPLIED MOLDINGS PINE, WITH GOLD LEAF. 28 x 50. 1740–70. JOHN H. BUCK, HARTFORD.

2938–39. BATTERSEA KNOBS. BLACK AND GREY, POSSIBLY MOURNING. GOOD EXAMPLE OF TRANSFER FROM COPPER ENGRAVED PLATES. CHRISTINE J. STEELE.

2942. Cross-Banded Frame, with Carved and Sawed Ornamental Additions at Top and Bottom. 16 x 27. 1730–60. John H. Buck.

2941. Handsome Applied Side Carving. Corners Usually Earlier than Chippendale. Three Feathers. 1730–60. Katrina Kipper.

2940. Early Chippendale. The Immediate Frame Is Cross Banded, and the Inside Member Carved and Gilded. Gilded Carved Decoration in Top. 22 x 40. John H. Buck.

2945. FRENCH. GILDED. EARLY CORNERS. 1780. KATRINA KIPPER.

2944. AN ENGLISH CHIPPENDALE WITH COAT OF ARMS SURMOUNTED BY AN EAGLE. GILDED. 1750–70. C. R. MORSON.

2943. WALNUT, FINE APPLIED CARVING. SALEM. QUEEN ANNE. 19 x 43. FLAYDERMAN & KAUFMAN.

2947. Mahogany. Herringbone. James Davidson.

2946. Mahogany. Carved. Gilded Bird. 1780.

2951. CARVED AND GILDED. 17 x 32. 1750-75. H. W. ERVING.

2948. (Opposite page.) RICH CHIPPENDALE. CARVED, GILDED. 1750-70. C. P. COOLEY.

2949. (Opposite page; right.) RICHLY GRAINED WOOD. CARVED ON THE WOOD AND ON APPLIED PINE DECORATIONS. GILDED.

2950. CHIPPENDALE, PIERCED SCROLL. 1750-80.

2953. CHIPPENDALE, SHAPED CORNERS. AUTHOR'S.

2952. LATE CHIPPENDALE. 16 x 24. JOHN H. BUCK.

2955. Carved. 1750–75. E. B. Leete Co.

2954. Carved. Gilded. 1750–75.

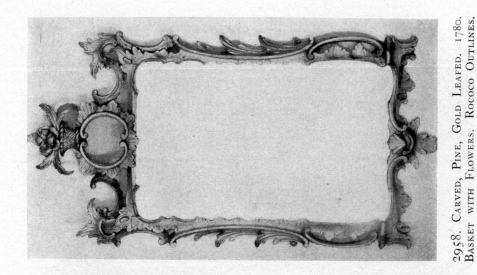

2958. Carved, Pine, Gold Leafed. 1780.
Basket with Flowers. Rococo Outlines.
Second Half 18th Century.
E. B. Leete Company, Guilford.

2957. Mahogany and Gold. Both Incised
and Applied Carving. Second Half 18th
Century. H. V. Weil.

2956. Chippendale. Eight Small Glasses
Surrounding Large. Gilt Phœnix and
Rosette. Second Half 18th Century.
Joe Kindig, Jr.

2961. Walnut. Carving in the Walnut and Applied Gilded Decoration. The Effort To Show All the Forms Would Be Hopeless. Second Half 18th Century. N. Cushing, Providence.

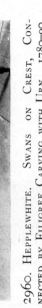

2960. Hepplewhite. Swans on Crest, Connected by Filigree Carving with Urn. 1780–90. Formerly the Author's.

2959. Chippendale. Sawed Fret, Enriched with Outlines of Foliage Scrolls. Four Feathers in Oval. Very Popular Type. 15 x 26. Latter Half 18th Century. E. B. Leete Company.

2962. Inlaid with Eagle. 19½ x 30½. 18th Century. Mr. and Mrs. George Shipley, Baltimore.
2963. (Right.) Inlaid with Shell. Dainty Scroll. Late 18th C. 24 x 56. John H. Buck.

2964. Label Found on Glass of Late 18th Century. Flayderman & Kaufman.

2965. STOOPING EAGLE ON SPIRALED SUPPORT. LATE CHIPPENDALE. STEARNS COLLECTION.
2966. (Right.) CHIPPENDALE. FEATHERS AND INNER BORDER CARVED AND GILDED.
SAMUEL WINECK.

2967. FULLY CARVED, CHIPPENDALE MANTEL GLASS. SECOND HALF 18TH CENTURY.
METROPOLITAN MUSEUM.

2968. THREE-PART MANTEL GLASS, FULLY CARVED AND GILDED. SECOND HALF 18TH CENTURY.
C. R. MORSON.

2969. CARVED WITH CREST OF BASKET AND FLOWERS. SECOND HALF 18TH CENTURY.
HOWARD REIFSNYDER, PHILADELPHIA.

2970. (Right.) CARVED WITH FRUIT CLUSTERS. THESE SHAPES ARE CALLED ROCOCO. SECOND
HALF 18TH CENTURY. CLIFFORD R. WELD, ROCK, MASSACHUSETTS.

2971. Carved with Birds and Flowers and Scrolls on a Plaque. English.
Second Half 18th Century. Mrs. Francis P. Garvan.

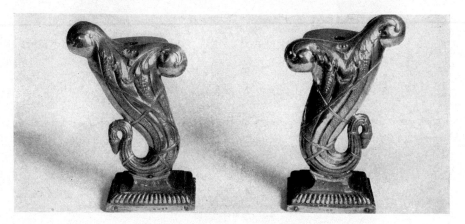

2972-73. Silver Candlesticks, Jacobean. Sheet of Hand-Beaten Repoussé.
Backed to a Wooden Base. Holder Also of Wood. They Bear Hallmarks.
Clifford S. Drake, North Hampton, New Hampshire.

2974. GEORGIAN GLASS, CARVED AND GILDED. LARGE. MID 18TH
CENTURY. C. R. MORSON.

2975-77. GLASS ON MANTEL WITH FESTOONS. 18TH C. STONE MANTEL. EMPIRE CHAIR. FENN COL.

2978-81. GEORGIAN GLASS. DUTCH SETTEE. ENGLISH CUPBOARD. OAK CHEST. C. P. COOLEY.

2982. ADAM OR BILBAO. INSET MEDALLION. ROSETTES ON CORNERS. MORRIS BERRY.
2983. (Right.) CHIPPENDALE WITH THE SAME MOTIVE REPEATED ON ALL SIDES. CLIFFORD R. WELD.

2984. MINIATURE QUEEN ANNE. VENEERED AS IF A SLAB OF WOOD WITH BARK. TWO PART.
EARLY 18TH CENTURY. BROOKS REED.
2985. (Right.) EARLY CHIPPENDALE. SMALLER GLASSES IN FRAME. 29½ x 53. PINE, GILDED.
MID 18TH CENTURY. FLAYDERMAN & KAUFMAN.

2986–87. Large Chippendale. Carved Pine with Gold Leaf. Plaque on Right Bas Relief.

2988–90. Early Rare Stamped Brasses from Queen Anne Lowboy. Henry A. Hoffman, Barrington, Rhode Island.

2991. LARGE, DELICATELY CARVED BIRD. SECOND HALF 18TH CENTURY. I. SACK.

These graceful glasses give much dignity to a room. On them seem to be expended some of the best talent of the 18th century. The applied carving of bits of wood wired together and all gilded running down the sides is done in various patterns. The scroll top is practically the same as that used in the Queen Anne and Chippendale time on high cabinet pieces and doorheads.

2992. (Right.) LARGE, WITH AN INLAID OVAL ABOVE AND BELOW. TWO PART. LANDSCAPE IN PAINTED GLASS ON THE UPPER SECTION. CARVED URN WITH WIRED GRASSES. LATE 18TH CENTURY.
C. SANFORD BULL, WATERBURY, CONNECTICUT.

2993. Richly Carved, and Gold Leafed. Mantel. 1750–75. C. P. Cooley, Hartford.
2994–95. (Below.) Pine Painted. Bigelow Collection.

2996. An Elaborate and Rich Glass Carved Throughout and Covered with Gold Leaf. Bigelow Collection.

2997. CARVED PINE, GOLD LEAF. SWAN ON NEST AT BOTTOM; BIRDS
FACING EACH OTHER ON UPPER CORNERS; BASKET WITH FLOWERS AT
CREST; FOLIAGE AND FRUIT AT SIDES. ROCOCO SCROLLS. LARGE.
1750–75. I. SACK.

By Chippendale's time, glass was somewhat cheaper, and larger examples are found. The use of two glasses, in the pier mirrors was merely
to save expense.

2998. BUTTERFLY INLAY. URN WITH FLOWERS AND WHEAT EARS. 1780–90. CHARLES P. COOLEY.
2999. (Right.) GOLD ON PINE. SCROLLS WITH FLOWERS. 1750–80. CHARLES P. COOLEY.

3000–01. TWO PETAL AND THISTLE BRASSES. 1790. A. H. EATON.

3004. Scrolls at Top with Delicate Ramp, So Sharp as To Reach the Vertical. Applied Decoration, Gilt. H. V. Weil.

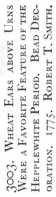

3003. Wheat Ears above Urns Were a Favorte Feature of the Hepplewhite Period. Bead Decoration. 1775. Robert T. Smith.

3002. Crane, Gilt, as Also All Applied Ornaments. 1770–80. C. R. Morson.

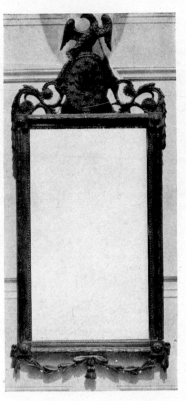

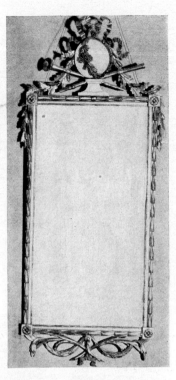

3005. "Tabernacle." 1790. Wickford Antique Shop.

3006. Thirteen Star. 1785–90. James Fenimore Cooper.

3007. Oak Leaves and Horn. 1790. Misses Foster.

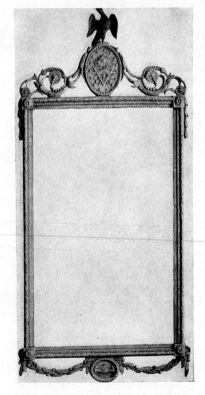

3008. Thirteen Star with Bird. Some Ornaments Gone. 1790. Alan Wright.

3009. (Right.) Masonic Glass. Fifteen Stars and Bird. 1790. Helen T. Cooke.

3010. Hepplewhite. Rope Mold, Urn and Husk. E. F. Sanderson.
3011. (Right.) 17½ x 20½. Gilt Inside and Out. Walnut. 1750–75. Bigelow Collection.

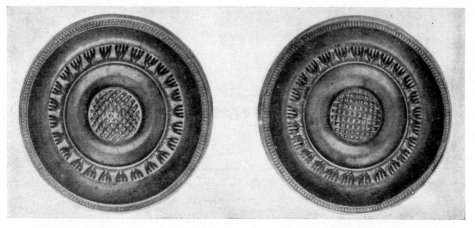

3012–13. Large Brass Knobs. This Sort Was Pressed in a Die, and Not Cast.

3014. JUTTING SQUARES, FESTOONS, URN, ETC. 26 x 61. JOHN H. BUCK.

3015. (Right.) RIBBON AND WREATH, URN AND DRAPERY. 1790. KATRINA KIPPER, ACCORD.

3016–17. BRASSES FOR WINDOW DRAPERIES. 19TH CENTURY. FRANK A. ROBART.

3018. Italian "Chippendale." All Gold on Wood. 1750-75.
3019. (Right.) In the Style of Bilbao Glass. Landscape in Oval. 1790. Both C. P. Cooley.

3020-21. Brasses for Draperies. 19th Century. Frank A. Robart.

3022. WHEAT EAR ABOVE URN; HUSK PENDANTS. 1790. SANDERSON COLLECTION.
3023. (Right.) PROFUSION OF ORNAMENT. ALL GOLD ON WOOD. CHAS. P. COOLEY.

3024-25. GILDED EAGLE BRACKETS. RESTS FOR CLOCKS OR VASES.

3026. "Agricultural." Carved on Wood. 1790. The Misses A. and E. P. Foster.
3027. (Right.) Implements and Fruits. Carved on Wood. 32½ x 71. 1790.

3028-29. Knobs for Glasses. Late 18th Century.

3030. Italian. Shows Larger Motives Than Chippendale. 1730.
3031. (Right.) Hepplewhite. Late 18th Century. Both, Chas. P. Cooley.

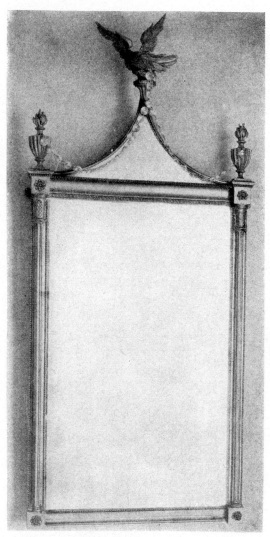

3032. HEPPLEWHITE. 23 x 50. 1790.
E. B. LEETE CO.

3033. 1790.

3034-35. BATTERSEA KNOBS. BRIDGE AND MILL. "ANTIQUES" MAGAZINE.

3038. Top Filled with Decorated Panel. Columns, Capitals, Rope Mold. E. C. Hall.

3037. Landscape in Oval. Architectural Half-Round Columns. 1790–1818. Katrina Kipper.

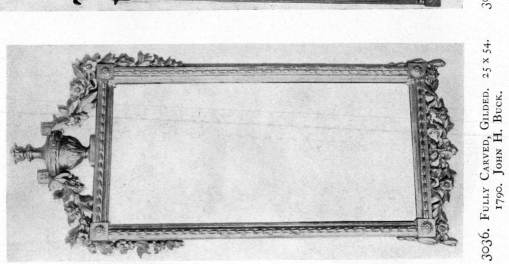

3036. Fully Carved, Gilded. 25 x 54. 1790. John H. Buck.

3041. Probably Venetian. "Cape Cod." Gold on Carved Wood. 1760–70. James Davidson.

3040. Large, French. 18th C. Clifford R. Weld.

3039. "Cape Cod." One of Many Types Brought in by Sea Captains. 1760–70. 14 x 32. Carved and Gilded. Newport. Flayderman & Kaufman.

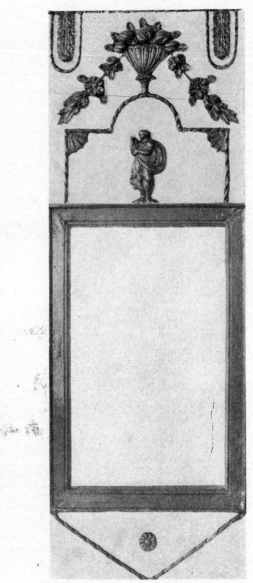

3042. ELABORATE. EAGLE ABOVE MEDALLION. 1790–1800. FRANCIS H. BIGELOW.
3043. (Right.) DIRECTOIRE. 1790–1800. 13½ x 38. FLAYDERMAN & KAUFMAN.

3044-45. EAGLE WITH ARROWS AND BIRD WITH FOLIAGE. A. H. EATON.

3047. Bilbao. Shell at Top. Rosettes and Inlay. Mahogany. 1790. Bigelow Collection.

3046. Seaman's Emblems in the Carving. Lantern, Spy Glass, Bell, Etc. Large. Gilded. 1790–1800. Nathanael Herreshoff.

3048. One of Pair. Latter 18th Century. Dutch or French. Carved and Gilded on Wood. Brass Sconce. 12 x 20. H. W. Erving. 3049. (Middle.) Carved on Wood. Gilded. 2nd Half 18th Century. Grotesque Face at Base. 23 x 36. John H. Buck. 3050. (Right.) Carved on Wood. Gilded. Sconces. This and Preceding, Perhaps Italian. 22 x 40. John H. Buck.

3051–53. ALL CARVED IN ONE PIECE. HEIGHT 10½ INCHES. CENTER: HEIGHT 11½ INCHES. THIS AND THE OTHER TWO, 3RD QUARTER 18TH CENTURY. ALL OF THE SAME PROVENANCE. THAT IS, THEY ARE CONTINENTAL, PERHAPS FRENCH OR DUTCH. ALL, H. W. ERVING.

3054. CARVED FROM ONE PIECE, NO MITERS. HEIGHT 20½ INCHES. 1750–75. H. W. ERVING.
3055. (Right.) CARVED ON WOOD. OUTSIDE 30½ x 56. MID 18TH CENTURY. THE MISSES A. AND E. P. FOSTER.

3056–57. TWO ITALIAN GLASSES. FORMERLY THE AUTHOR'S. MID 18TH CENTURY.

3058. CARVED ON WOOD IN ONE PIECE. NO MITERS. HEIGHT 21½ INCHES. 1750–75.
CHIPPENDALE TYPE. H. W. ERVING.

3059. (Right.) CARVED ON WOOD. GOLD. HEIGHT 34 INCHES. 2ND HALF 18TH CENTURY.
THE MISSES A. AND E. P. FOSTER.

3062. Carved on Wood, and Gilded. Height 15½ Inches. 1750–75. It Properly Belongs in Style with No. 3052. H. W. Erving.

3061. Carved on Wood. Helmeted Bust over an Oval Boss. Italian. 1740–60. Charles P. Cooley.

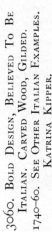

3060. Bold Design, Believed To Be Italian. Carved Wood, Gilded. 1740–60. See Other Italian Examples. Katrina Kipper.

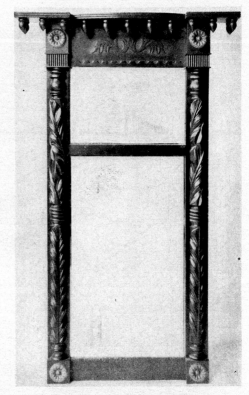

3063. THIRTEEN BALLS. 1800–10. NATHAN CUSHING.   3064. MAHOGANY. 1810–20. JAMES DAVIDSON

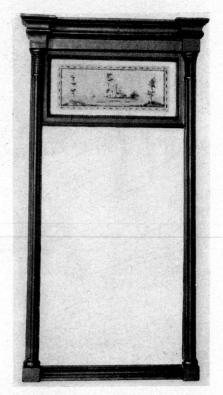

3065. HALF COLUMNS, GILDED. DOUBLE PANEL. PAINTED GLASS. 1800–10. BIGELOW COLLECTION.
3066. (Right.) EMPIRE. MODILLIONS ON FRAME. 1810–20. FRANK A. ROBART.

3067–68. ALL THIS CLASS CALLED ARCHITECTURAL. 1800–10. FLAYDERMAN & KAUFMAN.

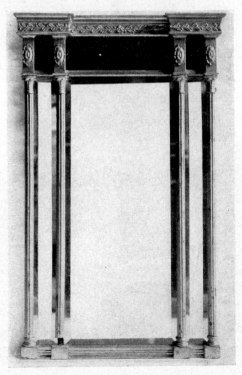

3069. SMALL GLASS ABOVE. S. PRESCOTT FAY.   3070. THREE GLASSES. 1800. C. R. MORSON.

3071. REVOLUTIONARY. NATIONAL FLAG AND ARMS. BELONGED TO A CONTINENTAL SOLDIER.
24 x 43. GILDED. JOHN H. BUCK.

3072. (Middle.) DOUBLE COLUMNS. STOOPING EAGLE, PAGODA CORNERS. GOLD. 1800–10. MRS. HARRY HORTON BENKARD.
3073. (Right.) PILLARS CARVED IN CORINTHIAN STYLE. INTERSECTING ARCHES. 1800–10. G. H. W. SMITH.

3074–75. Pine, Gilded. Original Label Shown Elsewhere. 1810–20. Flayderman & Kaufman.

3076–77. Curly Maple. Spindle Columns. 1810–20. McCarthy's Antique Shop, Cheshire.

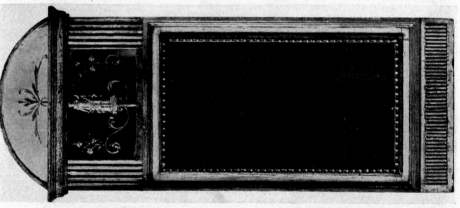

3079. Four Painted Glasses, in Black, White, and Silver. Reeding Black. Four Pillars with Acanthus Leaf Tops. 30 x 48. Pleasing Effect. 1800–10. Joe Kindig, Jr.

3078 A. Directoire. Figure on Colored Ground. 1790–1800. Bigelow Collection.

3078. All Glasses with Balls Sometimes Called Constitution, as Some Had Thirteen Balls. Architectural Is a Better Name. 1800–10. Charles P. Cooley.

3080–82. MAHOGANY. THE FIRST WITH A LYRE ABOVE THE COLUMN. 1820. FIRST AND SECOND, KATRINA KIPPER. THE THIRD, THE AUTHOR'S.

3083. UNUSUAL DESIGN. PINEAPPLES BOTH HORIZONTALLY AND VERTICALLY. REALLY ACORNS IN SHAPE. 1810–20. JOE KINDIG, JR.

3084. Ball Cornice with Unusual Columns, Carved Like Repeated Buds. 28½ x 36.
Thorp's Antique Shop, Plainfield, New Jersey.

3085. (Right.) Ball Cornice. Balls Recessed in Columns. Resting on Knobs. 1800–20.

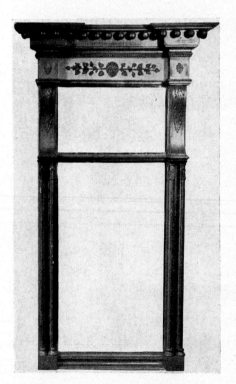
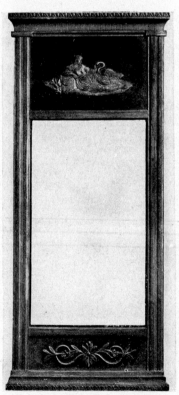
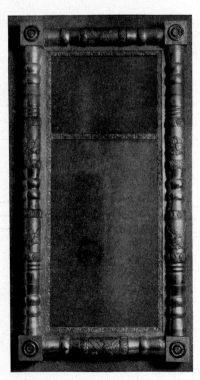

3086. Two Glasses, Modillions, Balls. Bigelow Collection.
3087. (Middle.) Directoire. Leda and Swan. Bigelow Collection.
3088. (Right). Plain. Late Half Spindle. Very Numerous.

3089. Half Column. Two Part. Upper Glass with Landscape. 1800–10. F. A. Robart.
3090. (Right.) Eagle in Flight with Scroll and Arrows. 1800–10. Estate of Harry W. Weeks.

3091. Six-Part. Three Upper Glasses, Painted in Five Designs. 1800–20. C. R. Morson.

Mantel glasses of a period earlier than this are very rare. The Chippendale glass scarcely ever seen, though we show some examples. Later than this the mantel glasses are very common.

3092-93. THREE-PART GLASS WITH THREE DISTINCTIVE SHELLS AND A LONG ARRAY OF ACORNS. 1800-20. AN ENGLISH CLOCK. THEY APPEAR IN SLIGHTLY VARYING DESIGNS. CHARLES P. COOLEY.

3094. McINTIRE GLASS, PEIRCE-NICHOLS HOUSE. GLASS PROBABLY MADE FOR ITS PRESENT POSITION. 1790– . ESSEX INSTITUTE.

3095-96. Eight Classical Figures, Dancing, in Central Panel. The Candles in Bronze with Hanging Crystals Are Decorative. 1800-20. Estate of Harry H. Weeks.

3097. Tasteful Columns. This Specimen Gains by the Simplicity of the Design. 1790-1810. Edward Crowninshield, Stockbridge.

3098. THREE-PART MANTEL GLASS. CLUSTERED COLUMNS WITH LARGE CAPITALS. 1800–10.
HELEN T. COOKE.

3099–3100. FOUR-PART GLASS. UNUSUAL DESIGN. MADE BY SOMEONE WHO LOVED TO PAINT
ON GLASS. CAPITALS AS MODILLIONS. FIGURES AT SIDES IN DECORATIVE POTTERY. 1800–10.
C. R. MORSON.

3101. FREE COLUMNS. EXCEEDINGLY RARE. 1800–10. BIGELOW COLLECTION.

3102. THREE-PART MANTEL GLASS. BIGELOW COLLECTION. 1800–20.
3102 A. CLOCK WITH EAGLE. FRENCH ORIGIN.

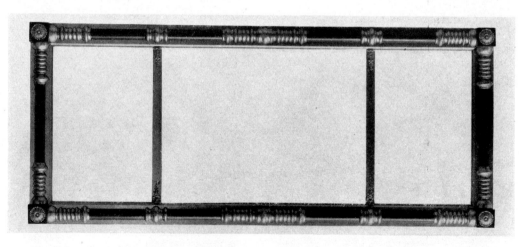

3103. SPLIT-SPINDLE GLASS. 22½ x 53. 1820–30.

3104. Corinthian Capitals. Spiraled Bead in Hollow Mold. 1800–10. Katrina Kipper.
3105. (Right.) Landscape of Connecticut River. 28 x 49. 1800–20. John H. Buck.

3106–07. Battersea. Late 18th Century. Diameter 3¾ Inches. Design Applied by Hand, in Lively Color Effects. Christine J. Steele. Courtesy of "Antiques."

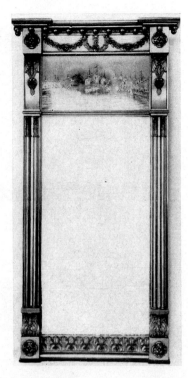

3108–09. EGYPTIAN MUMMY COLUMNS. RARE OR UNIQUE. 1796. MADE IN FRANCE. 23 x 36. WILLIAM B. GOODWIN. RIGHT: ARCHITECTURAL.

3110–13. SPIRALED COLUMN GLASS. MANTEL: READING TAVERN, NEAR CINCINNATI. ANDIRONS, OLD CHARTS, ADMIRABLE WALL DECORATION. WILLIAM B. GOODWIN.

3114. (Right.) BALL GLASS. 22 x 42. FOUND IN LYNN. 1800–10. FLAYDERMAN & KAUFMAN.

3115. Mantel Glass with Free Columns. A Variant of No. 3101. 1800–10. Bigelow Collection.

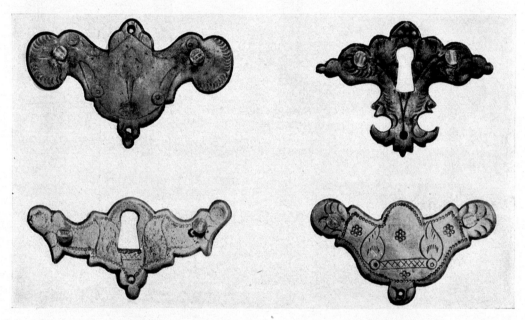

3116–19. Stamped Plates. 1690–1720. A. H. Eaton.

3120–21. Fair Faces on Old Knobs. Collection of A. H. Eaton, Collinsville.

3122–23. Bilbao Glasses. A Rare Pair. Marble and Gold. 1780–90. 22 x 50. Flayderman & Kaufman.

3124–25. Knobs in Black and Grey, Perhaps Mourning. Transfers from Copper Engraved Plates. Courtesy of "Antiques." Christine J. Steele.

3126–27. Bilbao Glasses, with Figures on a Blue Ground. Unusual Pair. 1780–90. Morris Berry.

3128–29. A Girandole and a Disk Glass. Perhaps Before 1780. 7 and 9 In. John H. Buck.

3130. MAHOGANY AND MARBLE. GLASSES FOUND AT BILBAO, BUT POSSIBLY FROM ITALY. SUGGESTIONS OF THE ADAM TYPE DO NOT INDICATE ENGLISH ORIGIN. FORMERLY THE AUTHOR'S. 3131. (Right.) BILBAO GLASS WITH FINE OPEN SCROLL. 1780–90. KATRINA KIPPER.

3132-33. A KNOB WITH THE NAME OF GENERAL STEUBEN. A SECOND, AN URN WITH PENDANTS, AND A FINE BORDER. THE FRAMES OF THESE KNOBS WERE OFTEN IMPORTANT AS WELL AS THE PICTURE. J. GROSSMAN.

3134. A RICH BILBAO GLASS NEARLY FOUR FEET HIGH. ELABORATE SCROLLS. 1780–90. C. R. MORSON.
3135. (Right.) MAHOGANY AND GILT, FROM PORTSMOUTH. 19 x 33½. CARVED GILT APPLIED ORNAMENTS. WAS OWNED BY COL. ABRAHAM DRAKE, WHO DIED 1781. INHERITED. CLIFFORD S. DRAKE.

3136. UNUSUAL FRETWORK. GILDED ROSETTES. 1780–90. MORRIS SCHWARTZ.
3137. (Right.) RESEMBLING BILBAO GLASS, BUT WOOD FRAME AND NO ROSETTES. 1790. C. R. MORSON.

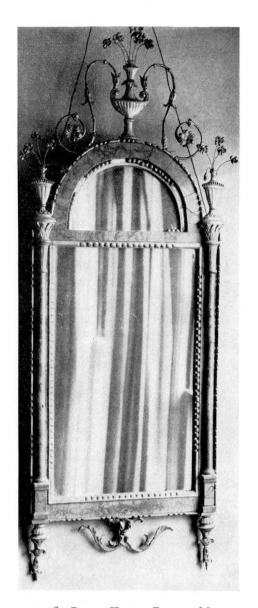

3138. ROUND-TOPPED BILBAO. MARBLE AND CARVED WOOD, GILDED. 1780–90. JOHN H. BUCK.
3139. (Right.) BILBAO GLASS, ORNAMENTS MISSING. MARBLE AND CARVED WOOD, GILDED. 1780–90.
MALCOLM A. NORTON.

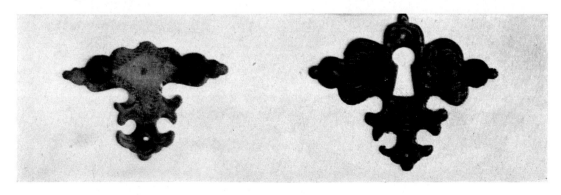

3140–41. QUEEN ANNE PLATE, AND ESCUTCHEON. 1690–1730. A. H. EATON, COLLINSVILLE.

3144. FINE GLASS AT TOP. FRAME
INLAID. 18 x 49. SALEM. 1790.
FLAYDERMAN & KAUFMAN.

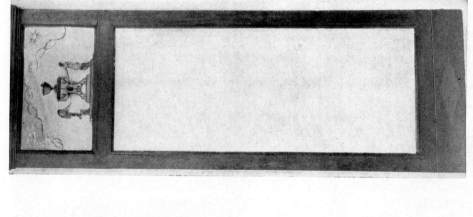

3143. DAINTILY CUT GLASS. FRAME
INLAID. 21½ x 60. 1780–90.
FLAYDERMAN & KAUFMAN.

3142. ALL CONTINENTAL. PERHAPS
GERMAN. INLAY AND CUT GLASS.
17 x 44. 1780–90. JOHN H. BUCK.

3147. Border Inlay. Conch-Shell. Mahogany Veneer. 20½ x 57¼. W. B. Goodwin.

3146A. Gilded Carvings. 26 x 62. Providence. Flayderman & Kaufman.

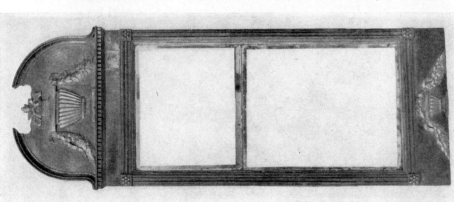

3146. Well-Shaped Top. Applied Gilded Carving. Mahogany. 17½ x 49. 1780–90. Flayderman & Kaufman.

3145. Inlaid Urn with Flowers and Diamond Inlay Below. 1780–90. John H. Buck.

3148. From Brooks Reed, Boston.

Here begin the courting glasses. They are so-called because they were carried in a shallow box with a cover when ladies went out calling. At the last moment they effected any necessary repairs to their countenances by inspecting themselves in the courting glasses. Their date is about 1800, and, like most glasses, they were brought from foreign parts, probably in the first place from China. The greater part of them are somewhat crude in workmanship. The frames are formed of glass decorated in the Chinese manner, or in other fashions which do not at all suggest that origin. Most of them are small and appropriate for carrying about. Occasionally one like that above is of pretty large size. It would seem that the fancy for them called for a size now and then proper for hanging on the wall.

3149. Unusual Courting Glass in that the Frame Is Mostly Molded. 18th Century. William F. Hubbard.

3150. (Right.) The Glass at the Top Is Masked. 18 x 26. John H. Buck, Hartford.

3151. Glass in Original Box, Cover Removed. This and the Following, William B. Goodwin.

3152. (Right.) Peregrine White Glass. 7 x 9¼. Pedigree on Back. Peregrine Died 1704. Pedigree Indicates Glass Belonged to His Parents.

3153. ARCHITECTURAL GLASS WITH DOUBLED COLUMNS. 1800–20. SANDERSON COLLECTION.
3154. (Right.) WELL PAINTED AND HARMONIOUS. THE ART OF PAINTING ON GLASS PERSISTS. C. P. COOLEY.

3155–57. GLASSES OWNED BY KATRINA KIPPER. THOSE AT THE SIDES FOLLOW THE CONVENTIONAL COURTING GLASSES IN DESIGN. CENTER; A DEAR LITTLE PIECE, RESEMBLING CAPE COD GLASSES.

3158. The Usual Type Which Indicates the Close Holding to a Copy. Perhaps Because of Chinese Habit. 12 x 16. John H. Buck.

3159. (Middle.) Beginning the Class of Convex Glasses, Otherwise Called Girandole. It Belonged to the End of the 18th Century, and It Is Said Was Designed so that a Hostess Could Take in at a Glance All That Was Occurring in a Room Full of Guests. Thorp's Antique Shop, Plainfield, New Jersey.

3160. (Right.) Courting Glass in Original Box. The Cover Was Attached by Small Hooks. Estate of Harry W. Weeks.

3161-63. GLASSES AS ARRANGED ON THE WALL OF MRS. CHARLES P. COOLEY, HARTFORD. THOSE AT THE SIDE ARE ITALIAN, AND STRONGLY DECORATIVE. THE CENTER GLASS IS A GIRANDOLE WITH EAGLE. CENTER, 1800. SIDES, 1750-75.

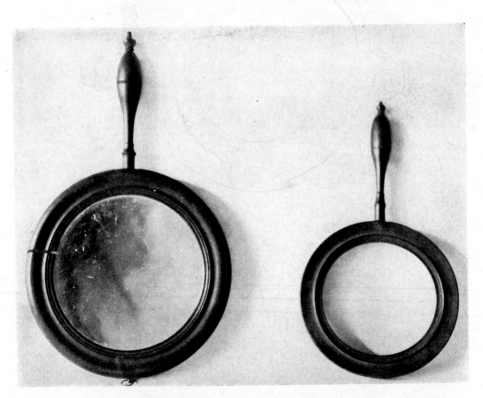

3164-65. BEAUTIFUL LITTLE HAND GLASSES, IN ONE OF WHICH THE GLASS IS CURVED. POSSIBLY THE ATTACHMENT SEEMED FRAGILE, OTHERWISE WE WONDER THAT THE STYLE WAS NOT POPULAR. WILLIAM F. HUBBARD.

3166. A Very Large and Ornate Girandole. St. George and the
Dragon. The Sconces Afforded Good Light, Since It Was Radiated
at Many Angles. c. 1800. Francis Hill Bigelow.

3167. An Elaborate Glass with Four Sconces Carrying Crystals. Decoration with a Grapevine. Eagle Above and Foliage Below. One Sees Here the Same Balls as in the Architectural Glasses. Rhode Island School of Design.

3168. (Right.) Elaborate and Unusual Glass with Rests for Lights Arranged in an Irregular Form. The Misses A. and E. P. Foster.

3169 and 3171. The Two Glasses, One on Either Side of This Page, Are a Pair, but the Eagles Are Differently Poised for Variety's Sake. Wired Sconces, Gilded. These Girandoles Are Commonly Gilded. C. R. Morson, New York.

3170. (Center.) An Example with Four Spiraled Sconces. The Inclusive Reflection, All in Focus, Indicates the Advantage of the Style. Flamboyant Foliage. Charles P. Cooley.

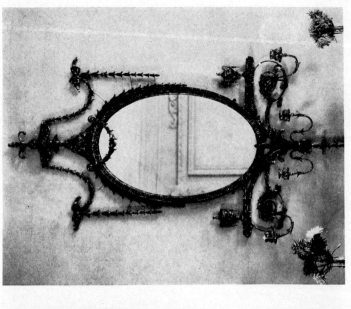

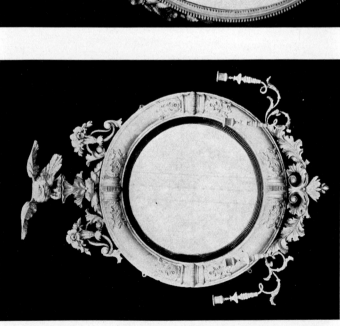

3172. A Four-Sconce Girandole with Foliage Scrolls on the Sconces, and Urns of Flowers on Either Side of the Boldly Carved Eagle. Reeded Black Border Next the Glass. H. H. Valentine Company, Richmond.

3173. (Middle.) Beginning a Class of Glasses of the Hepplewhite Period, Specifically Designated Filigree. Wired Carvings above the Oval Glass, Topped by Three Carved Feathers. English. C. R. Morson.

3174. (Right.) A Glass upon Which the Maker Expended No Little Ingenuity. Four Sconces, Two Good Urns above Them, Surmounted by Large Urns and Festoons.

3175. A High Spike Rising from the Top to a Broad Canopy with Wheat Ears. 1780–90. Katrina Kipper.

3176. (Right.) A Shield-Shaped Glass with Vase, Floral Scrolls, and Sconces. 1780–90. Morris Berry.

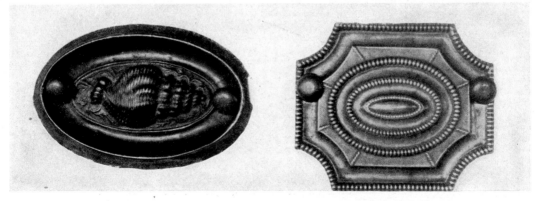

3177–78. A Good Snail Shell Brass, and a Brass with Band upon Band of Pearl-Shaped Ornaments. 1790–1800. A. H. Eaton.

3179–80. Two Glasses from Katrina Kipper, Accord. Such Pieces Are Not Meant To Be Moved Once They Are Placed on the Wall. They Are Most Effective against a Plain Wood or Paper Panel. 1780–90.

3181–82. A Pair of Drapery Holders, 19th C. F. A. Robart.

3183. A Panel or Mantel Glass with Very Sketchy Decoration of Wheat Ears and Festoons. Webb House, Colonial Dames, Wethersfield, Connecticut.

3184. An Unusual Horizontal Glass for Mantel. Three Part, the End Sections Being Cut. Mid 18th Century. Katrina Kipper.

3185-86. Stamped Brass Drapery Hooks. 19th Century. F. A. Robart.

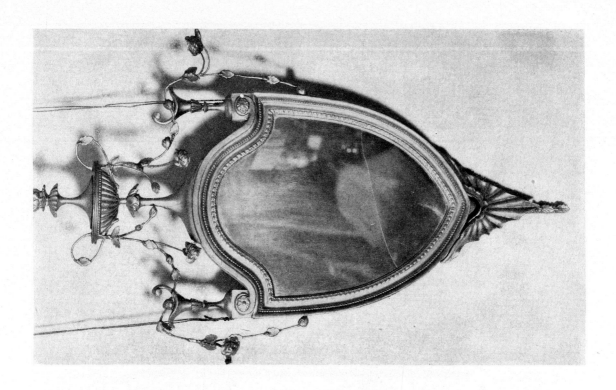

3187 and 3188. (Opposite, left.) 3187 Has Grapevine Decoration with a Knotted Cord and Tassel, Urn and Artichokes. Samuel Wineck, Hartford. 3188. (Opposite, right.) A Shield Glass with Pitchers and Urn Connected by Wired Traceries. 1780–90. John H. Buck.

3189–90. American Glasses, Late 18th Century. Carved, Gilt with Sconces. Metropolitan Museum.

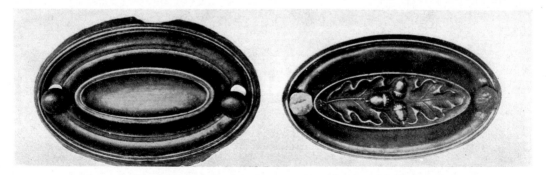

3191–92. Brasses of 1790–1800, the Right Being an Oak Leaf with Acorns. A. H. Eaton.

3193. Hepplewhite, 1780. Gilded, as Always. 19⅜ x 32⅜. Robert T. Smith, Hartford.
3194. (Right.) Pheasants Sustaining Festoons from an Urn. Cupid Below. Shelves and Sconces. Height 45 Inches. 1780-90. Misses A. and E. P. Foster.

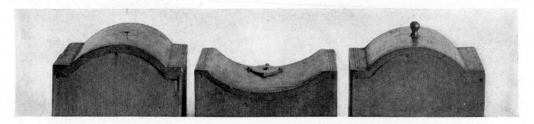

3195-97. Detail To Show Edge of Drawers on Queen Anne Glass, No. 3205.

3198. QUEEN ANNE GLASS, PINE. 17 x 12 x 8. SALEM. 1740–60. FLAYDERMAN & KAUFMAN.
3199. QUEEN ANNE GLASS, WITH A CURVED BASE IN THE DRAWERS, AND DAINTY FINIALS. 1750–70.

3200. A PIECE CALLED BY THE OWNER A FIRE SCREEN, BUT OF ABOUT THE HEIGHT OF A DRESSING GLASS
AND OBVIOUSLY USABLE FOR THAT PURPOSE. ENGLISH. 30 x 25. MAHOGANY. 1780–1800. INLAID.
3201. (Right.) ANOTHER ENGLISH GLASS. WALNUT. 22 x 42. ALL ORIGINAL. 1730–50.
BOTH, MRS. FRANCIS P. GARVAN.

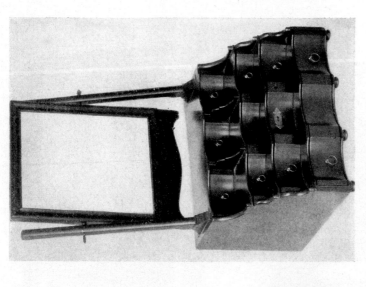

3202. Shaving Glass, Original Condition. 18 x 12 x 7. Mahogany. Connecticut. Very Good Lines. 1750–75. Robert P. Butler.

3203. (Center.) American Empire, Mahogany. Connecticut. c. 1825. H. W. Erving.

3204. (Right.) Shaving Glass with Four Tiers of Drawers, All Concave with Flat Connection. All These Drawers Have Precisely the Same Contour as the Concave Central Drawer in the Next Piece. 1750–70. Frank A. Robart.

3205. (Opposite.) Most Remarkable Shaving Glass. A Recent Find. A Walnut Block Front. The Wood Is Light in Color, like the New England White Walnut. Pine Is Used in the Back and Bottom of the Stand, and Bottom and Three Sides of the Drawers, and Back and Frame of the Glass Itself. The Top and the Front as Well as the Crest Are Crotch Walnut. 6 x 20 x 28. This Piece Indicates Very Early Use of the Block Front, at Least in This Arc Form. Probably Before 1750. A Delightful and Important Piece. Rhode Island. William B. Goodwin.

3206. (Opposite, right.) Kettle Base Glass. Pierced Circle with Ornament, like Chippendale Glass. 1750–75. "Antiques," March, 1923.

3207. Shaving Glass, Mahogany, Hepplewhite. Inlaid Fan. 21½ x 21. 1780–90. Flayderman & Kaufman.
3208. (Right.) Mahogany, Inlaid. 1790–1800. James Davidson.

3209. American Hepplewhite, Mahogany. Slight Inlay. Opalescent Glass Knobs. Silver Trimmings. Glass 16 x 20. c. 1800. H. W. Erving.
3210. (Right.) American Mahogany Glass, 17 Inches Long. Spiral Carved Posts, and Finials. Kettle Base. Front and Ends Cut from the Solid. 1790–1800. H. W. Erving.

3211. MAHOGANY AND SATINWOOD. AMERICAN. C. 1800. H. V. WEIL, NEW YORK.

These glasses are indiscriminately named shaving glass, toilet glass, also glass with a box. The earliest are in the Queen Anne time, and the latest are degraded Empire.

3212-13. TWO GLASSES, THE FORMER DATING ABOUT 1820, AND THE LATTER ABOUT 1800. MORRIS BERRY.

3214. WALNUT, SHIELD SHAPE. HEPPLEWHITE. HEIGHT 16½ INCHES. TRESTLE FEET. IVORY
ROSETTES. STRING INLAY. 1785–95. H. W. ERVING.

3215. (Right.) OVAL, HEPPLEWHITE. THESE STANDARDS LEAN BACKWARD. 1790. SAMUEL WINECK.

3216. DAINTY SIDE SUPPORT. MAHOGANY. 24 x 21. NEW HAMPSHIRE. 1810–20. RUDOLPH P. PAULY.

3217. (Right.) REEDED. IVORY KNOBS. SMALL SPINDLE GALLERIES. 1820–30. FLAYDERMAN & KAUFMAN.

3218. Only Glass Shown without a Base, Suggests the Back of a Hepplewhite Chair. Braces Behind. 1790. Mrs. Francis P. Garvan.

3219. (Right.) Oval. Serpentine Drawers. Ivory Buttons. 1800. Morris Berry.

3220. Mahogany, Reeded Posts, String Inlay. Embossed Brass Knobs and Feet. New York State. Sheraton Type. c. 1800. H. W. Erving.

3221. (Right.) Mahogany, Line Inlay. Connecticut. c. 1800. James Davidson.

JOHN ELLIOTT,
At his LOOKING-GLASS STORE,
the Sign of the *Bell* and *Looking-glass*, in *Walnut-street*, PHILADELPHIA,
IMPORTS and SELLS all Sorts of *English* Looking-glasses, at the lowest Rates.
He also new Quickfilvers and Frames old Glasses, and supplies People with new Glass to their own Frames.

Johannes Elliott,
In feinem Waarenlager (oder Store) wo die Glocke und der Spiegel aushängt, in der Walnuß-strasse, zu Philadelphia, Hat jederzeit einen grossen Vorrath von allerley Englischen Spiegeln, welche er herein bringen läßet, und um den wohlfeilsten Preis verkauft. Er macht auch neu Queckfilber an alte Gläser, und setzt sie in neue Rahmen, versiehet auch die Leute, mit neuen Gläsern zu ihren eigenen Rahmen.

3222. A LABEL ON THE BACK OF A QUEEN ANNE GLASS.
J. STOGDELL STOKES.

3223. THE WOOL SPINNING WHEEL. OPERATED BY FINGER OR SPINNING STICK.

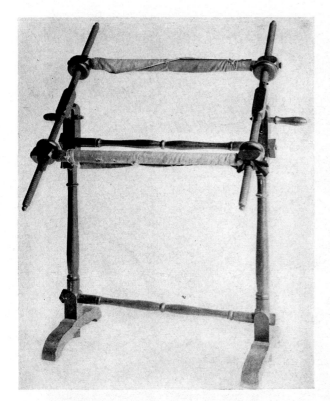

3224. EMBROIDERY FRAME, ADJUSTABLE. 18TH CENTURY. EDWARD C. WHEELER, JR.

3225. (Right.) YARN REEL, WITH CLICKING COUNTER. 18TH CENTURY. WADSWORTH ATHENEUM.

3226. A REEL WHICH REGISTERS THE REVOLUTIONS AND SO MEASURES THE YARN.

3227-28. (Right.) BOBBIN WHEEL AND CARD. THE WHEEL WAS TO PREPARE THE YARN FOR THE LOOM. THE CARD WAS TO PREPARE THE WOOL FOR SPINNING.

3229–32. A Rag-Carpet Loom in Operation. The Lady Is Wearing One of the Marvelous
Old Silk Quilted Petticoats. On Top of Highboy: Washington and Silver Luster Pitcher.

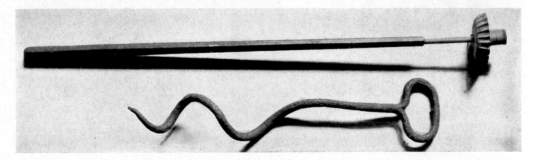

3233–34. A Candle Torch, and a Twisted Article No Longer Used. Fuessenich Collection.

3235. SPINNING JENNY OR FLAX WHEEL. HANK OF FLAX READY FOR SPINNING.
3236. (Right.) REEL WITH ADJUSTABLE ARMS FOR SHORTER SKEINS.

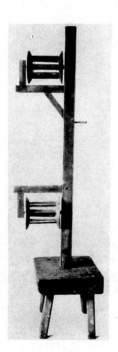

3237. A DOUBLE JENNY FOR SPINNING TWO YARNS AT ONCE. 3238. ADJUSTABLE, VERTICAL WHEEL.
3239. A JENNY OF THE CONNECTICUT CHAIR-FRAME TYPE. ADJUSTMENT FOR TIGHTENING BELT.
ALL: WADSWORTH ATHENEUM.

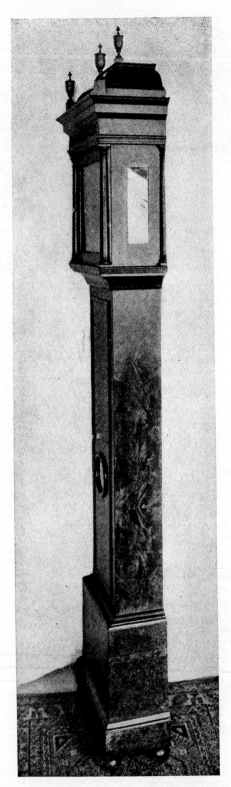

3240. BY BENJAMIN BAGNALL, CHARLESTOWN, MASSACHUSETTS. BURL VENEER ON PINE.
c. 1730. ONE OF THE EARLIEST MAKERS. JOHN M. MILLER, PROVIDENCE.

3241. (Right.) SIDE VIEW OF THE SAME. BALL FEET. ENGLISH INFLUENCE.

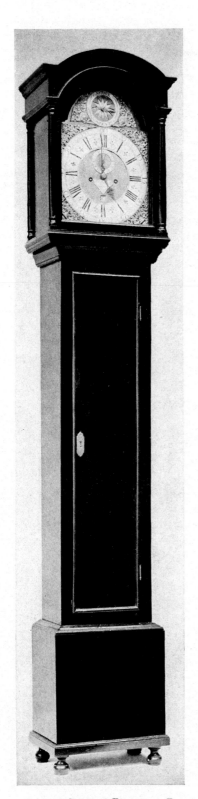

3242. Samuel Bagnall, Boston, 1740–60. Mahogany. Metropolitan Museum.
3243. (Right.) Benjamin Bagnall, Boston, 1725–50. Walnut on Pine. Beautiful Frets. Metropolitan Museum.

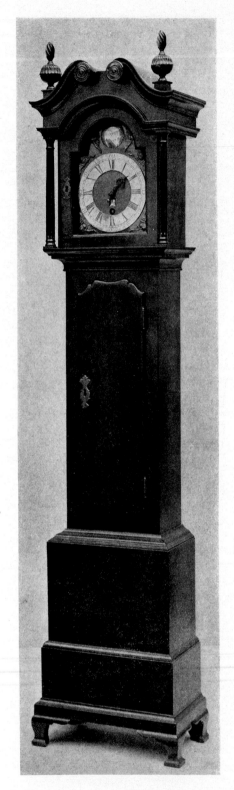

3244. THOMAS CLAGGETT, NEWPORT. 1730–49. MINIATURE, MAHOGANY. METROPOLITAN MUSEUM.
3245. (Right.) WILLIAM CLAGGETT, NEWPORT. 1730–49. CHINESE LACQUER. WALTER H. DURFEE.

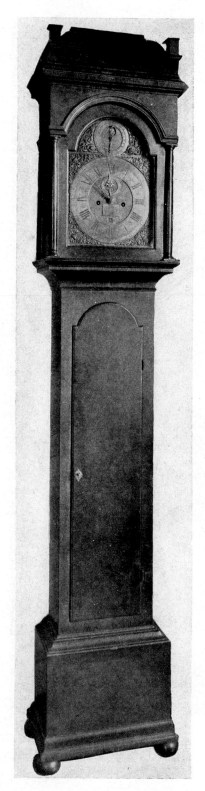 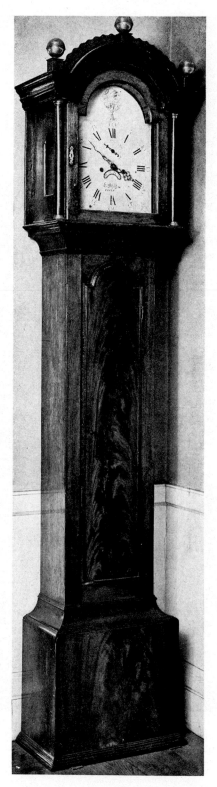

3246. W. Claggett, Newport, 1730–49. Mrs. Stanley Bristol, Newport.
3247. (Right.) "E. Willard Fecit," 1777–1805. Rare. Bigelow Collection.

3248. WILLIAM CLAGGETT DIAL. HE MADE THE BEST. NAME SPELLED HERE WITH T DOUBLED. IN NEXT NUMBER SPELLED WITH ONE T. NOTHING LIKE VARIETY! HEIRS OF WILLIAM G. RUSSELL, LATE OF PROVIDENCE.

3249. WILLIAM CLAGGETT DIAL. CLOCK BURIED AT KINGSTON, R. I., DURING THE REVOLUTION.
G. WINTHROP BROWN, BOSTON, 1730–49.

3250. By Contrast There Is Shown Above a Fromanteel & Clarke. 1710. Name on Outside
Edge of Circle. Below on Dial, A. Fromanteel. One of Best Early English. Rhode Island
School of Design.

3251-52. Oval and Round Brasses, General Washington. Quite Dissimilar.
Bigelow Collection.

3253. E. Willard Dial. Brass; Iron Painted Top, "Boston Light." Important. Clocks of Ephraim Willard Were Rare. Usually Dials Were Painted White on Iron. The Brass Is Better but Not So Legible. W. G. A. Turner, Malden, Massachusetts.

The purpose of the tall clock was to protect the long pendulum. When the short pendulum applied to Willard clocks came in tall clocks soon went out of fashion. But so great is their decorative and sentimental value that a generation ago they again became popular. The ancient short pendulum clock of the 17th century was not a good timekeeper.

3254. FROMANTEEL DIAL. MARSDEN J. PERRY, PROVIDENCE.

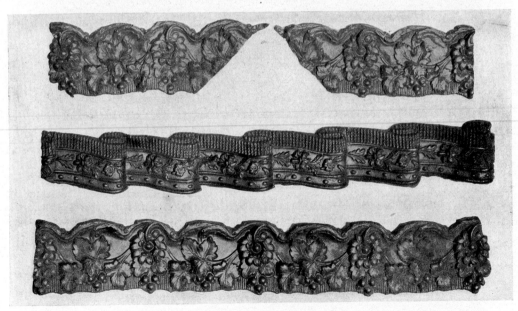

3255-58. BRASS CORNICES FOR WINDOWS. 19TH CENTURY. FRANK A. ROBART.

3259. S. Taber. His Date and Place Are Uncertain. S. M. Taber Is Traced to Providence in 1824. Mahogany, Inlaid. 1800–10. Leonard M. Robinson, Providence.

3260. (Right.) Benjamin Willard, Grafton, 1743–1803. Mahogany. c. 1790. Brass Band around Columns Halfway Up. W. L. Mulligan, Springfield.

DIRECTIONS FOR PUTTING UP THE TIMEPIECE.

Drive a brad in the wall where it is to be placed and Suspend the Time piece upon it. Open the lower door which is unfastened by turning the button a little forward with the key. Loosen the pendulum by which the Timepiece may be plumbed, observing that it hangs free of the case and in a line with the point where it was confined: then screw it to the wall with two screws thro' the back. Put the pendulum in motion. The weight is already wound up. Set it with the minute hand which may be moved backwards or forwards. To make the TIMEPIECE go faster raise the pendulum ball by the screw at the bottom. to make it go slower. lower the ball with the same screw.

These Timepieces are an improvement upon all others. as they go by a Weight instead of a Spring, and the pendulum being of a longer calculation than in any other small Pieces. renders it more accurate and has proved to keep better time. The President of the United States having granted a Patent for them. they are made by licence from the Patentee by Aaron Willard Jun.r Washington St. Boston.

near Roxbury.
MASSACHUSETTS

3261. AARON WILLARD, JUNIOR'S, LABEL.

3262. NEEDLEWORK PICTURE, 21 X 42, IN EARLY FRAME. FRANCIS H. BIGELOW.

3263. A Block Front with Shell. Scrolled Top, Fretwork and Fine Fluted and Spiraled Finials. 1760–75.

3264. (Right.) Curly Maple, Connecticut. 84 x 22½ x 12. Asahel Cheney, East Hartford. He Was Known To Be in Northfield in 1790, but This Clock Is Earlier. Carved Quarter Columns. Inlaid Spandrels. Both: Mrs. Francis P. Garvan.

A considerable number of block clocks is known. The writer has tallied seven, and has heard of others. So far as traced they go back to Newport or Providence. They were undoubtedly made by John Goddard or his father-in-law, Job Townsend. The blocking and the shell are precisely like those found on his secretaries. The same motive is in the hood. They prove that the fret was used on American pieces. It should be observed that the pillars are not as attenuated as in most clocks. Also that in this fine early period, no brasses were used for the bases or capitals of pillars, nor for top ornaments. All is in wood. In these clocks the case is far more important than the works.

3265. (Opposite.) Block and Shell, Stop Flute Quarter Columns, All Wood Including Ornaments. Works by William Tomlinson, London. Before 1760. Metropolitan Museum.

3266. (Right, opposite.) Cherry and Pine, Satinwood Inlay. 111 x 20½ x 11½. Was Capt. Thomas Marshall's, Washington, Kentucky, Son of Col. Thomas of the Same Place and Virginia, and Brother of Chief Justice Marshall. Large Survival about Cincinnati of Cherry, and Inlays of Veneer, Satinwood, Bird's Eye Birch, in Desks, Sideboards, Et Cetera. Weights Left Behind in Virginia. 1775–1810. William B. Goodwin.

3267. (Above.) Beautifully Inlaid and Cross-Band Veneered. Eli Porter, Williamstown, Massachusetts.

3268. (Right.) Mahogany, No Name. 96 x 19 x 10. c. 1790. Mrs. Francis P. Garvan.

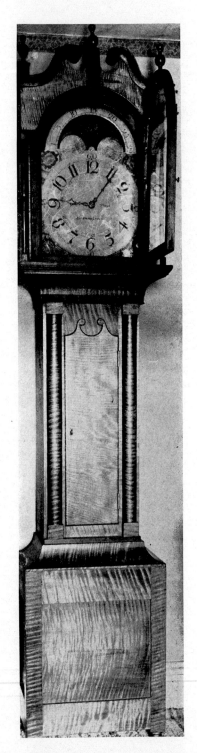

3269. BLOCK FRONT WITH SHELL. JOHN GODDARD. ALL WOOD, NO BRASS ORNAMENTS. NO NAME, AND THE SAME IS TRUE OF SOME OTHER GODDARD CLOCKS. FEET ALWAYS FINE OGEE. 1760–75. G. W. H. SMITH, PROVIDENCE.

3270. (Right.) BEAUTIFULLY CURLED MAPLE. CLOCKS OF THIS CLASS IN PENNSYLVANIA HAD, USUALLY, TURNED FEET. MADE BY SHEID, PENNSYLVANIA. FRANCIS MIREAU, DOYLESTOWN.

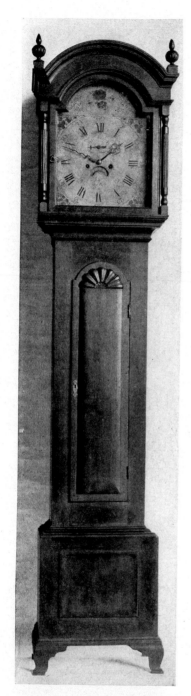

3271. Block Front Shell. Height 84 Inches. Apple Wood. David Williams. 1825, Given as His Date, Is Obviously Too Late. The Shell Is Not Quite Equal to No. 3263, and the Quarter Columns Are Omitted.

3272. (Right.) Very Rare Turned Columns, Repeated on Hood. 1790–1800. Both: Mrs. Francis P. Garvan.

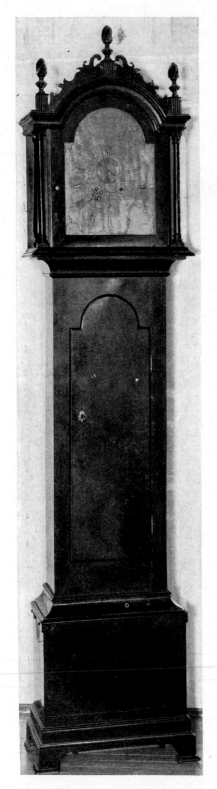 

3273. SOLID MAHOGANY. 87 x 18 x 9. BRASS WORKS AND DIAL, ENGRAVED, "TIME FLIES AND DEATH COMES." 1775. BY THOMAS HARLAND, NORWICH, CONNECTICUT. ROBERT T. SMITH, HARTFORD.

3274. (Right.) BLOCK FRONT AND SHELL CASE BY JOHN GODDARD, NEWPORT. CASE VERY SIMILAR TO TOWNSEND'S No. 3265. WILLIAM H. PUTNAM, HARTFORD.

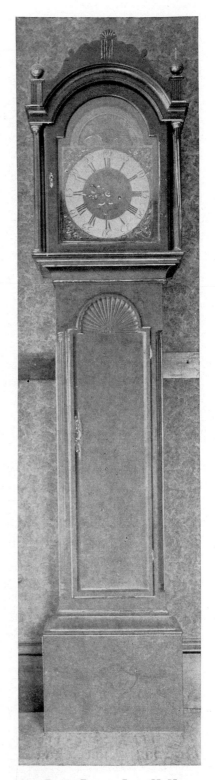

3275. HANDSOME VENEERED CASE. NEW ENGLAND FRET, WITH BRASS BALLS. JOHN H. HALFORD, NORRISTOWN, PENNSYLVANIA.

3276. (Right.) SUNBURST, CONCAVED DOOR. ENOS DOOLITTLE, NEW HAVEN, 1772. OWNED IN PLYMOUTH, MASSACHUSETTS.

3277. (Opposite.) DAVID RITTENHOUSE. OWNED BY DREXEL INSTITUTE AND IN PENNSYLVANIA MUSEUM, PHILADELPHIA. RICHEST AMERICAN CLOCK. CASE OBVIOUSLY MADE IN THE SAVERY TIME, AND IN PHIL-ADELPHIA. THIS CLOCK MECHANICALLY IS A WORK OF GENIUS. OF COURSE, THE CASE, FROM THE NATURE OF THE WORKS, APPEARS TOO BROAD.

3278. (Above.) A DAVID RITTENHOUSE DIAL ON THE GENERAL WAYNE CLOCK. WAYNE'S FIGURE APPEARS DIMLY IN THE BRASS CIRCLE ABOVE. ESTATE OF WILLIAM E. MONTAGUE, NORRISTOWN.

Dav. Rittenhouse

3279. David Rittenhouse Was a Great Clock Maker, Astronomer, and Friend. He Shares with Franklin the Features of the Early Ideal American. The Beauty and Quality of His Clocks Are Unsurpassed. He Was a Notable Figure, Politically, Socially, and Mechanically. His Home Was Norriton, from Which Norristown Is Taken.

 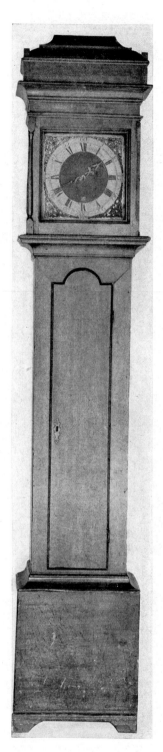

3280. CURLY MAPLE, THREE BULL'S EYES IN THE DOOR. PLAIN TOP. BY HENRY G. MOLBROW.
3281. (Right.) DAVID RITTENHOUSE. CASE SUGGESTS ENGLISH INFLUENCE. PLAIN BELOW.
PHILIP MEREDITH ALLEN, BROAD AXE, PENNSYLVANIA, OWNS BOTH.

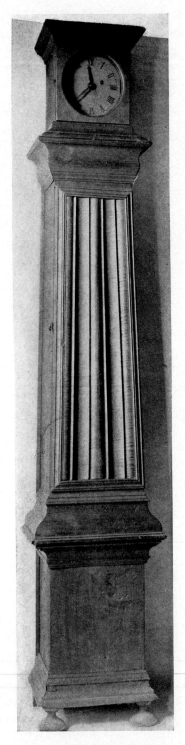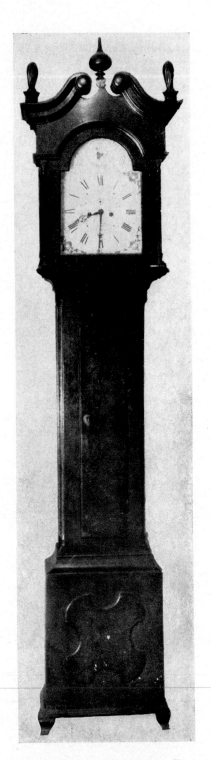

3282. A Rare Pattern like a Monument. Bun Feet, Called in America, Onion Feet.
Fuessenich Collection.

3283. (Right.) Unusual Arch with Plain Boss. Finials in Wood.

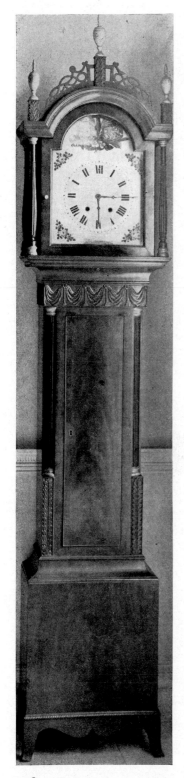

3284. Carved Base of Quarter Columns and Finials.   Drapery under the Hood.
1785–1800. Mrs. Harry Horton Benkard.

3285. (Right.) Carved Shell and Foliage. Reversed Spiral Flames. Plain Columns.
Richly Featured Grain in Door. W. Gedney Beatty. Both at Metropolitan Museum.

3286. By Thomas Harland, Norwich. Good Spiral Flames. Scalloped Mold on Upper Section of Base. Large Ogee Feet. 1773-1807. He Advertised that He Made a Great Variety of Watches and Clocks and Parts "Neat as Is In London, and at the Same Price." Taught Apprentices, among Them, Eli Terry. Wadsworth Atheneum.

3287. (Right.) "S. Willard." Case with Rich Mahogany, Featured, and Inlaid Bands. Fret over Arch, Also Second Fret Immediately over Dial. From E. A. Locke, M.D., Boston.

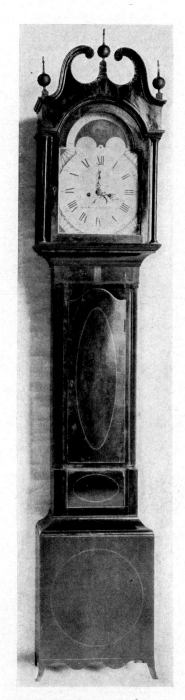 

3288. LINE INLAY, SLENDER ARCH. BRASS BALLS. 94 x 19 x 9½. MAHOGANY.
3289. (Right.) FINE INLAID BAND ABOUT DOOR, BASE OF QUARTER COLUMNS CARVED.
BY JAMES DOULL, CHARLESTOWN. BOTH: MRS. FRANCIS P. GARVAN.

3290. Featured Grain, Carved Chamfer on Base. Fret under Hood, and over Arch. Mrs. Francis P. Garvan.

3291. (Right.) Carved Door Top. Good Light Inlaid Scrolls in Spandrel. By Peter Clark, Manchester, England. Charles P. Cooley.

3292. PHILADELPHIA TYPE. BEAUTIFULLY CARVED HOOD WITH DENTILS AND SPIRAL ROSETTES FOLIATED. RICH GRAIN DOOR IN BASE. PENNSYLVANIA MUSEUM, MEMORIAL HALL, PHILADELPHIA.

3293. (Right.) PHILADELPHIA PATTERN, GOOD PIERCED SCROLL WITH DENTILS. MRS. ELLSWORTH SPERRY, EAST WINDSOR HILL, CONNECTICUT.

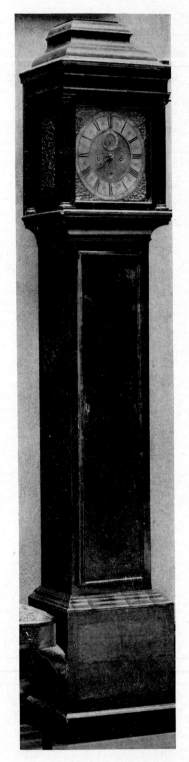

3294. DANIEL QUARE, ENGLAND. c. 1700. HE WAS A CELEBRATED MAKER. CHARLES F. WILLIAMS COLLECTION, PENNSYLVANIA MUSEUM, PHILADELPHIA.

3295. (Right.) MINIATURE, OTHERWISE CALLED A GRANDMOTHER CLOCK. BY J. WILDER, HINGHAM, 1780–1800. THIS MAKER SPECIALIZED ON MINIATURES. C. PRESCOTT KNIGHT, PROVIDENCE.

3296. Brass Face, Plain Columns. The Contour of the Hood Is Found in Few English and American Examples. Mrs. Charles P. Cooley, Hartford.

3297. (Right.) Bull's-Eye Door, Engaged Columns Front and Back on Hood, Heavy Cornice. E. S. Macomber, Providence.

3298. Simple Case, Applied Carved Heart in Base, Carved Rosette at Center of Arch. Nathan Cushing, Providence.

3299. (Middle.) Inlay on Door and Base. Remarkable Top, Square with Fretted Gallery and Fans. Unusual Hands. Found by the Author in Portsmouth. c. 1800.

3300. (Right.) Applied Half Spindle, Spool Turned. Carved Rosettes. Four Star Inlay. Cherry and Satinwood, and Mahogany Trim. By Jacob Cope, Pennsylvania. Name Engraved on Pendulum. Cope Is an English Name. The Case Is Undoubtedly American. Very Slender Waist. Malcolm A. Norton.

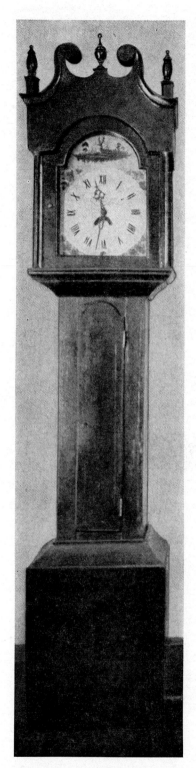

3301. GRANDMOTHER'S CLOCK WITH SHARP RAMP. 1780–1800.

3302. (Right.) COL. WILLIAM TERRY CLOCK, OLD GARRISON HOUSE, TRENTON. BY JOHN WOOD, PHILADELPHIA.

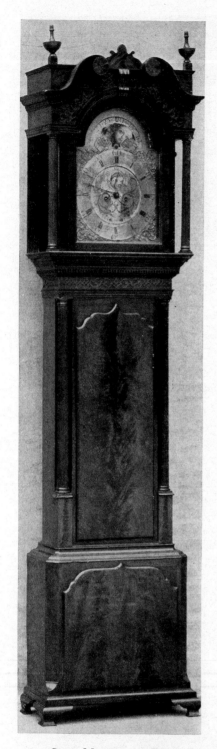 

3303. Solid Mahogany. Front Beautifully Marked Crotch. Fret and Dentil under Hood and over Arch. Urns Carved, Works Brass. By Barker Wigan. H. C. Valentine & Company.

3304. (Right.) By Thomas Harland, Norwich. c. 1790. Brass Face on Which Are the Name and Place. William H. Putnam, Hartford.

3305. BY WILLIAM CUMMENS. c. 1825. FLUTE STOPPED WITH BRASS. CROTCH GRAIN MAHOGANY ON DOOR AND INLAID PATERA BELOW. D. J. STEELE, EAST MILTON, MASSACHUSETTS.

3306. (Right.) A DRY-BATTERY ELECTRIC CLOCK, ESSEX INSTITUTE, SALEM, MASSACHUSETTS.

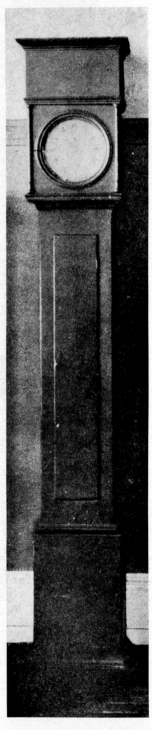

3307. Arch Unusually Open. Very Light Spindling Columns. Pagodaed Finials. Estate of Wm. E. Montague.
3308. (Middle.) Quarter Column in Base and on Waist. Rhode Island School of Design.
3309. (Right.) By David Rittenhouse. Early. Markedly Simple and Narrow. Estate of Wm. E. Montague.

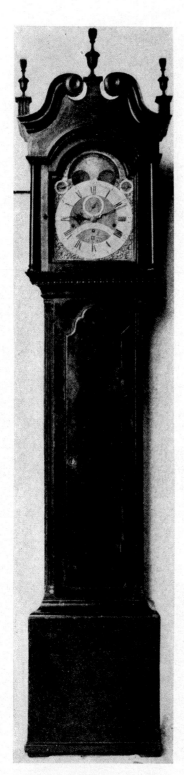

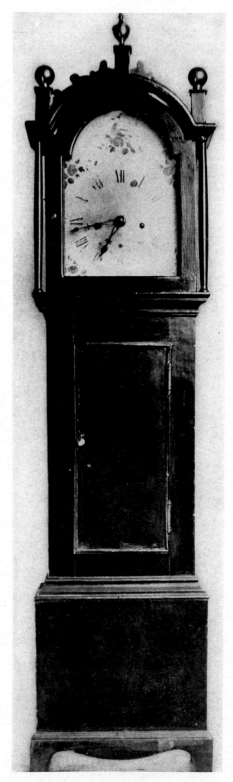

3310. By Henry Flower, Philadelphia. Fine Cabinet Work. Flying Finials. Mrs. C. Wheaton Vaughn.

3311. (Right.) Miniature, 48 Inches High. Essex Institute. Too Large in Waist!

3312. ENGLISH CLOCK WITH PEDIMENT CLOSED. CARVED PENDANTS. GREEK MOLD ON
ARCH. CARVED MODILLION. I. SACK, FROM PALMER COLLECTION.

3313. (Right.) BY GAWEN BROWN, OF JAMES STREET, BOSTON, 1750–76, BUT BY RECORD
WAS IN BROOKLYN, CONNECTICUT, IN 1742.

3314. THE DIAL: "PRESERVED CLAPP, NEW ENGLAND." DIALS PRINTED FROM ENGRAVINGS. ESSEX INSTITUTE, SALEM.

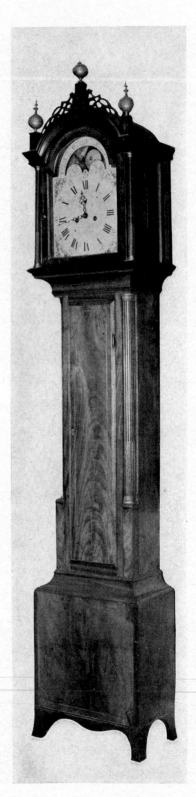

3315. David Rittenhouse, Twenty-Four Hour. The Shell and Door Almost Approach a Block.
John H. Halford, Norristown.

3316. (Right.) Simon Willard, Inlaid Mahogany. 94½ x 19 x 10. Bigelow Collection.
Sometimes Rear Columns on Hood Were Engaged, Sometimes Omitted Entirely.

3317–18. Miniature or Grandmother Clocks, Owned by Mrs. M. B. Cookerow, Pottstown, Pennsylvania. That at the Left Has No Name. That at the Right Reads "Hy. Bower." They Are Probably Both Pennsylvania Clocks. Like the Grandmother Clocks Made in Pennsylvania, They Have a Small Waist, Good Dials with a Ship Motion, or Other Good Features. The Hoods Are Artistic, but the Feet Are Not Attractive.

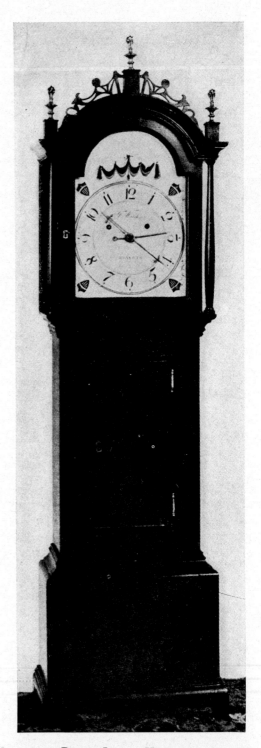

3319. William Claggett, 1730–49, Newport. Mahogany. Rhode Island Historical Society, Providence.

3320. (Right.) Joshua Wilder, Hingham, Massachusetts. c. 1790. Pine. Time and Alarm. The Shield Corners on Dial Are Common in His Clocks. Miniature. C. Prescott Knight, Providence.

3321. David Williams, Newport. 1800–10. Mahogany. The Fret Is Unusual. Brass Bases
and Capitals and Finials. Dr. Emory M. Porter, Providence.

3322. (Right.) Caleb Wheaton, Providence. c. 1800. Mahogany with Fret on Bonnet.
Mrs. Guy Metcalf Keating, Pinehurst, North Carolina.

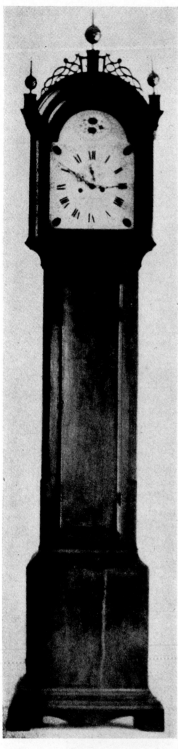
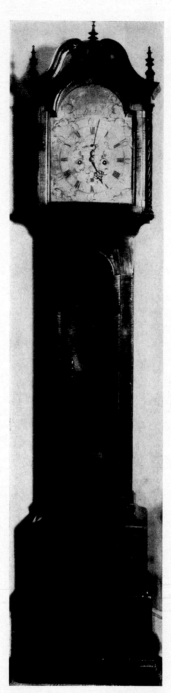
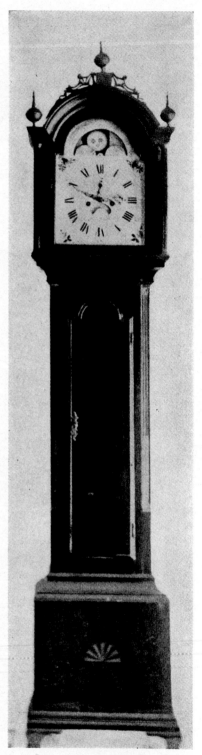

3323. By Nathan Edwards, Acton, Massachusetts. Mahogany. Height 88 Inches. Hood 18½ Inches Wide. Waist 17⅝ Inches. Base 17¾ Inches. Warren W. Creamer, Waldoboro, Maine.

3324. (Middle.) Zebra Grain Curly Maple; Spiraled Columns on Hood. Rosettes at Crest of Arch. Unusual Finials. Preston, England. Mrs. Francis P. Garvan.

3325. (Right.) Aaron Willard, Roxbury. Mahogany with Inlay. 76 x 18½. On Back of Dial in White Enamel: "By William Prescott," Who Was a Decorator. Warren W. Creamer.

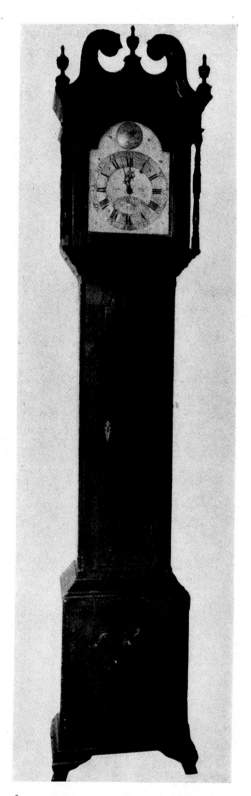

3326. By Daniel Rose, Reading, Pennsylvania. 1820–40. Mrs. M. B. Cookerow, Pottstown. 3327. (Right.) "Richard Simestree, Birmingham." Mahogany, Brass Mounts. Brass Dial with Cast Cherub Spandrels, On Boss, a Flying Mercury. 95 x 21 x 11½. *See* Britten, p. 745.

3328. LIGHTHOUSE CLOCK. ROSENBACH COMPANY, PHILADELPHIA. THESE ARE NOW MUCH SOUGHT FOR.

3329. (Right.) MAHOGANY WITH MARQUETRY, CONNECTICUT. c. 1803. METROPOLITAN MUSEUM, NEW YORK.

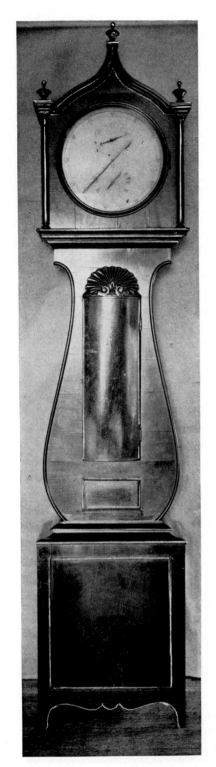

3330. Pennsylvania. A True Block Shell. Bombé Center. Gothic Arch Top.
Estate of William E. Montague, Norristown.

3331. (Right.) "Benjamin Rittenhouse, Worcester, Fecit." Quarter Columns.
Carved Rosettes.

3332. "D. H. Salliday, Sy. Town." Glass in Door Not Original. Small Waist, Chamfered. Estate of William E. Montague.

3333. (Right.) David Rittenhouse. It Is Obvious that His Cases Were Made by Different Persons. This Clock Once Sold for Twenty Cents. Same Owner.

3334. By Timothy Chandler, Concord, N.H., c. 1800. Unusual Urn Finials. Essex Institute, Salem.

3335. (Right.) By Hoadley, Plymouth, Connecticut. Numerous and Simple Clocks by This Maker. Essex Institute, Salem, Massachusetts.

3336. To Show the Movement, Time, and Alarm Weight of Miniature; Joshua Wilder. They Mostly Have a Door in the Back, Running Full Length as Here. C. Prescott Knight, Providence.

3337. (Right.) By Simon Willard. Self Clock Invented by Him. Attractive Case, as of One Piece Imposed on Another. Clarence H. Allen, Portland, Maine.

3338. WATCHMAN'S CLOCK, ANCHOR ESCAPEMENT. BY AARON WILLARD. ESSEX INSTITUTE, SALEM.
3339. (Right.) ENGLISH STYLE, WITH PANELS. SPIRALED PILLARS. BRASS CAPITALS. FRET UNDER
CORNICE.

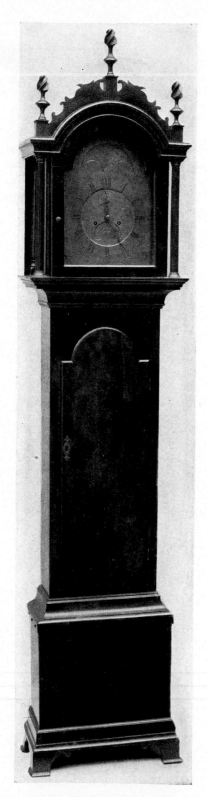

3340. THOMAS HARLAND, NORWICH. 1775-1800. A SLIGHT VARIANT FROM THOSE PREVIOUSLY SHOWN. METROPOLITAN MUSEUM.

3341. (Right.) INLAID CURLY MAPLE. E. STORRS, UTICA, NEW YORK. VERY HANDSOME. EARLY 19TH CENTURY. METROPOLITAN MUSEUM.

3342. Anchor Escapement, One Day. 1792. English. Good Outlines, Well Carved.
Foreign. Probably Dutch.
3343. (Right.) Lacquered with Plain Dome. By Thomas Wagstaff, 1766–94. He Was a
Quaker, and American Quakers Often Bought His Clocks. Base Molding Should Be Removed.
Estate of Harry W. Weeks, Framingham.

Dr. Sir

Dec.r 7.th 1792

In my accounts for the Year 1778 as settled by
Committee of Assembly, and printed, you will see how the 35,000
Dollars was disposed of. Whether there was any receipts with the
Extracts I can't say, for I think all the Vouchers are in your
hands. It seems likely that there was one or two receipts, for
my receipt for the money is dated March 28.th And I find three
Entries of payments on the 24.th and 27

I am Dr Sir

most respectfully

Your very humble serv.t

Dav.d Rittenhouse

Comptroller Gen.l

3344. This Letter Speaks for Itself. Rittenhouse Was State Treasurer, Professor of Astronomy in Pennsylvania University, Director of United States Mint, and President of American Philosophical Society. His Work Dates from 1751 to Near the End of the Century.

3345. German, by Jacob Strausser, Nuremberg, 1737. New England Case, c. 1800.
Essex Institute, Salem.

3346. (Right.) By Sam Stevens, London. Scrolled Brackets Are Very Unusual.
Essex Institute, Salem.

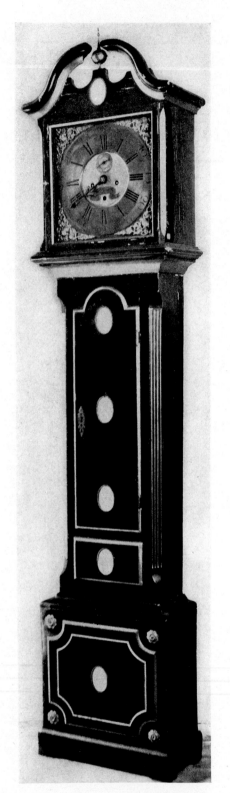

3347. IRISH, BY THOMAS CORNWALL, DUBLIN. WEDGEWOOD MEDALLIONS. ESSEX INSTITUTE, SALEM.
3348. (Right.) BY EDWARD FAULKNER, LONDON, 1710–35. LACQUERED. HENRY FORD, WAYSIDE INN.

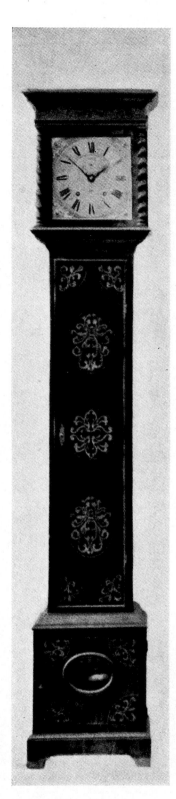

3349. By Christopher Gould, London. c. 1695. Burl Walnut. John H. Halford, Norristown.

3350. (Middle.) By Edward East, London. Inlaid Walnut. c. 1690. Rare Month Movement. 54 Inches High. Rapid Beat, Rather Short Pendulum.

3351. (Right.) By Thomas Tompion, Famous Maker. c. 1690. Both: Wetherfield Collection.

3352. BY CHARLES GRETTON, LONDON. C. 1795. FINE INLAY. THIS AND NEXT: WETHERFIELD COLLECTION.

3353. (Middle.) BY JOSHUA WILLSON, LONDON. C. 1705. EXQUISITE INLAY.

3354. (Right.) BY GEORGE PEACOCK, ENGLAND. C. 1700. OWNER IS UNKNOWN.

3355. ENGLISH, VERY EARLY. MOVEMENT, DIAL, ETC., NEXT PAGE. ENGAGED SPIRAL COLUMNS.
3356. (Middle.) BY ESAYE FLEUREAU, LONDON. C. 1810. MARQUETRY, ARABESQUE. WETHERFIELD COL.
3357. (Right.) BY JONATHAN LOUNDE, LONDON. C. 1705. A GOOD SCROLL IN MARQUETRY.

3358. Showing the Dial and Works of No. 3355, Also Two Excellent Hands.

3359. (Opposite.) Beautiful Case, Carved on Base, Fret under Hood, and Interlacing Scrolls above the Arch. Spiral Finials. Pointed Rosettes. Corners Cut Away above and below Quarter Columns. Rhode Island School of Design.

3360. (Right.) By Dieco Evans, London. Cast Brass Feet, and Finials, Very Decorative. Brass Trim Throughout. Fan Inlay, besides Lines and Cross Bands. Rhode Island School of Design.

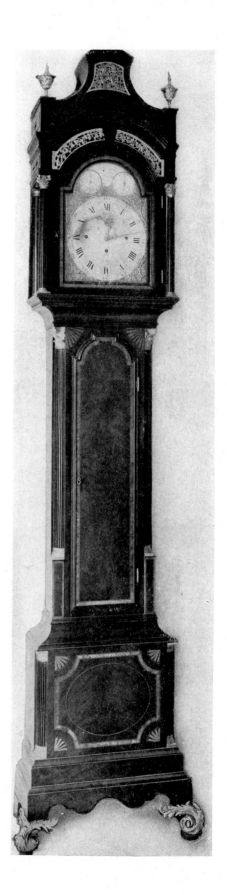

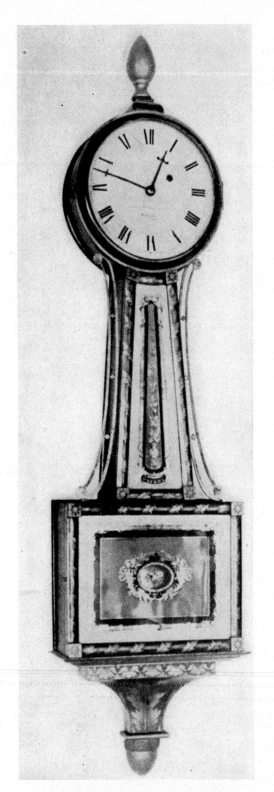

3361. Stenciled Banjo, by Simon Willard & Sons, Boston. Mahogany Period. Stencil Work on the Moldings, Center, and Bottom Bracket. c. 1820–25. Rare. Dr. Emory M. Porter, Providence.

3362. (Right.) By L. Curtis, Concord, Massachusetts. A Mahogany Lyre Case, with Carved Bottom Bracket and Center Panel, and Leaf Ornament at the Top. Strikes Hours on Two Piano Wires. J. Winthrop Brown.

 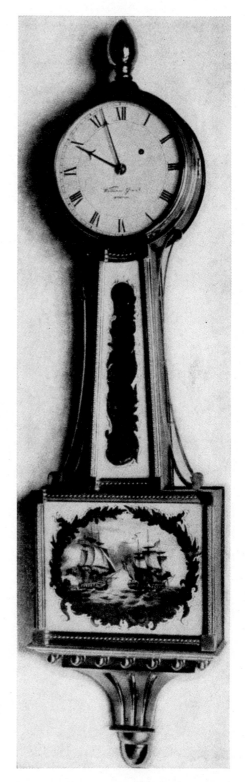

3363. By L. Curtis, Concord. Front Panels Pine, Gilded. Case, Mahogany. Rare.
Philip A. Johnson, Norwich.

3364. (Right.) By William Grant, Boston. Mahogany, Pine Panels of Front Gilded. 1815-25.
Robert C. Johnson, Norwich.

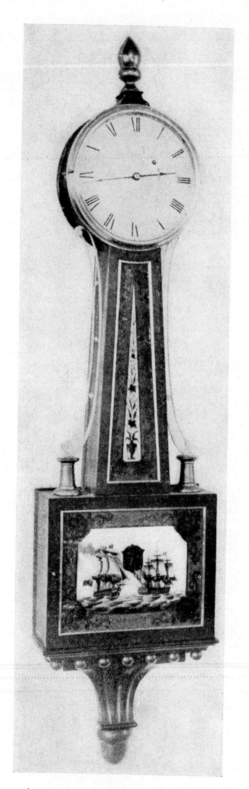

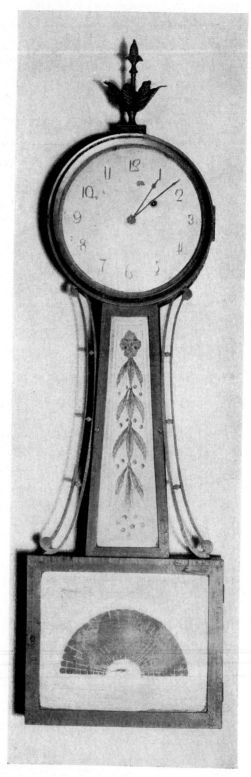

3365. By William Cummens. Spool Banjo. Mahogany; Brass Moldings on Inside of Lower and Central Panels. c. 1815. Large. C. Prescott Knight, Providence.

3366. (Right.) A Simon Willard. Original Bottom Glass. "S. Willard Patent." F. L. Dunne, Boston.

3367. SIMON WILLARD, IN PINE CASE. BANJO MOVEMENT. CASE ORIGINAL. COVER REMOVED. ESTATE OF HARRY W. WEEKS.

3368. (Right.) SIMON WILLARD, PICTURE ON LOWER GLASS, TELEMACHUS. ESTATE OF HARRY W. WEEKS. FRAMINGHAM.

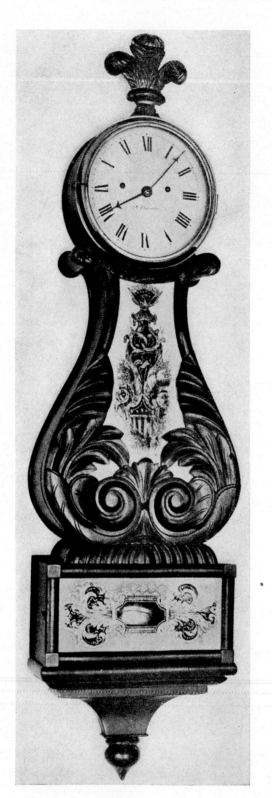 

3369. By A. Chandler, Concord, N. H. Mahogany Lyre, Carved Center Panel and Feather Finial. c. 1835–40. A Bottom Door. Striking Movement with Count Wheel. Benjamin A. Jackson, Providence.

3370. (Right.) Similar Clock, with Different Carving and Gilded Panel on Door. Sawin & Dyar, Boston. 1800–20. H. V. Weil.

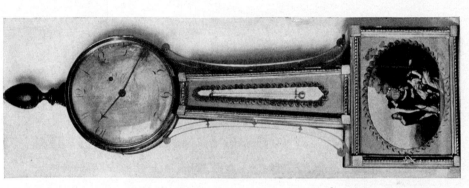

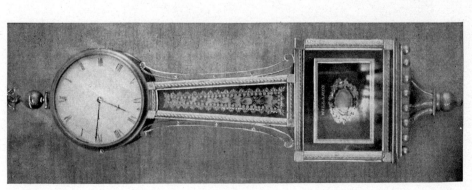

3371. By Simon Willard. Gilded Panel Outlines. Estate of William E. Montague, Norristown.
3372. (Middle.) Simon Willard; with a Barometer. Rare. Estate of Harry W. Weeks, Framingham.
3373. (Right.) By David Wood, Newburyport, Massachusetts. 1800–25. Mahogany on Pine. Metropolitan Museum.

3374. SAWIN AND DYAR, BOSTON. THIS MAKER IS SUPPOSED TO
HAVE ORIGINATED THE FORM. MAHOGANY. 1800–20.
METROPOLITAN MUSEUM, NEW YORK.

3375–78. Beautiful English Clock Hands from Early Clocks. c. 1700. Walter H. Durfee, Providence.

3379. The Works of a Simon Willard Timepiece or Banjo. He Used the Former Name and Possibly Did Not Use the Bracket Below. The Piece Was Made as a Mantel Clock or To Screw to the Wall. This Finial of Gilded Wood Is Probably the Earliest. The Works Have His Peculiar Escapement. Wallace Nutting.

3381. By Z. Gates. Note the Hands.
Estate of William E. Montague.

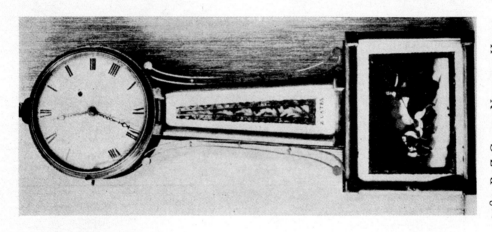

3382. The Ornament Is Used Often.
c. 1802. Estate of Wm. E. Montague.

3380. Mahogany. Somewhat Late.
Estate of William E. Montague.

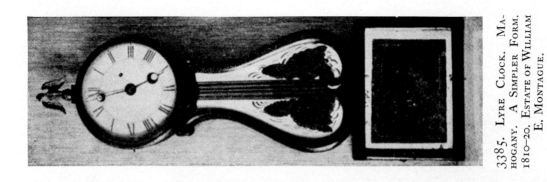

3385. LYRE CLOCK. MA-
HOGANY. A SIMPLER FORM.
1810–20. ESTATE OF WILLIAM
E. MONTAGUE.

3384. AARON WILLARD REGULATOR.
MAHOGANY. EARLY 19TH CENTURY.
DISH DIAL. BANJO MOVEMENT. LIKE
"ACT OF PARLIAMENT" CLOCK.
DR. EMORY M. PORTER.

3383. AARON WILLARD. "PATENT" ON
UPPER GLASS. SIMON'S INVENTION WAS
FREELY PIRATED. ESTATE OF
WILLIAM E. MONTAGUE.

3386. Good Design of Lyre. Formerly the Author's. Has Strike. No Name on Dial.

3387. (Right.) The Escapement of a Simon Willard, Showing the Curved Teeth of the Wheel. Simon Senior Invented This Clock, and the Escapement Also Is Peculiar to Him. It Required Great Skill and Was Not Copied. Wallace Nutting.

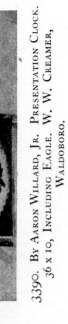

3390. By Aaron Willard, Jr. Presentation Clock. 36 x 10, Including Eagle. W. W. Creamer, Waldoboro.

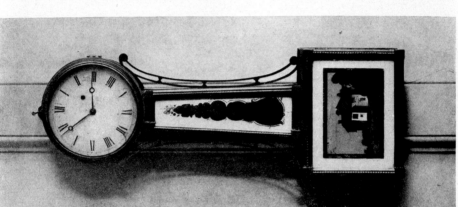

3389. By David Wood, Newbury- port. Rare. W. H. Douglas. 1790–1824.

3388. Alarm Clock, Plain Outlines, John Sawin, Boston. 1823–63. W. H. Douglas, Plymouth

3391. CARVED, MAHOGANY LYRE. NO GILDING. ACORN TOP. ESTATE OF WILLIAM E. MONTAGUE, NORRISTOWN.

3392. (Right.) "MASSACHUSETTS PATTERN." JOHN SAWIN, BOSTON. MAHOGANY WITH PAINTED GLASSES AROUND THE DIAL, AND LOWER PANEL. c. 1830. DIAL IS DISHED, THE USUAL TERM FOR CONVEX. EDWIN P. ANTHONY, PROVIDENCE.

3393. Painted Glass Below, Bas Relief Cupids. Above All a Lyre Pattern. Beautiful and Very Rare Specimen. I. Sack, Boston.

3394. (Middle.) Connecticut. Mid 18th Century. An Immense Number of This Type or Somewhat Simpler Were Made. Charles P. Cooley, Hartford.

3395. (Right.) Rare Pattern. All Gilded, on Pine. 35 x 13½ x 3⅛. Face Diameter 12½ Inches. Early 19th Century. Probably Swiss. Flayderman & Kaufman.

3396. Beautiful Rare Design. Bracket with Doubled Shells. Fine Carved Scroll Above. Old Garrison House, Trenton, New Jersey.

3397. (Right.) By John Winkley, England, c. 1760. Brass, Engraved with Maker's Name. Banjo Works. Cherry. William G. A. Turner, Malden.

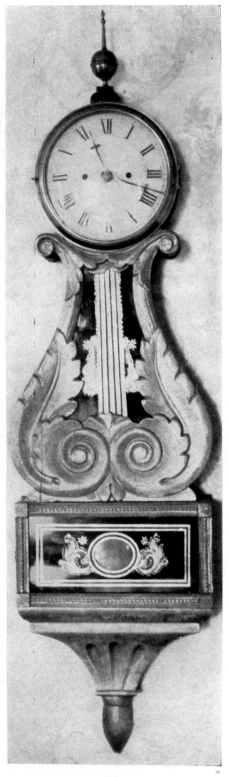

3398. By John Sawin. Mahogany with Carved Panel. Carved Eagle of Pine, Gilded. 1830–35.
Mrs. Emma A. Taft.

3399. (Right.) Gilded Lower Panel, Painted Glass. Upper Panel Carved and Gilded. Estate
of Harry W. Weeks.

3402. SIMON WILLARD. PANELED BELOW. PRESENTATION. CHARLES F. WILLIAMS COLLECTION. PENNSYLVANIA MUSEUM.

3401. MINIATURE. QUARTER COLUMNS. FLAYDERMAN & KAUFMAN.

3400. BY JAMES FERGUSON, LONDON. 1710–76. THE DATE SEEMS DOUBTFUL FOR THE STYLE. TWENTY-FOUR HOUR DIAL. ESSEX INSTITUTE.

3403. Regulator, by George D. Hatch. Rosewood, Date Uncertain. Unusual Shape. Striking Banjo Movement. Dr. Emory M. Porter, Providence.

3404. (Right.) By J. D. Custer, Norristown, Pennsylvania. 1805–72. Design Suggests Connecticut Pillar and Scroll. Estate of William E. Montague.

3405. Curtis, Girandole. Pine, Painted White. Bracket, Lower Door, Center Panel and Top, Gilded. Rare. By Lemuel Curtis, Concord. 1810–18. Mrs. L. F. O'Neil. Auburn, New York.

3406. English Chippendale, Chinese Pattern. Elegant Example.
Benjamin M. Jackson, Providence.

3407. By Aaron Willard, Boston. Mahogany, Inlaid, French Foot, c. 1800.
Kidney Dial. C. Prescott Knight, Providence.

3410. By Boston Clock Company. Essex Institute, Salem.

3409. Lyre, Carved. Name Indistinct. Boston. 1820-30.

3408. Familiar Sea Fight Design. Essex Institute, Salem.

3411. By Jerome & Darrow, 1825–30. Mahogany, Black and Gold Stenciled Columns and Top. Quite Usual. Thirty-Hour Wooden Works. Richard E. Wheeler, Providence.

3412. (Right.) Tower Clock from Church in Morristown, N.J. Colonial Date. Washington Headquarters Museum in That Town.

3413. Forestville Mfg. Co., Bristol, Connecticut. Acorn Pattern. Mounted Like a Looking-Glass. 1830. Estate of William E. Montague.

3414. (Right.) By Joseph Ives, New York City, 1818–30. Fine Wagon-Spring Movement, 30 Days. Movement Now in Another Clock. C. Prescott Knight, Providence.

3415. CHIPPENDALE, THREE URNS WITH FLAMES; SHELL BELOW AND ABOVE DIAL. BALL-AND-CLAW FEET. RICH SPECIMEN. HOSTETTER COLLECTION, LANCASTER, PENNSYLVANIA.

3416. By E. Taber. Mahogany Inlaid, c. 1800. Kidney Dial; Good Example. Massachusetts Pattern. C. Prescott Knight, Providence.

3417. (Right.) By Simon Willard. Mahogany, 1770–80. Very Rare. Thirty-Hour Movement and Brass Dial. G. Winthrop Brown, Boston.

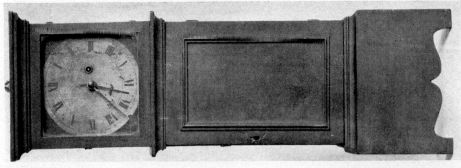

3420. MINIATURE. 27 x 10 x 5.
MAHOGANY. MRS. FRANCIS P.
GARVAN.

3419. LIGHTHOUSE CLOCK, WITH SUPERIMPOSED
BELL. ESSEX INSTITUTE, SALEM.

3418. BEAUTIFUL DESIGN, QUARTER COLUMN.
OWNER: CLARENCE H. ALLEN, PORTLAND.

3423. Lighthouse. Ball Feet. Applied Leaf. F. L. Dunne.

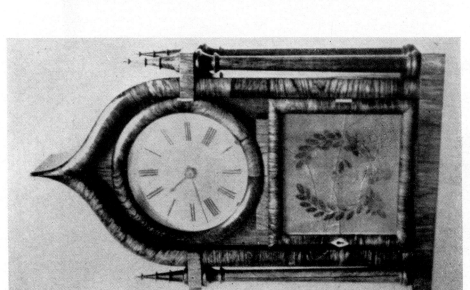

3422. Gothic. Designed by Elias Ingraham, Founder of the Firm Who Made It, Brewster & Ingraham. 1843–48. E. Ingraham Company, Bristol, Connecticut.

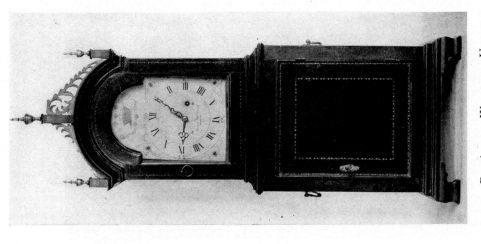

3421. By Aaron Willard. Unusual Fret. Case Carved. Pennsylvania Museum, Philadelphia.

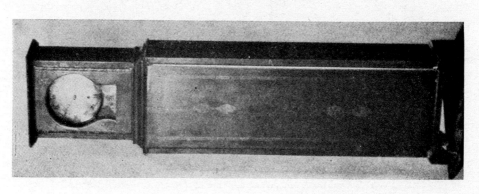

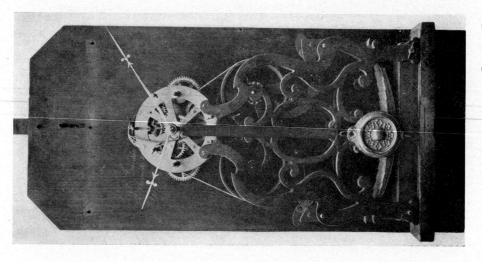

3424. JOSEPH IVES. CART SPRING MOVEMENT. C. PRESCOTT KNIGHT, PROVIDENCE. 1811-25.

3425. (Middle.) GRANDMOTHER CLOCK, PROBABLY BY S. MULLIKEN. CHERRY, 21½ x 10. DIAL 5½ INCHES, SILVERED BRASS. KIDNEY DIAL. PALLET ARBOR WITHOUT SUSPENSION SPRING. BRASS INLAY. P. H. SAFFORD, FITCHBURG.

3426. (Right.) BILL OF AARON WILLARD, JR, BOSTON, MARCH 21ST. 1829. G. W. A. TURNER, MALDEN.

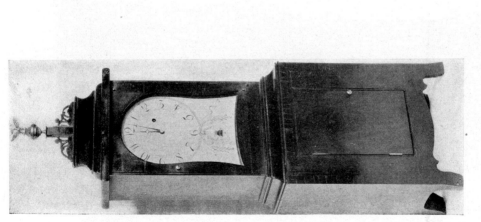

3427. MAHOGANY, 40 x 12½ x 6½. PROBABLY BY E. TABER. MARY M. SAMPSON, BOSTON.

3428. (Middle.) BY SETH THOMAS, PLYMOUTH HOLLOW, CONNECTICUT, c. 1860. INTEREST CHIEFLY IN HEAVY SCROLL OF BASE, AS IN DEGRADED EMPIRE. ESSEX INSTITUTE.

3429. (Right.) BY J. WILDER, HINGHAM. QUARTER COLUMNS, GOOD FRET AND BALLS. F. L. DUNNE, BOSTON.

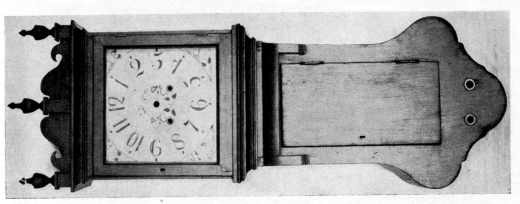

3430. BY DAVID WOOD, NEWBURY PORT [sic]. GOOD DESIGN. KATRINA KIPPER, ACCORD.
3431. (MIDDLE.) PINE, URNS NEW. ODD DESIGN. ORIGIN UNKNOWN. WALLACE NUTTING.
3432. (RIGHT.) BY AARON WILLARD, JR., BOSTON. PAINTED GLASS AROUND THE DIAL. KATRINA KIPPER.

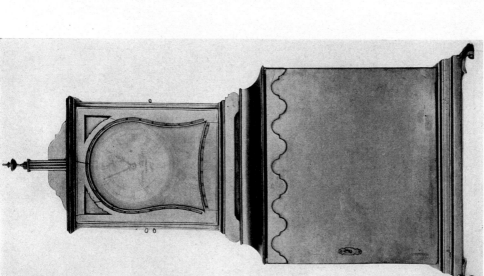

3433. By David Studley, Hanover, 1806–35. F. L. Dunne, Boston, as Also the Others on This Page.

3434. (Middle.) "By Simon Willard, Grafton. N. 2." Probably It Means That This Is the Second Clock of This Kind That Willard Made. Effect of One Cabinet Piece on Another. Kidney Dial. Scrolled Mold on Base Like Those on Harland's Clocks of Norwich. Places Not Far Apart. About 1776.

3435. (Right.) David Wood, Newburyport. Inlaid with Snail Shell and Fan. Inlay on Base.

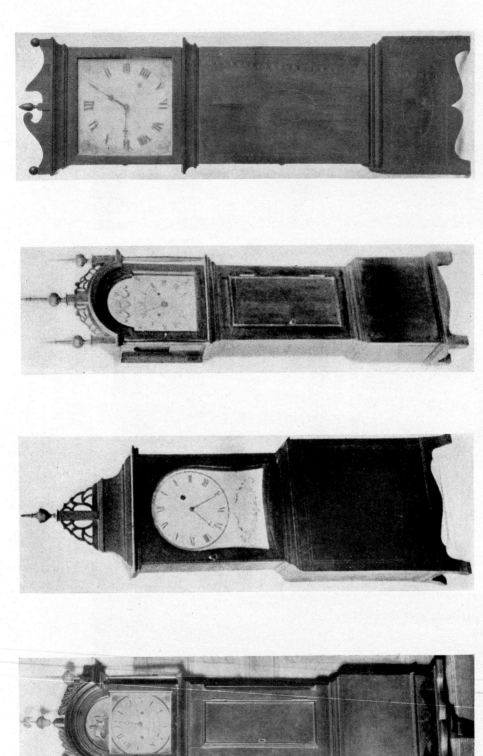

3436. By John Bailey, Jr., Hanover. Beautiful Fret of Imbricated Leaves. Fine Brass Urns. Rocking Horse above Dial.

3437. (Second.) By Ebenezer Belknap, Boston. 1823. Bigelow Collection. F. L. Dunne, Boston.

3438. (Third). By Reuben Tower, Kingston, Massachusetts. Delicate Finials. 1812–20.

3439. (Right.) Miniature, Benjamin Willard, Lexington. 30 x 9½ x 4½. Mahogany. 1768–1770. Mrs. Francis P. Garvan.

3440. MASSACHUSETTS PATTERN. PINE. THIRTY HOUR. MAKER UNKNOWN. 1780–90.
ELISHA C. DURFEE, PROVIDENCE.

3441. (Right.) WAS OWNED BY MARY WILLARD HAZEN, DAUGHTER OF SARAH WILLARD, AND EDWARD
HAZEN, LANCASTER, THIRD COUSIN OF THE WILLARD CLOCK MAKERS. SHE MARRIED JOSEPH RUGG,
AND HER DAUGHTER JULIA GAVE THIS CLOCK TO MRS. HENRIETTA GATES. OLD FURNITURE SHOP,
WORCESTER, MASSACHUSETTS.

3442. BY DAVID WILLIAMS, NEWPORT. MAHOGANY. KIDNEY DIAL.
WELL DECORATED. FINE HANDS. TOP UNUSUAL. 1820–30.
BENJAMIN A. JACKSON, PROVIDENCE.

3443. Beautifully Inlaid, and Fine Shape. Savin Make.
Design Possibly Suggested from the French. Cross-Banded
Border. Ogee Feet. I. Sack, Boston.

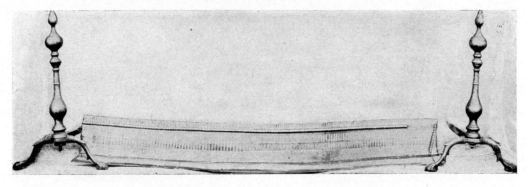

3444. Ball-and-Claw Foot Andirons. Spiraled Tops. Cut-Brass Serpentine Screen.
J. K. Beard, Richmond, Virginia.

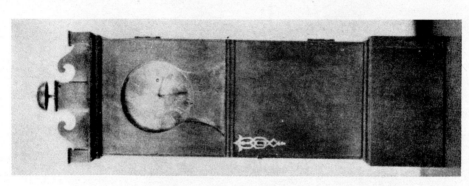

3445-46. Same Clock Open and Closed. Odd Weight To Gain Longer Run. Interesting. Original Ornaments, Kidney Dial. William G. A. Turner, Malden.

3447. (Right.) Grandmother Clock, 48 Inches High. Cherry. Marked by Small Waist, as Often in Pennsylvania Miniatures. Quarter Columns on Both Sections. Good Hood. Philip Meredith Allen, Broad Axe, Pennsylvania.

3448. By Aaron Willard, Boston. Characteristic Ball and Eagle. Landscape with Cattle, Sheep, Dog, Man, and Woman. Beautiful Example. F. L. Dunne, Boston.

3449. (Middle.) Early Advertisement of Benjamin Willard, Whose Clocks Are Rare. First Work at Grafton. Walter H. Durfee, Providence.

3450. (Right.) By Ezekiel Jones, Boston. Feet Quite Unusual. Good Painting about Dial.

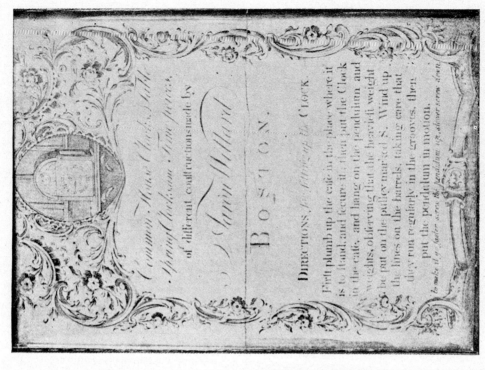

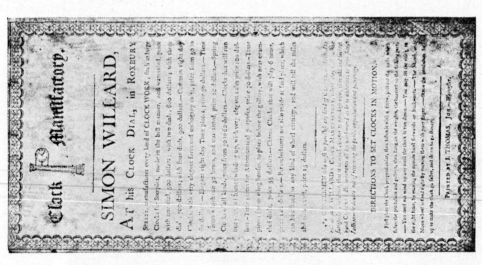

3451-52. Labels of Simon and Aaron Willard, with Directions for Setting Up. Picture from W. G. A. Turner, Malden. Interesting Engraving in Second Label of English Shelf Clock.

SIMON WILLARD,

BEGS leave to inform the publick, that he has opened a Shop in ROXBURY-STREET, nearly opposite the road that turns off to PLYMOUTH, where he carries on the Business of

Clock Making

in all its branches.——Gentlemen may be supplied at said shop on the most reasonable terms, with CLOCKS of different constructions, to run either a day, eight days, one month, or a year, with once winding up; common eight-day repeating Clocks, Spring Clocks of all sorts, among which are, common spring table, spring chime, and spring tune Clocks, which will play different tunes every hour; also large tune clocks which run with weights, will play every hour, repeat the quarters, &c.——Also, may be had, said WILLARD's new constructed Astronomical TIME KEEPER, ascertaining the 60th or 20th part of a minute, by a second hand from the centre of the large circle, made upon a most simple plan, in which the friction and influence of the oil is almost annihilated; and has proved to keep time with the greatest accuracy, with a new constructed pendulum, from the centre of the ball, shews the different degrees of expansion of the bars, and answers, in some degree, as a thermometor, &c. those that oscilate half seconds are portable, and are easily moved to any part of the room, or where it is convenient for to make observations; to the pedestal of which is affixed (without obstructing the movement) a perpetual calender, newly engraved, which shews at one view, the day of the month, the true and comparative time of the sun's rising and setting forever; as well as the age, increase, decrease, rising and setting of the moon, time of high water, &c. the whole globe with its rotation every twenty-four hours, shewing the longitude, latitude, the hour and minute upon the most noted places on the globe.—Such gentlemen or ladies as will favour the said Willard with their commands in the above business, may depend on having their work done in the neatest manner, and may be supplied with MEHOGANY CASES in the newest taste.—Those who live at a distance may have Clock Work sent them, with direction how to manage and set them up, without the assistance of the Clock-Maker.

Watch Work

of all sorts is done in the neatest manner, and carefully cleaned and regulated, with Crystals, Keys, Seals, Chains, Springs, &c. &c. Also, is made by said WILLARD, and COMPANY, a new invented

Roasting Jack,

in which is containe. a compleat apparatus of Kitchen Dripping-Pan, Spit, Skewers and Baster, &c. which is so constructed with tin plates as to reflect back upon the meat all the heat the tin receives, which occasions the saving of almost one half of that important article fire-wood; it is also recommended for its being portable, which can be placed to any small fire-place, in any room, and which is made upon so simple a plan that it is not subject to get out of repair, and the friction upon every part being so trifling, that it will continue for longer duration than any mechanical performances of that kind is known to do.

Roxbury, February 24. 1784.

N. B. The above JACKS may be had of Col. PAUL REVERE, directly opposite Liberty-Pole, Boston.

Copied from
THOMAS'S
MASSACHUSETTS SPY, Or
WORCESTER GAZETTE
Thursday, March 11, 1784

3453. SELF EXPLANATORY.

3454. By Seth Thomas, Plymouth Hollow, Connecticut. "Pillar and Scroll" Design. Became Wonderfully Popular. Mahogany, c. 1820. Veneer under Ornaments Is Satinwood. Painting Original and Excellent. Glass Slightly Curved, as in All the Originals. Concave. Mrs. Harrison B. Huntoon, Providence.

3455. (Right.) Said To Be by Simon Willard, but No Name Appears. William E. Montague, Norristown.

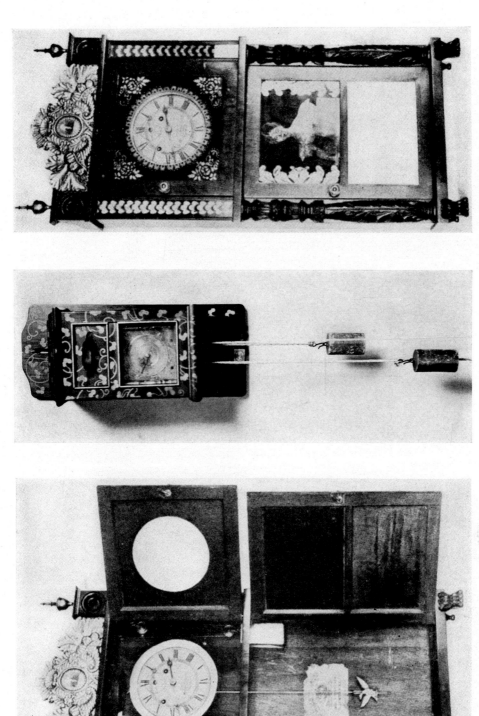

3456. Interior of No. 3458, by Munger & Benedict, Auburn, New York. "A. Munger" on Paster. Carved, with Plaster Top and Painting of Washington.

3457. (Middle.) Japanese Wall Clock. Scrolled Design Carried Over to the Wall Board. Essex Institute, Salem.

3458. (Right.) Stenciled Design, Perhaps Unique. 1833 Engraved on Hammer. Eagle Pendulum Bob. C. Prescott Knight.

3459. By C. & N. Jerome, Bristol. Mahogany, 1830. Heavy Late Empire. Brass, Eight Day. Unusual Dial, Black and Gold. Pierced To Show Movement. Dr. Charles H. Chetwood, Massachusetts.

3460. (Right.) By Eli Terry, Plymouth. Mahogany, 1793–1818. Deservedly Popular. Thirty-Hour Wood Movement.

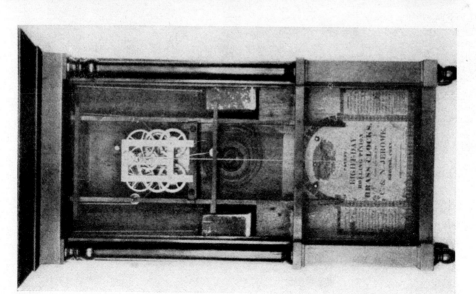

3461. (Left.) INTERIOR OF No. 3459.

3462. (Middle.) AN AARON WILLARD, WITH SHIELDS ON SPANDRELS OF THE DIAL.

3463. (Right.) BY ATKINS & DOWNS, BRISTOL, CONNECTICUT, MAHOGANY CARVED COLUMNS, FEET AND TOP. c. 1830.
MRS. GEORGE L. SHATTUCK, PROVIDENCE.

3464. By Eli Terry, Plymouth. Mahogany, c. 1818. Early, with Escape Wheel in Front of Dial. Francis E. Gates, Oak Lawn, Rhode Island.

3465. (Right.) Japanese. Odd Oriental Scrolls and Frets. Essex Institute, Salem.

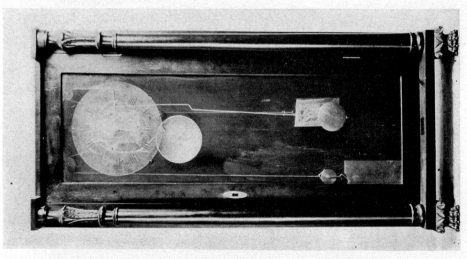

3466. Original Dial Removed. Interesting, Architectural Design Like a Looking-Glass. Essex Institute, Salem.
3467. (Right.) By Burnham Terry. Balance Escapement. Sold by J. J. & W. Beals, Boston, Essex Institute, Salem.

3468. By Joshua Wilder, Hingham. English Type Top. Pine. S. Prescott Fay, Boston.
3469. (Middle.) Line Inlay, Arched Top. James Davidson, New London, c. 1800. Found in a Bristol Factory Some Years Ago.
3470. (Right.) Miniature. Kidney Dial. Unusual Base Scroll. S. Prescott Fay, Boston.

3473. Kidney Dial. Basket Fret. Data Mislaid. c. 1800.

3474. (Middle.) English Lantern. 1650-90. The First Popular Short Clock. Formerly the Author's.

3475. (Right.) Looking-Glass Front. Maple Leaf Painting, c. 1830. W. F. Hubbard, Hartford.

3476. Movement, Weights, and Center Panel of L. Curtis. 1814–53. C. Prescott Knight.

3477. Chest Lift. Chippendale Brass, from
Philip Meredith Allen, Broad Axe, Penn.

3478. Looking-Glass Clock, Eight-Day Movement and Strike. Wheels Show in Top. From E. S. Macomber, Providence.

3479. (Right.) Toby Clock. It Is Said that a Man in Good Health Can Tell Time by His Stomach. An Iron Man. W. F. Hubbard, Hartford.

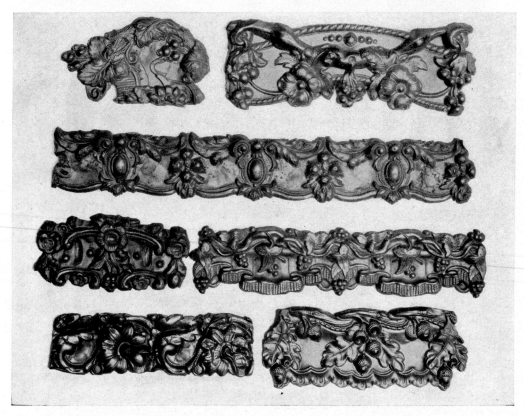

3480–86. Drapery Cornices of Stamped Brass. 19th Century. Frank A. Robart.

3487. AMERICAN CASE, FRENCH WORKS. FINE OGEE BRACKET FEET. GOOD SCROLL TOP. FRANCIS D. BRINTON, WEST CHESTER, PENNSYLVANIA.

3488. (Right.) SHOWS WORKS THROUGH LARGE CUT-OUT. BEADED ORNAMENTS ON SIDE. W. F. HUBBARD, HARTFORD.

3489. METAL CLOCK, PAINTED ORNAMENTS. W. F. HUBBARD, HARTFORD.

3490. (Middle.) CURIOUS SMALL WALL CLOCK. PINE. 18½ x 8¾ x 4¼. FOUND BY MRS. MINNIE BROWN, ROCKLAND, MASSACHUSETTS. WAG-ON-THE-WALL, C. 1820. FLAYDERMAN & KAUFMAN.

3491. (Right.) SMALL METAL CLOCK, PAINTED DECORATION. WILLIAM F. HUBBARD, HARTFORD.

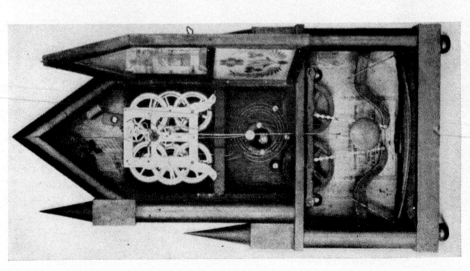

3492. Cathedral Case, Otherwise Called Gothic. Sometimes a Double Decker, or Steeple Clock. By Birge & Fuller, Bristol. Mahogany. 1830–35. Wagon Spring. J. Ives Pattern. Dr. Emory M. Porter, Providence.

3493. (Middle.) Kidney Dial. Shelf Clock. About Same Date as Similar Dials Previously Shown. Essex Institute.

3494. (Right.) Steeple, with Crotchets. E. Ingraham Company, Bristol, Connecticut.

3495-96. GOTHIC CLOCK, WITH DOORS OPENED AND CLOSED. "IMPROVED STEEL SPRINGS, EIGHT-DAY BRASS CLOCK, BIRGE & FULLER, BRISTOL, CONN." GLASS IS ESPECIALLY GOOD.

3497. BY WAY OF SURPRISE, A BECKET IS SHOWN. THIS IS THE HANDLE WORKED BY SAILORS FOR THEIR CHESTS. THE TEST OF AN ANTIQUARIAN IS THAT HE KNOWS THE NAME OF THIS AND A FEW OTHER THINGS. SANDERSON COLLECTION, NANTUCKET.

3498. A "Solar Time Piece," by Timby, Baldwinsville, New York. Essex Institute, Salem.
3499. (Right.) Late Type by Atkins Clock Company, Bristol, Connecticut, 1820— .

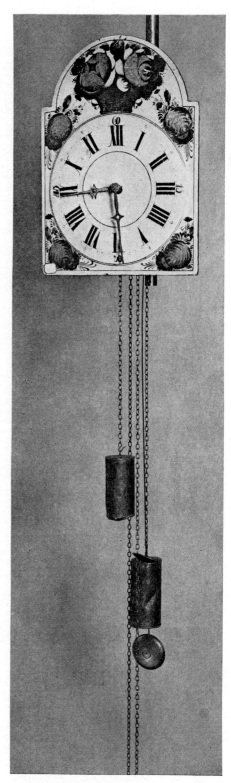

3500. Wag-on-the-Wall. Dutch or German. Essex Institute, Salem.
3501. (Right.) Wag-on-the-Wall. German. Essex Institute, Salem.

3502. Clock with a Musical Instrument in Back, a Zither. Two Tunes Are Played. Spanish Netherlands or Spain. 18th Century.

3503. (Right.) Wag-on-the-Wall, Probably German. Essex Institute, Salem.

3504. ASTRONOMICAL CLOCK. "IT SHOWS THE TIME ALL OVER THE GLOBE, AND THE POSITION OF THE STARS AT ALL TIMES." BALANCE ESCAPEMENT, UNIVERSUM CLOCK CO., BOSTON. ESSEX INSTITUTE, SALEM.

3505. LABEL IN CLOCK OF HENRY A. HOFFMAN, BARRINGTON.

3506. BY PEREGRINE WHITE. 1774– . DIAL OF COLONIAL CHIME CLOCK,
PLAYS TUNES EVERY THREE HOURS. DIFFERENT TUNE FOR EACH DAY OF THE
WEEK, AND A PSALM TUNE ON SUNDAY. THE LATE EX-GOVERNOR ELISHA DYER,
PROVIDENCE.

3507. Bracket Clock. "Jam^S Stevens, London," the Name Being Repeated on Engraved Brass Back. 15¾ x 10¼ x 6¼.

3508. "Jno. Perins, London." Mahogany. Battersea Enamel Dial, Pink Scrolled Spandrel with Birds. Back Plate Engraved. Bigelow Collection.

3509-10. Unusual Brass Escutcheon; (Reversed) 1700. Eagle and Shield 1790. Bigelow Collection.

3511. The English Shelf Clock Like the Above Is a Handsome Well-Made Article and Is Likely Always To Be Much Sought for in America. The Works Are Very Good. These Are Largely London Make.

3512. (Right.) Mahogany, Inlaid, Beautiful Open Fret in Ends. G. Winthrop Brown, Boston.

3513. By Alexander Cummings, London (b. 1732, d. 1814).

3514. (Right.) Two-Day, Fusee Movement, by Edward Smith, Dublin, c. 1810. It Is Supposed the Plain Lettering "Two Days," on the Dial Was an Advantage in Selling. Essex Institute, Salem.

3515. (Opposite.) By John Martin, London, c. 1700. Very Rare. Wetherfield Collection.

3516. (Opposite, right.) By Daniel Quare. Ebony, Brass Mounted, c. 1700. Three Chimes and a Quarter Chime on Six Bells. The Maker Invented a Repeating Watch. Wetherfield Collection.

3517. (Above.) By Thomas Parker, Philadelphia. Whether This Means that He Imported It or Not Does Not Appear. But Dealers Had Their Names Placed on the Clocks, as Was Probably the Case Here. Miss Susan P. Wharton.

3518. (Right.) Italian, 17th Century. Pennsylvania Museum, Philadelphia.

3519. T. G. Moore, Worthington, England. Mahogany with Brass Frets under the Dial and Brass Ogee Feet, c. 1830. Owner Unknown.

3520. (Right.) By Mummery, Dover, England. Name Not Given in Britten. Probably a Dealer. Mahogany with Brass Inlay, Finely Done, c. 1830. Beautiful Specimen. Stephen O. Metcalf Providence.

3521–22. TWO ENGLISH SHELF, OR BRACKET CLOCKS.

3523. By Stephen Rimbeault, London. Ebony, c. 1760–80. Sixteen Hammers, Chimes at Three Quarters, and Plays at the Hour. Musicians in the Arch of the Dial Play with the Tune. Marsden J. Perry, Providence.

3524. By J. Smith & Sons, London, c. 1800–10. Case in Red Chinese Lacquer. Picture from Walter H. Durfee, Providence

3525. (Right.) From Soltykoff's "Horologerie," 1858, Plate XVIII. Original Plates in Steel. Soltykoff Says This Piece Has Neither Signature nor Date, but He Believes It German of the Time of Ferdinand of Austria.

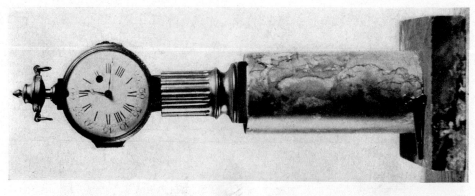

3526. GERMAN, 16TH CENTURY. PENNSYLVANIA MUSEUM, PHILADELPHIA.

3527. (MIDDLE.) GERMAN SWORD CLOCK. ESSEX INSTITUTE, SALEM, MASSACHUSETTS.

3528. (RIGHT.) BY W. OAKES, OLDHAM, ENGLAND, FUSEE ANCHOR ESCAPEMENT. ESSEX INSTITUTE, SALEM.

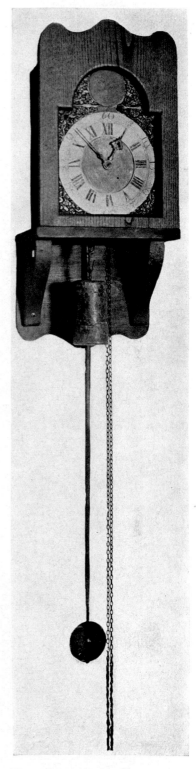

3529. Friesland. These Hooded Clocks, with Pewter or Brass Filigree, All Follow the Same Type. The Figures Often Hint at the Date. Essex Institute, Salem.

3530. (Right.) Wag-on-the-Wall, by R. T. Manning, 1767. Essex Institute, Salem.

3531. Italian, by Arcangelo Mayereffer, Rome, 1794. Essex Institute, Salem.

3532. From Soltykoff's "Horologerie," 1858, Plate XX. "The Monogram
G. G. Proves that the Beautiful Piece Belonged to Gaston of Orleans,
Son of Henry IV."

3533. From Soltykoff's "Horologerie," 1858, Plate XI. By Andreas Müller, in the Reign of
Ferdinand, Brother and Successor of Charles V.

3534-35. From Soltykoff's "Horologerie," 1858, Plate I. Constructed by Louis David, Period of Henry III. The Plaque Above Is a Satire of the Huguenot Time against the Papacy.

3536. French. Ormolu and Gilt Bronze, with Sèvre Mounts. Essex Institute, Salem.

3537. Probably English. Pendulum Stimulates the Piston Rod of an Engine.
On the Other Side Is a Barometer.

3538. Perhaps French. Essex Institute, Salem.

3539. Probably Swiss, Possibly German. A Number of Such Clocks Have Been Found. Essex Institute, Salem.

3541. French, Essex Institute.

3540. Japanese, Essex Institute, Salem.

3542-43. French Fusee Clock. They Usually Have White Stone Bases with Ball Feet, and Are Raised on Bell-Shaped Piers. Sometimes There Is an Arrangement for Leveling. Essex Institute, Salem.

3544. Empire, Maker Unknown, c. 1825–30. An Imported Repeating Movement, Striking on the Hour and Quarter, Very Rare. The Case Is American. Warren R. Fales, East Providence.

3545. FRENCH, 16TH CENTURY. PENNSYLVANIA MUSEUM, PHILADELPHIA.

3546. From Soltykoff's "Horologerie," 1858, Plate VII. Dimensions in Centimeters: 34 High, 23 Across at the Base, 13 Across in the Main Part of the Clock, and 7 Deep. This Shows the Annunciation, the Adoration of the Magi, and Various Other Scenes from the Life of Christ. A Very Elegant Example. Date, 1521.

3547. FRENCH, 16TH CENTURY. PENNSYLVANIA MUSEUM, PHILADELPHIA.

3548. FRENCH, 16TH CENTURY. PENNSYLVANIA MUSEUM, PHILADELPHIA.

3549. FROM MEDICI PALACE, VIA SERVI, FLORENCE. ESSEX INSTITUTE, SALEM.

3550. Hall Clock Movement, by Johannes A. Fromanteel, 1675, London. Alarm Dial Is on the Side of the Movement instead of in Front. The Wheel of the Winding Arbor Is Separate from the Winding Drum. These Are Held Together by the Movement Plates. Very Unusual.

 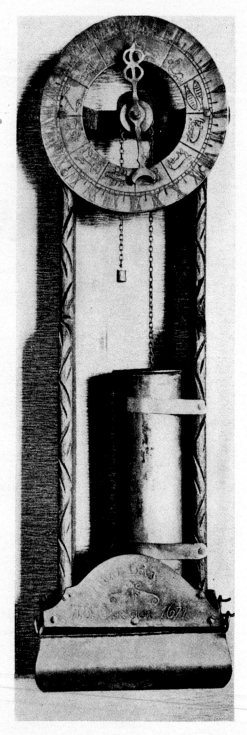

3551. Swiss, or German. Movement of Pendulum Seen in the Opening Below. Estate of William E. Montague, Norristown, Pennsylvania.

3552. (Right.) By Albert Davis, Norwich, 1671. This English Water Clock Was One of the Earliest Known Forms. Water Clocks Were in Use in Classical Times.

3553. Unknown Origin. Certainly Foreign. The Pendulum Is In Front of the Dial. Father Time in Somewhat Fresh Paint. Possibly Patched Up. Wadsworth Atheneum.

3554. Foreign. The Only Instance Shown of a Base Like a Table Frame for the Support of a Clock. Essex Institute.

3555. NORWEGIAN. THE FIGURES DANCE. THE CARVING OF THE FACE IS SIMILAR TO SPANISH EXAMPLES.
ESSEX INSTITUTE, SALEM.
3556. (Right.) SWEDISH. O. I. DAHL, ARTMARK. ESSEX INSTITUTE, SALEM.

3557. WAG-ON-THE-WALL. WINGED HORSE REPRESENTING THE FLIGHT OF TIME.
ESSEX INSTITUTE, SALEM.

3558. (Right.) WAG-ON-THE-WALL. CONTINENTAL. SAME OWNERS.

3559. FRIESLAND CLOCK. 18TH CENTURY. FORMERLY OWNED BY L. C. FLYNT, MONSON, MASSACHUSETTS.

3560. (Right.) BY THOMAS MOORE, IPSWICH, C. 1610. THE LANTERN CLOCK IS VERY DECORATIVE AND SHOULD BE POPULAR. JOHN H. HALFORD, NORRISTOWN, PENNSYLVANIA.

3561. Reported as Made in Bensburg, Prussia, Early 14th Century. Taken to Dalsband County, Sweden. Found in the 16th Century in Ruins of Church Abandoned, 1347–48. This Description Is Not Vouched For. Essex Institute, Salem.

3562. (Right.) Flemish, by J. B. Bandeream, Braine-l'Alleud, Near Brussels. Essex Institute, Salem.

3563. "Father Time," Lakeport, California, from a Type Patented in 1808 by John Schmidt of London, a Dane, Who Was Taken Prisoner in Copenhagen and Brought to England. He Called It "The Mysterious Circulator of Chronological Equilibrium." This Clock Is Now the Property of the Essex Institute, Salem.

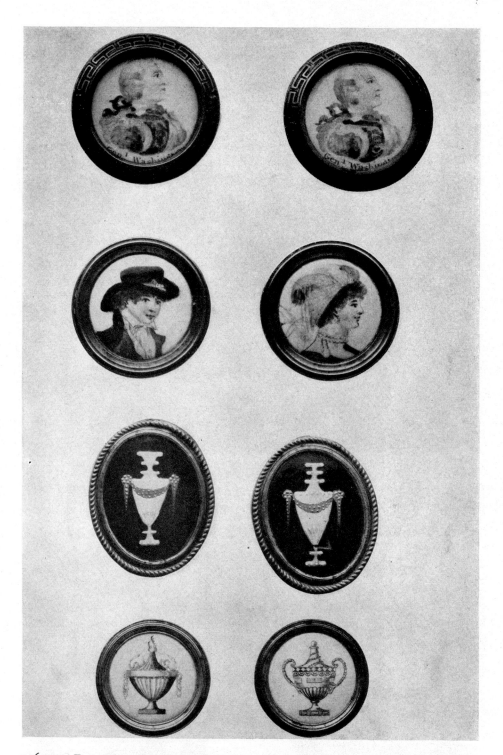

3564–71. EIGHT KNOBS FOR LOOKING-GLASSES. PICTURE SUPPLIED BY IRVING P. LYON, M.D. ALL BELONGED TO HIS FATHER DR. LYON, WHO MADE THE FIRST GOOD BOOK ON FURNITURE, EXCEPT THE SECOND SET FROM THE TOP. THEY ARE FROM HOUSES IN NEWBURYPORT. THE OTHER SETS ACQUIRED BY DR. IRVING P. LYON IN MASSACHUSETTS. GENERAL WASHINGTON APPEARS VERY YOUNG HERE. IS IT POSSIBLE THAT PERSONS SOMETIMES HAD THEIR PORTRAITS MADE FOR KNOBS, AS IN THE SECOND SET? THEY ARE IN PLAIN BLACK, THEN IN SEPIA, OR MORE OFTEN PAINTED IN COLORS. THE GREATEST DIAMETER IS 1¾ INCHES INSIDE. ABOUT 1800.

3572–77. The Top Pair of Knobs Is Very Beautiful, the Second Pair Are of
Huntington, and Governor Morris. J. Grossman, Boston.

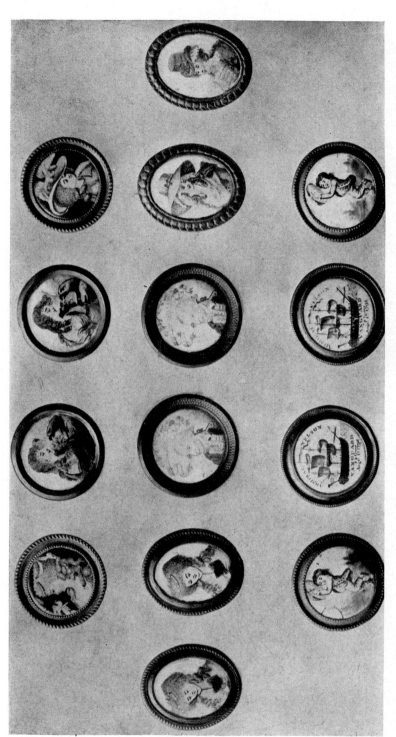

3578–91. A Series Supplied by the Courtesy of "Antiques." Nelson's Vanguard Is Dated 1798. Those of Washington Are Next in Importance. The Two Members of the Pair of Knobs Are Not Necessarily the Same. From George C. Flynt, Monson, Massachusetts.

The fashion of these knobs ought to be revived because they supply individuality to a home. Pictures of subjects of special interest to the family or of local importance would enshrine a history and make a permanent record and add a pleasing and useful decorative feature. The same is true of furniture brasses. There is an abundant field for design of modern brasses, which could be made most interesting. Why do we leave to our fathers all such matters?

The author has endeavored to make a representative showing of brasses, partly owing to the intrinsic interest of the subject, and partly in the hope of stimulating the revival of a neglected art.

3592–98. Picture Supplied by Irving P. Lyon, M.D. All Belonged to His
Father Dr. Lyon, Except the First Set. These Knobs or Sets Are All
Enamel on Copper, Mounted in Brass Frames with Screw Posts Generally
about 2½ Inches Long. Most Are Printed on the Enamel from Paper
Transfer Prints from Copper Engraving.

3599–3602. Knobs of a Lady Leaning on an Anchor, and of a Lady with Long Curls. J. Grossman, Boston

3603–06. Fine Brasses of the First and Second Period, 1690–1710. Rudolph P. Pauly.

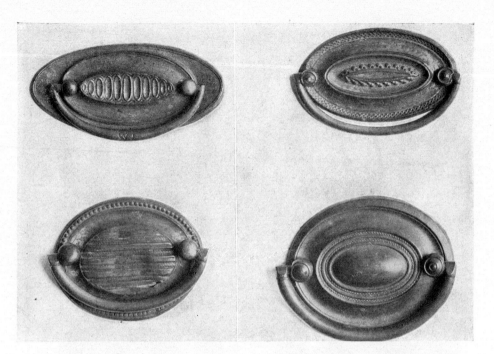

3607-10. Brasses from the Goodwin and the Norton Collections. The Stamped
Initials W. J. Are on the Top Left Brass. Late 18th Century.
Figure 3611 has been omitted in the numbering.

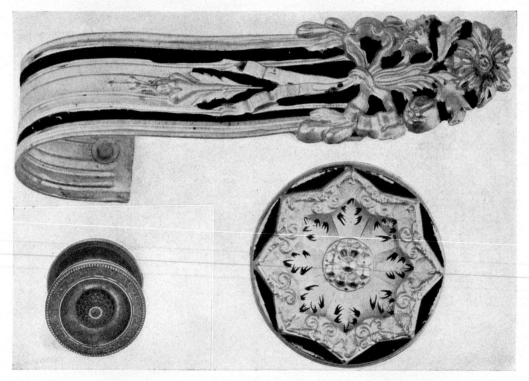

3612-14. The Rich Knob and Pull in Blue, Pink, White, and Gilt. Knob Diameter
3 Inches. Pull 2¼ x 12. The Smaller Knob, as the Others, Are from the William B.
Goodwin Collection.

3615–22. The Most Interesting Are the First of the Third Line, Which Is Called Thomas Jefferson, and the Beehive with the Legend "Nothing without Labor." This Set Is One of the Complete Equipment of a Sideboard, Hepplewhite Period. James Davidson Collection.

3623-31. Fine Chippendale Open Handles, with Three at the Top of an Earlier Period. Collection of Frank A. Robart

The teardrop is the earliest brass handle, about 1690. The stamped William and Mary and Queen Anne handles run from about 1700–1730. The open scroll, or the closed scroll handles, usually called willow handles, are of the Chippendale time, ranging from 1740–80. In America the scroll handle like the bottom left example, or at least a handle which is not cut out with interior scrolls, has proved to be more popular. Handles in the first period were attached by wires clinched on the inside. The posts came a little later, with handmade nuts always of irregular form on the outside. Brasses have been, and are, imitated so closely that only an expert, whoever he may be, can detect the difference.

3632–39. CHIPPENDALE BRASSES. THE LOWER ONES ON THE LEFT SHOW THE EVOLUTION FROM
THE EARLIER QUEEN ANNE TYPE. COLLECTION OF FRANK A. ROBART.

    These brasses all have a beveled edge, which was cleaned up by a file. They are invariably cast and
not cut out by a stamp. They are also very thin, about a 32nd of an inch.
    Thick brasses, or brasses with a rounded edge, or a square edge are modern. It is only recently
that two American firms have arrived at the skill necessary for the copying of the ancient brasses.

3640–47. ALL EXCEPT THE OPENWORK BRASS ARE OF THE EMPIRE PERIOD, AND RANGE FROM
1800 TO 1830. COLLECTION OF FRANK A. ROBART.

By this time the cutting of threads by machine was developed. Brasses before this period had all their threads cut by hand. The detection of the machine-cut thread is the readiest method of learning that the brass is modern. The Empire brasses were all of them stamped in dies. The work on them is not to be confused with the stamping of the Queen Anne time which was done with a series of small tools, each cutting a minute section, and combining in an endless variety.

3648–55. This Sheet of Chippendale Brasses, from the Collection of Frank A. Robart, Represents the More Popular and Usual Pattern Found on Furniture between 1760 and 1775.

These brasses all had plain surfaces, and it was considered poor housekeeping to neglect the polishing of the brasses. These were highly burnished, and the woodwork about them on old pieces shows a polish where the material used overran the edge of the brass.

3656–63. COLLECTION OF HENRY WOOD ERVING.

The brass most commonly found, and of a design that has appealed to the greatest number of old furniture buyers, are those on the left of this sheet. Messrs. Erving, Goodwin, Bigelow, Norton, Eaton, Pauly, and others have been most kind in allowing individual brasses to be removed for pictorial use. The matter of matching up old brasses is often of great annoyance, and a test of serenity of character. A set of good brasses is now worth, in many instances, more than the piece of furniture to which they are affixed.

3664-71. THE OLDER SPECIMENS HERE ARE AT THE TOP, RIGHT, AND THE FIRST AND LAST IN THE SECOND ROW. THE FIRST IN THE SECOND ROW REPRESENTS A NUDE FIGURE PLAYING A FIFE. THE PUFFED-OUT CHEEKS ARE FUNNY. THE CREATURE HAS WINGS AND APPEARS TO BE SITTING ON A CLOUD WHICH CONSISTS OF SPIRALS. IT MAY BE PRESUMED THAT HE IS SUPPLYING THE MUSIC OF THE SPHERES. ON THE RIGHT IN THE SAME ROW, IS AN URN WITH DRAPERY. THE LARGEST BRASS, WITH THE LION, SHOWS ALSO IMPLEMENTS OF WAR. THE LION WAS THE MOST POPULAR AND THE LEAST ATTRACTIVE OF ALL THE STAMPED BRASSES OF THE EMPIRE TIME. COLLECTION OF FRANK A. ROBART.

3672. UNIQUE COMBINED LATCH AND KNOCKER. THE AUTHOR'S.

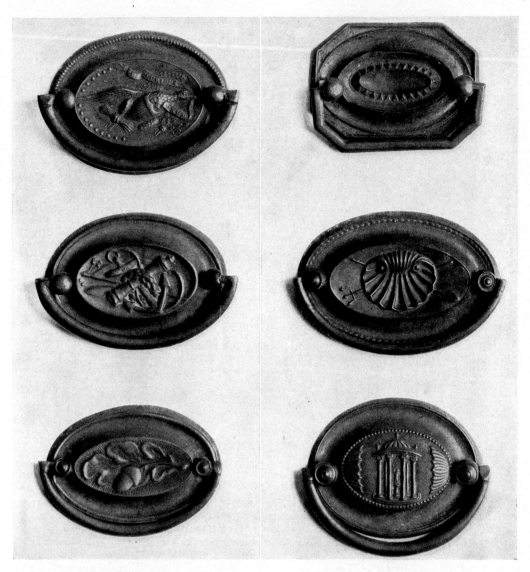

3673-78. The Flying Eagle Carries the Scroll with E Pluribus Unum in the Beak, and a Sheaf of Arrows with the Olive Branch in the Claws. Fifteen Stars for the States, Which Give the Date. In the Second Row There Are Naval Emblems in the Left-Hand Brass, and Fine Shell with Trident and Spear in the Right-Hand Brass. At the Bottom We Have the Acorn Leaf and Acorn Which Appear in Various Forms. On the Right at the Bottom There Is a Small Classical Temple with a Figure. Collections of William G. Goodwin and Malcolm A. Norton.

In these volumes the author has appealed to those who desire compacted information. It is not feasible in the limits of the work to write sketches of notable cabinetmakers, all of which information may be found in any library. The thought is, first, the picture, then the mention of its salient features.

3679–86. Chippendale on the Left, Hepplewhite and Sheraton on the Right. Collection of Henry Wood Erving, Hartford.

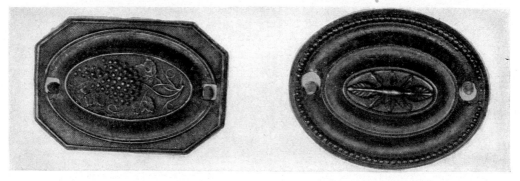

3687–88. An Octagon and an Oval Brass, from Francis Hill Bigelow, 1790–1800.

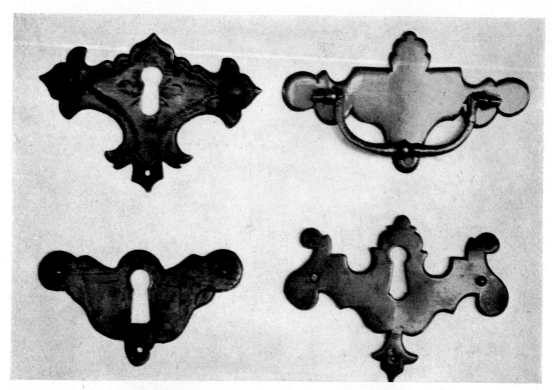

3689–92. Two Queen Anne and Two Chippendale Brasses. Both of the Queen Anne Specimens
Are Very Rare. A. H. Eaton, Collinsville.

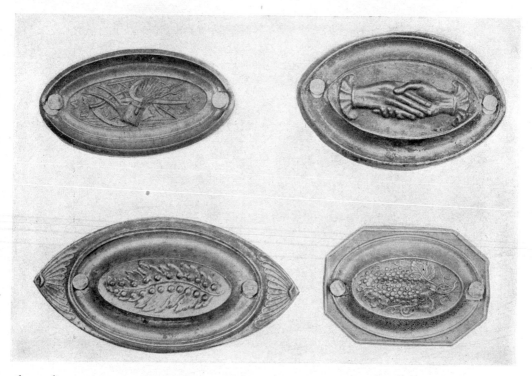

3693–96. Agricultural Brass, Top Left. Clasped Hands on the Right. The Others Are a
Leaf and a Grape Pattern. Rudolph P. Pauly, Boston.

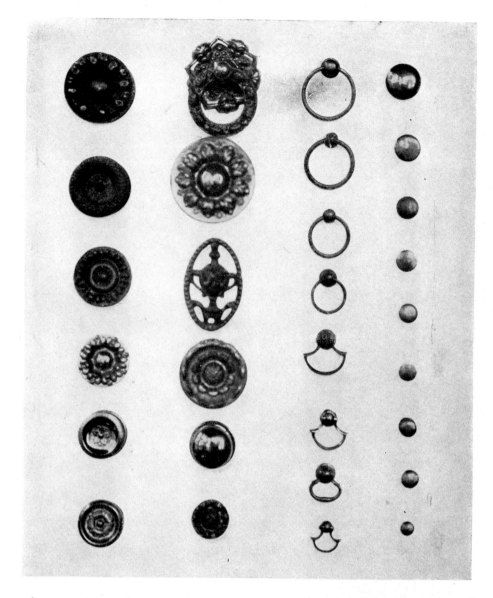

3697-3725. A Sheet of Brasses Prepared by the Patience of Henry Wood Erving.

The first and second columns represent the Empire period. The third column is earlier; the four shaped drops on the right being very dainty and some of them small, used on little cabinet drawers. For the fourth column the knobs were used in the 18th and early 19th Centuries. These small drops are similar to and a hold-over from the first half of the 18th century. They appear in larger form on box locks. In smaller forms we find them on the doors of cupboards. The knobs were used on the sustaining slides for desks and on any small drawer or cupboard door.

Most hardware was imported for old types of furniture and is still imported, but during the last five years American firms have learned to supply all our needs.

3726–30. Late 17th and Early 18th Centuries. All Probably English, but Found on American Furniture.

The teardrops were sometimes flat on the back, and sometimes round, as in the bottom left example. In the top left example, it is easy to see that a round punch mark is used several times in the center of the flower. A second tool was perhaps all that was necessary to complete this brass.

3731–32. A Pair of Knobs Showing an Eagle on a Perch. Unusual.
J. Grossman, Boston.

3733-41. NINE BRASSES OF THE EARLIEST AND LATEST PERIODS. THE
BAILS WITH PLAIN ROSETTES ARE FOUND ON VARIOUS PIECES AND ON SMALL
BLOCK FRONTS. THE ESCUTCHEONS ARE QUEEN ANNE. OCTAGON BRASSES
ARE LESS USUAL, AND THEREFORE NOTICED. TWO LATE EMPIRE RING
BRASSES COMPLETE THE LOT. H. W. ERVING.

3742-43. LADIES WITH HATS OF THE GAINSBOROUGH TIME, ON LOOKING-
GLASS KNOBS WITH BRASS FRAMES. J. GROSSMAN, BOSTON.

3744–50. SEVEN BRASSES FROM RUDOLPH P. PAULY.
A CABIN ON THE LOWER LEFT IS VERY RARE. SHEAF
OF GRAIN IS GOOD. THE BASKET AND SHELL BRASS,
WHILE NOT COMMON, WERE FOUND IN THE EMPIRE
PERIOD. ON THE CENTRAL BRASS IS AN URN WITH A
WREATH. THE OTHERS ARE EMPIRE TIME.

DETAILS

There begin here a large number of detail and turning parts.

3751. A FINE HEPPLEWHITE BEDPOST WITH SPADE
FOOT. J. K. BEARD, RICHMOND, VIRGINIA.

3752. (Right.) A VERY LATE POST OFTEN CALLED
WEST INDIAN FROM THE FACT THAT SO MANY WERE IM-
PORTED FROM THAT REGION. TWISTED REEDS. 1820–30.
ANNE S. HOUSTON, CHATTANOOGA, TENNESSEE.

3753. A Curly Maple Trencher, Size of a Large Dinner Plate. Wadsworth Atheneum.

3754. (Right.) A Candle Rack. When the Candle Was Dipped, the Wick Was Doubled and a Small Loop Left at the Top; When This Loop Was Removed from the Stick the Candles Could Be Hung Up Separately To Prevent Them from Sticking Together. Mrs. De Witt Howe.

3755. A Carved Foot Stove. Very Rare. 18th Century. On One Side There Is a Slide To Admit a Box of Iron, for Coals. Wadsworth Atheneum.

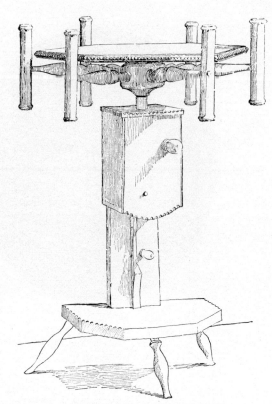

3756. THE HEAD OF A TAPE LOOM, WITH PENNSYLVANIA-GERMAN TULIP DECORATION AND INSCRIPTION. DATED 1794. WILLIAM B. MONTAGUE, NORRISTOWN, PENNSYLVANIA.

3757. (Right.) A COMBINED TABLE AND WHEEL. DELAWARE VALLEY. WADSWORTH ATHENEUM.

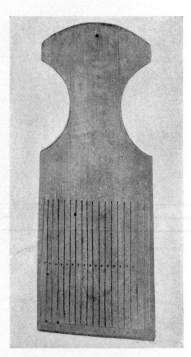

3758-60. TAPE LOOMS. LEFT: W. F. HUBBARD, RIGHT: WADSWORTH ATHENEUM.

3759. (Middle.) A DISH TOP TABLE. WIFE OF DR. SAMUEL COOPER. BIGELOW COLLECTION.

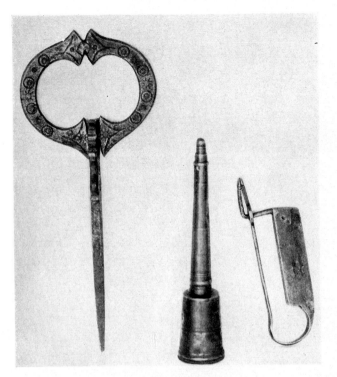

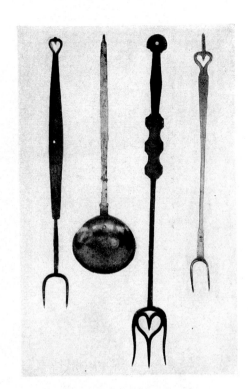

3761–63. A Remarkable Wrought Drop Handle, Stamped. Ink Horn, the Top of Which Unscrews and Releases a Pen. A Miniature Steel for Striking Flint Combined with a Pair of Tongs for Holding the Lighted Material to a Pipe. Wadsworth Atheneum.

3764–67. (Right.) Culinary Articles Decorated. Usually Votive Offerings at the Shrine of a Maiden, and Hung by Her in the Fireplace. All 17th or 18th Century. J. Stogdell Stokes.

3768. A Smoke Jack, of Which One or Two Others Are Known, Notably That at Mount Vernon. It Is in the Kitchen Chimney of the Wentworth-Gardner House, Portsmouth. The Author Took It Out and Repaired the Fans, Oiled It and Restored It to Its Place, and Made It Workable. It Is Operated by the Draught of the Chimney to Turn the Spit.

3769–70. (Right.) A Toddy Iron, and a Basket for Pitch Wood. Wadsworth Atheneum.

3771. The Finest Burl Bowl at Present Known. There Are Larger, but This Specimen Has the Ears Cut upon It. Diameter 23 Inches. These Bowls Were Made in America, Canada, Ireland, and the Philippine Islands. In Ireland They Are Often of Ash. In America They Are More Often Walnut, Maple, or Other Woods. Cut from the Burl, They Would Not Split. Wadsworth Atheneum.

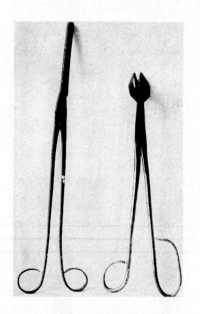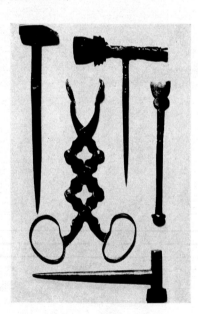

3772-73. Curling Irons. Wadsworth Atheneum.

3774-78. (Right.) An Extension Toggle Pipe Tongs, and Sets of Buttonhole and Eyelet Cutters. Pennsylvania. Mrs. M. B. Cookerow.

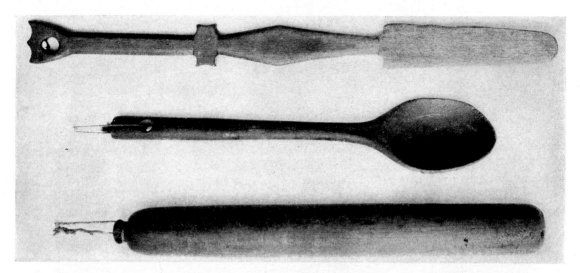

3779–81. Hasty Pudding Stick, Wooden Spoon, Roller. 18th Century. Wadsworth Atheneum.

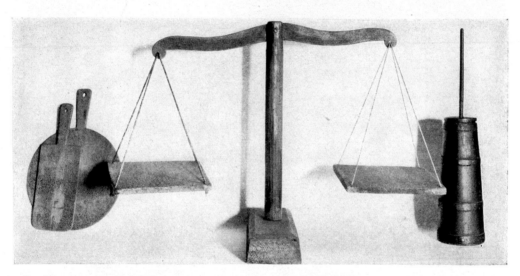

3782–85. Two Butter Pats or Shapers, a Primitive Butter Scale all of Wood, and a Dash Churn. 18th Century. L. P. Goulding, Sudbury.

3786. Goose Yoke, Imitated from an Ox Yoke. Nine Inches. 18th Century. Chetwood Smith.

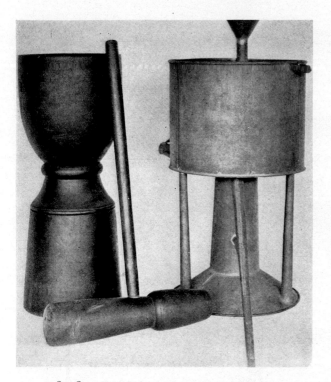

3787-89. Fine Large Mortar and Huge Pestle. 22 Inches High. An Ancient Still.
Wadsworth Atheneum.
3790. An Odd Instrument Probably for Working Down the Nap of Hats. William B. Montague.

3791-97. Three Mortars, One of Them Enormous. A Hand-Wrought Burl Bowl. A Froe
Held by the Wooden Part, and Struck with a Sledge on the Iron Part for Splitting Clap-
boards. A Great Shovel Worked from One Piece of Wood, and a Piggin Made of Staves.
Wadsworth Atheneum.

3798–99. Decorative Pennsylvania Foot Scrapers, To Be Set into a Stone at the Door. Francis D. Brinton.

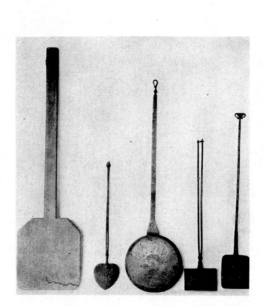
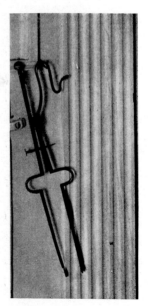

3800. A Standard for Embroidery with a Ball and Socket Joint, Adjustable.

3801–05. A Wooden Slice for the Brick Oven. Two Waffle Irons, One of Heart Shape. A Brass Warming Pan, with the Early Iron Handle, and an Iron Shovel or Slice, Decorative D.

3806. The Best Pair of Pipe Tongs Known to the Author. Taken by a Member of the Williams Family at the Capture of Fort Henry, 1756. South Easton.

3807–11. A Huge Mortar High Enough To Operate as It Stood on the Floor. It Stands Higher than a Table. A Pestle Which Did Not Go with It. An Ancient Beehive, Which Was Waxed on the Interior by the Bees To Make It Water Tight. The Second Mortar, Hand Worked from a Log, with a Handle, and All in One Piece, Has Also an Enormous Pestle of One Piece. These Are the Finest Examples the Author Has Seen. Left: Wadsworth Atheneum. Right: J. J. Sullivan, Woodbury, Connecticut.

3812–15. An Early Pair of Snowshoes. A Huge Shovel of Quartered Oak. The Author Has Used This in Clearing Paths. An Ancient Churn with a Scheme for Preventing the Overflow of the Cream, and a Log Barrel. It Is Probable that Advantage Was Taken of a Hollow Log, and the Shaping Was Finished by Burning. A Wooden Bottom Was Pinned In.

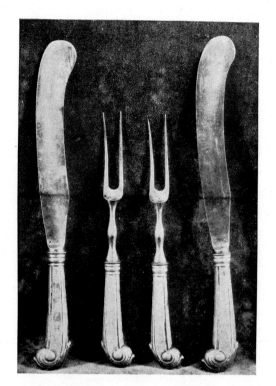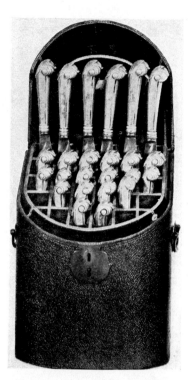

3816–19. Knives and Forks, Some Shown in Detail, with Silver Pistol-Grip Handles, Scimitar-Shaped Blades, and Two-Tined Forks, Bearing the Silversmith's Mark. J. L. Attributed to John Le Roux, New York City, 1732. Original Shagreen Case. W. Lanier Washington, Wakefield, Westport, Connecticut.

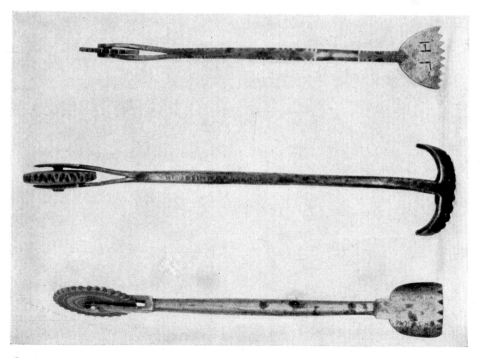

3820–22. Decorative and Initialed Pie Edgers and Cutters. These Also Were Presented by Swains to Their Sweethearts. Wrought Iron, Delaware Valley. Wadsworth Atheneum.

3823-24. Sheraton Period Standards, Carrying Respectively a Terrestrial and a Celestial Globe, with a Compass at the Bottom. Joe Kindig, Jr., York, Pennsylvania.

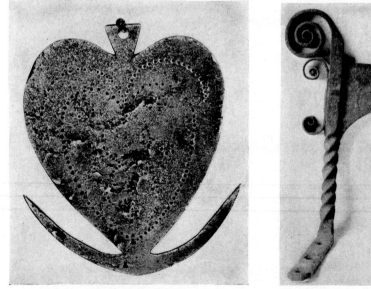 

3825. A Heart-Shaped Skewer Holder. The Giver of It Was So Enamored that He Outlined Two Other Hearts with a Punch.

3826. Decorative Scraper of Twisted and Scrolled Iron. 18th Century. Wadsworth Atheneum.

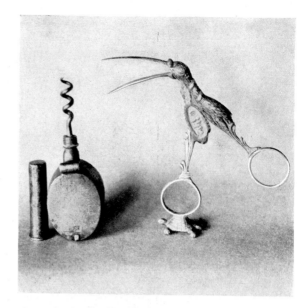

3827. A Burl Bowl with a Turned Cover. These Articles Are Much Sought For, and with a Cover They Are Very Rare. J. Stogdell Stokes.

3828-30. (Right.) A Cork Screw, the Head of Which Opens. It May Have Contained Wafers or Snuff. The Article on the Right Is a Pair of Silver Forceps, Which, When Opened, Disclose in the Cavity a Swathed Figure. Perhaps the Use Was Surgical. Why, However, the Arrangement To Stand It Erect Was Added Is a Puzzle, Unless It Was for Cleanliness. Wm. B. Montague, Norristown, Penna.

3831-32. Combined Spoon Rack and Knife Box. The Hinges Are Shaped from Dowels Formed on the Lid, Which Is Molded as Well as the Other Cross Pieces. The Spoons Are Pewter in Various Patterns. Wadsworth Atheneum.

3833. (Right.) An Ancient Caster, Prettily Turned with a Colonial Drop Handle. The Glass Is of an Early Pattern. Bigelow Collection.

3834. Corner Fireplace in the York Jail.   3835. (Right.) A Cheese Press. L. P. Goulding.

3836. Trammel with a D-Shaped Handle for Adjustment. J. Stogdell Stokes.
3837. (Right.) Brass, Foot Stove, Washington Headquarters, Morristown, New Jersey.

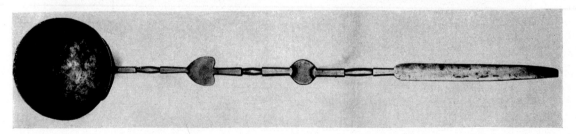

3838. Very Fine Gift Ladle with a Wrought Heart, Copper Bowl Attached by a T-Shaped Welding.
Best So Far Found. Pennsylvania. Wadsworth Atheneum.

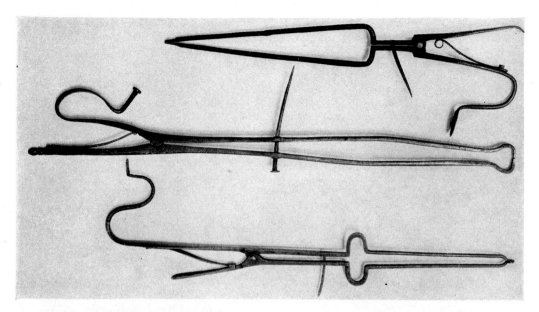

3839-41. THREE FINE TYPES OF PIPE TONGS, WROUGHT. 18TH CENTURY. THE FLATTENED THUMB PIECE AT THE END OF THE SCROLL WAS USED TO PRESS THE TOBACCO DOWN IN THE PIPE, AS THE FINE GENTLEMEN WHO USED THESE ARTICLES HAD NO CALLUSES ON THEIR THUMBS. THE SPIKE WAS USED TO CLEAN OUT THE BOWL. WADSWORTH ATHENEUM.

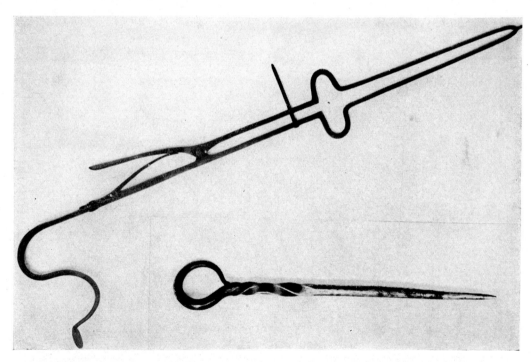

3842. FINE PIPE TONGS, SQUARE SECTION. SPRING ENDING IN AN ACORN. HENRY FORD.

3843. (Right.) ORNAMENTAL SKEWER WITH A DOUBLE TWIST. IT STOOD IN THE JOINT AS IT WAS BROUGHT TO THE TABLE. PRESENTED TO THE AUTHOR BY CHETWOOD SMITH.

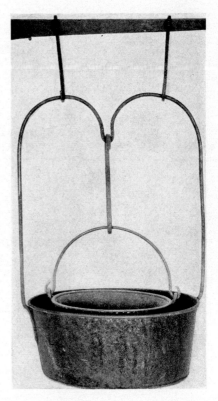

3844. A Double-Ended Trivet. It Had a Wooden Handle. Used over the Coals for a Porringer.

3845. (Right.) A Double Boiler. One of Two Known To Hang on Crane. It Proves that Our Ancestors Worked Out Some of Our Inventions without Patenting Them. Both: 18th Century. Wadsworth Atheneum.

3846–47. A Kettle with a Wrought Frame and Trivet with Wooden Handle. The Top Has Pierced Work. 18th Century. H. W. Erving.

3848. Cast Hessian Andirons. The Mustaches Reach the Ears. Intended To Be Ironical. Cast with Flat Backs in the Early Fashion. 1780–90. J. Stogdell Stokes.

3849–51. Hessian, and General Washington Andirons. The Middle Pair Are Wrought with Square-Turned Brass Tops. Present Owners Unknown.

3852. Wrought Twisted Pipe Tongs, 18th Century. Wadsworth Atheneum.

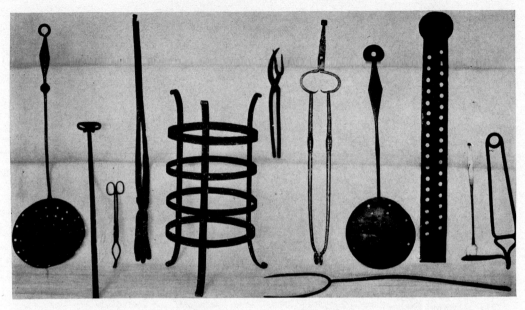

3853-64. Large Shaped Skimmer, Shovel Handles, Cast Pipe Tongs, Forceps, Trivet, Kettle Lifter, Tongs, Skimmer, Skewer Post, Small Slice, Pipe Tongs, and Pie Plate Lifter for the Great Oven. Doylestown Tavern, Pennsylvania.

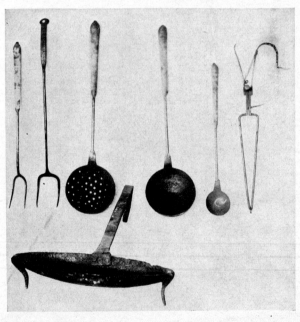

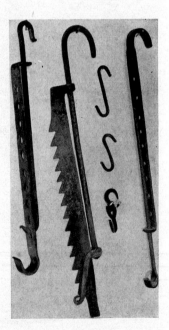

3865-71. In the Foreground Is a Long, Narrow Wrought-Iron Tray for Dipping the Rush. Very Rare. The Other Articles Have Decorations or Initials on the Handles.

3872-77. (Right.) Trammels, the Second of Which Is the Best, with Saw Teeth. The Other Articles Are Pot Hooks of Different Sizes, That at the Bottom Being Made with a Swivel.

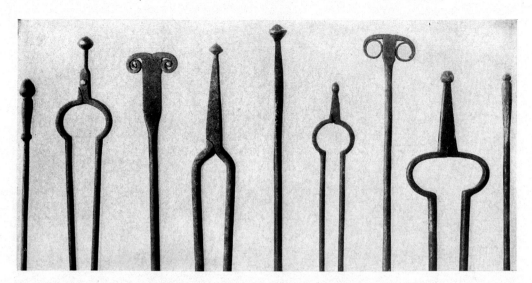

3878–86. Handles of Tongs or Shovels, All Wrought, Showing the Various Designs of Scrolls or Octagons. The Author's.

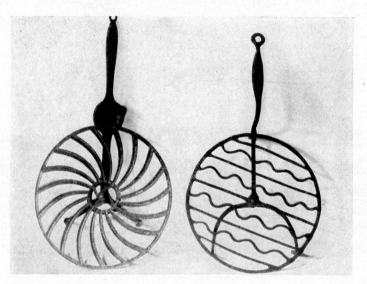

3887–88. Whirling Broilers. The Second Being Wrought. 18th Century. H. W. Erving.

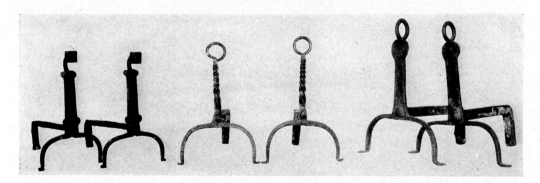

3889–91. Three Pairs of Andirons, the First Having a Goose Neck with Squares, the Second Being Twisted with Rings, and the Third Flattened. Wadsworth Atheneum.

3892-95. Four Broilers, All Wrought. Straight, Serpentine, and Scrolled. The Third Was a Nice Piece of Work. 18th Century. Wadsworth Atheneum.

3896-97. Fine Brass Andirons, Spiraled. Both with Ball Feet. The First Pair Has the Fender Posts. The Second Pair Has Octagon Sections. Bigelow Collection.

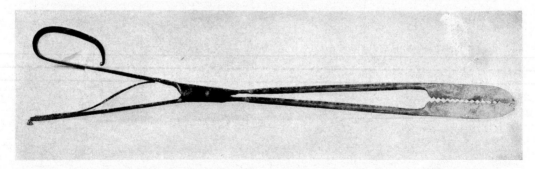

3898. Long, Large Ember Tongs. For Handling Partly Burned Logs in a Fireplace. Mark M. Henderson, Norwalk, Connecticut.

3899-3903. Five Styles of Andirons, the First and Last Being Cast. On One a Bust, the Other a Hessian with a Handle Hat Like a Mitre. The Second Is Wrought with a Brass Cap, the Third and Fourth Are Rare Designs, All Wrought. Rudolph P. Pauly, Boston.

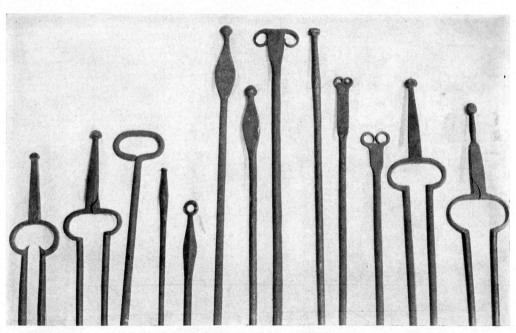

3904-16. Tong and Shovel Handles, All Wrought. The Best Is the Last, Since It Was Decorated with Tool Work on the Handle. 18th Century. The Author's.

3917-54. 17TH CENTURY. L. P. GOULDING, SUDBURY.

The best-furnished fireplace known to the author. Birch broom, carved spoon, gourd, long-handled spider, flapjack turner, S hanger, slice, two skewer holders with skewers, hasty-pudding stick, culinary forks, two kettle lifters, three patterns of broilers, toaster, two trivets, a charcoal stove, andirons with spit rods, swivel teakettle, brass kettle, trammel chain, two trammels, toddy iron, very large skimmer, firkin, dipper, sugar toddy stick, and on the floor the largest toddy iron ever found, hanging spider, bean pot, door for oven, stone fireplace.

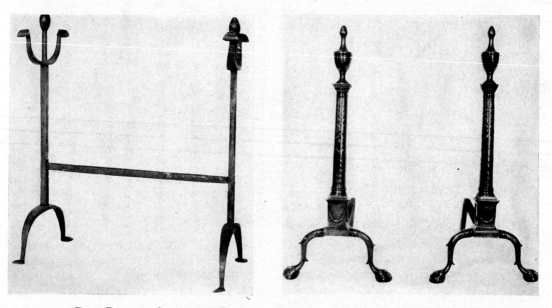

3955. RARE REST FOR SKEWER, OR POSSIBLY FOR SHOVEL AND TONGS. J. STOGDELL STOKES.
3956. (Right.) RARE PAIR OF BRASS ANDIRONS, BALL AND CLAW, DECORATED WITH SEVERAL CLASSICAL MOTIVES. I. SACK, PALMER COLLECTION.

3957-59. THREE PAIRS OF ANDIRONS, THE GOOSE HEAD WITH BALL, THE FLAT SCROLL, AND THE COLONIAL PIGTAIL. WADSWORTH ATHENEUM.

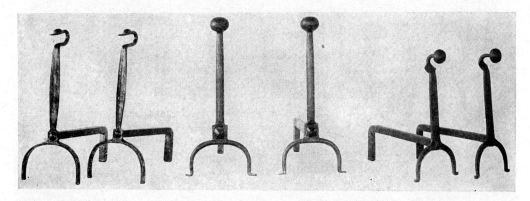

3960-62. THREE PAIRS OF ANDIRONS, A GOOSE HEAD WITH THE BILL, EYE, AND NOSTRIL MARKED, THE STRAIGHT BALL, AND THE GOOSE-HEAD BALL. FORMERLY THE AUTHOR'S.

3963-65. THE FIRST A HEART MOTIVE ANDIRON. E. W. SARGENT, PROVIDENCE. THE SECOND AND THIRD TRESTLE-FOOT ANDIRONS, WITH BALL AND SCROLL HEADS. FORMERLY THE AUTHOR'S.

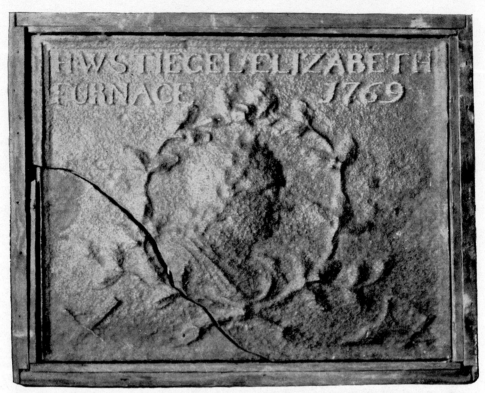

3966. Chiefly Interesting from the Inscription "H. W. Stiegel, Elizabeth Furnace, 1769." Philip Meredith Allen, Broad Axe, Pennsylvania.

3967–81. Fireplace with Equipment. Francis D. Brinton.

3982–84. THREE STYLES OF ANDIRONS, OF WHICH THE FIRST IS PROBABLY ENGLISH. 3985. (Right.) A KETTLE LIFTER TO REMOVE HEAVY ARTICLES FROM THE CRANE. VERY RARE. J. STOGDELL STOKES.

3986–90. BEAUTIFULLY PATTERNED IRON FIRE FRAME, UNUSUAL FIRE DOGS, BETTY LAMPS, SKILLET, SHOVEL AND TONGS, IRON TOASTER, LANTERN, PIPE TONGS. E. S. MACOMBER, PROVIDENCE.

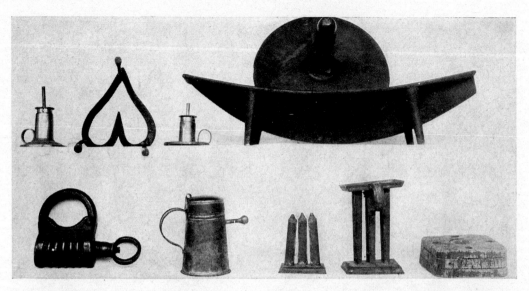

3991–99. Utensils from Doylestown Tavern. Two Sperm Oil Lamps, Trivet for Sad Iron,
a Remarkable Cast Chopping Bowl, the Edged Roller Moving in the Bottom of the Trench
Only, a Padlock, Tin Nursing Bottle, Candle Holder, and an Ink Well.

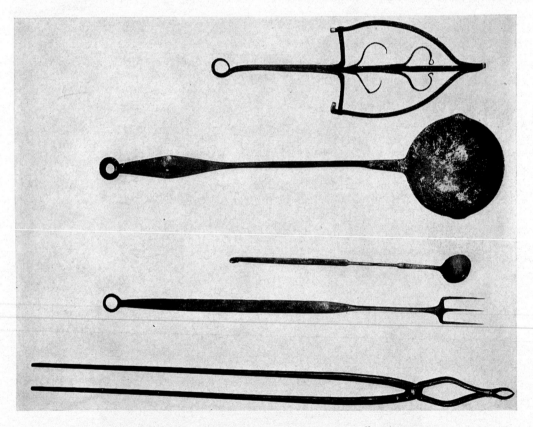

4000–04. Wrought Flatiron Holder, Double-Nosed Wrought Ladle, Light Wrought Spoon,
a Fork Long Enough To Sup with a Certain Individual, and Odd Pipe Tongs.
Wadsworth Atheneum.

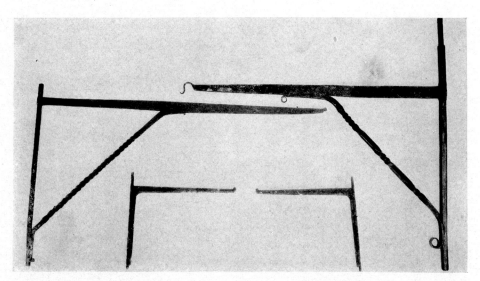

4005-08. Two Unusual Cranes, and a Pair of Cranes.

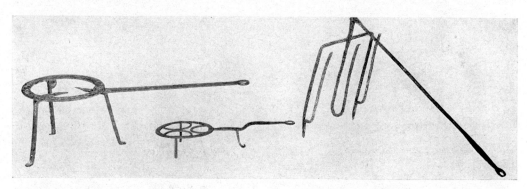

4009-11. A Common and an Unusual Trivet, and a Jointed Bread Toaster. Pennsylvania.

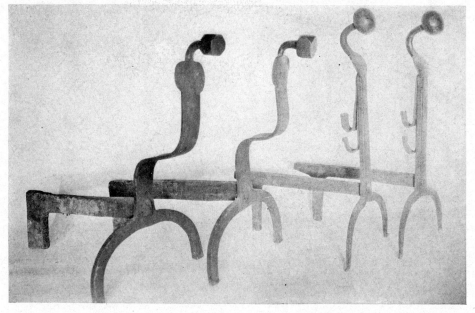

4012-13. Rare Pair of Ogee Andirons, and a Pair with Hooks for the Spit.
All on Page Wadsworth Atheneum.

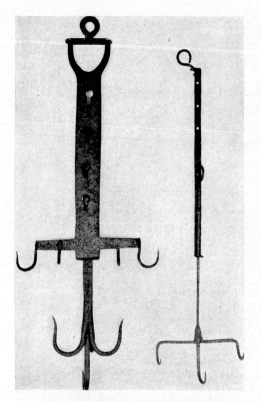
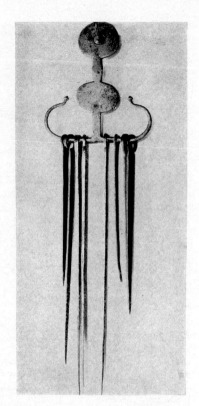

4014–15. Two Trammel Bird Spits, Both Very Rare. Wadsworth Atheneum.
4016–17. An Excellent Skewer Holder with Ball Terminations. L. P. Goulding.

4018. Clockwork Jack with Brass Face and Weight. Wadsworth Atheneum.
4019. (Right.) A Wrought-Iron Beetle Built for a Bootjack. 18th Century. Perhaps the
Original of the Cast, and Late, Jacks. Francis D. Brinton.

4020–28. COLLECTION OF MRS. J. INSLEY BLAIR, TUXEDO PARK. THE BROILER AND TOASTING FORK ARE GOOD. THE SKEWER HOLDER IS VERY FINE. AN ODD WAFFLE IRON, OR PERHAPS WAFER IRON, AN ADJUSTABLE BIRD SPIT, TWO PAIRS OF PIPE TONGS, A CAKE TURNER, AND A TIN PIPE BOX, PERHAPS UNIQUE, CARRYING A LEGEND.

4029–38. IN THE FOREGROUND A SLATER'S HAMMER AND AN S CHOPPER. BEHIND, AN ANCIENT THERMOMETER, SPIRALED BROILER, KETTLE LIFTER, COLANDER, RAT TRAP, MILK WARMER, AND CHOPPER. FRANCIS MIREAU.

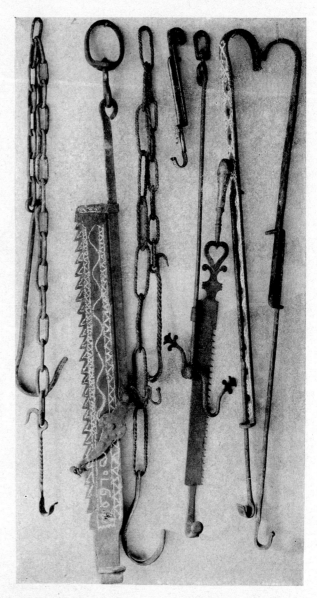

4039–46. REMARKABLE ASSEMBLAGE OF DECORATIVE TRAMMELS. THE FIRST HAS AN ODD SAW TOOTH, WITH PUNCH MARKS AND SCROLLS. THE SECOND AND FOURTH ARE CHAIN TRAMMELS, TWISTED, WITH HOOKS ATTACHED. THE THIRD IS THE OLDEST DATED, NAMELY 1697. THE SIXTH IS FANCIFUL WITH HEART MOTIVE AND WOODEN HANDLE. THE SEVENTH HAS PUNCH MARK DECORATION.

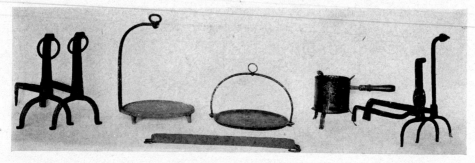

4047–53. THREE STYLES IN ANDIRONS, TWO IN GRIDDLES, A CHARCOAL STOVE, AND IN THE FOREGROUND A SCROLLED FENDER BAR TO LIE ON THE FLOOR. WADSWORTH ATHENEUM.

4054–57. A Good Fireplace, Late 18th Century. A Fender with Brass Turned Ornaments. Very Rare. Fine Pair of Brass Andirons, a Handsome Brass Fire Set. Henry A. Hoffman, Barrington, Rhode Island.

4058. Rare Burl Tray, Wrought from One Piece. A Most Attractive Article in This Material. Joseph Skinner, Holyoke.

4059–64. Fine Scroll Hinge with Scroll Brace, Scrolled Latch Bar. Well-Designed Escutcheon. A Unique Scraper for Attaching to the Side of a Wall, a Fish Held by a Dog, as a Fish Broiler, a Swivel Candlestand. All Wrought Iron. William B. Montague.

4065–66. Broilers with Swivel Braces To Hold Them at an Angle Against the Fire. Very Rare. William B. Montague, Norristown.

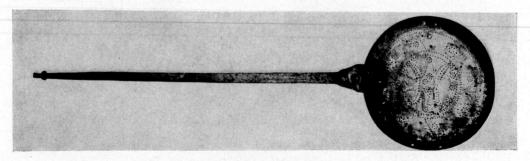

4067. Engraved Brass Warming Pan, Iron Handle, with Crook Top. Earlier than the Wooden Handle. 18th Century. Wadsworth Atheneum.

4068. Rare Pair of Cast Andirons. One Is Welcome to Suppose
Them To Be Any Fair Lady of the Olden Day. E. C. Hall,
Longmeadow, Massachusetts.

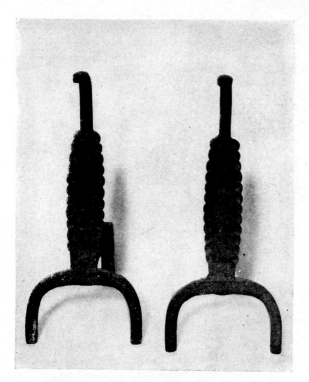

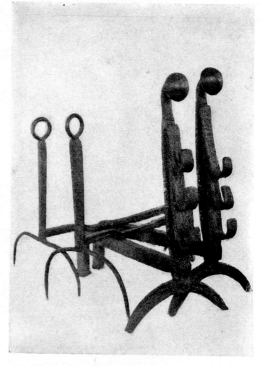

4069. Rattlesnake Andirons, Probably Unique. 17¼ Inches High. 1780. Perhaps These Are All
That Is Left To Mark the Recovery of the Blacksmith from Seeing Things.

4070–71. (Right.) Very Light Andirons and a Crude Pair with Three Sets of Hooks for the Spit.

4072. Excellent Design in Andirons. Pad Feet. A Floral Motive Is Worked on the Square above the Branch, the Legs Are Riveted into the Post.

4073. A Camp Kettle, Copper. Iron Scrolled Legs and Wooden Handles. Used by an Officer in the Revolution. Washington Headquarters. Morristown, New Jersey.

4074. Sunflower Andirons. Unique. Formed by Twisting the Sections into One. Bigelow Collection. 18th Century.

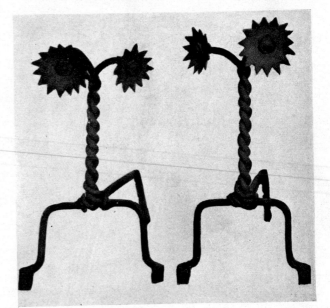

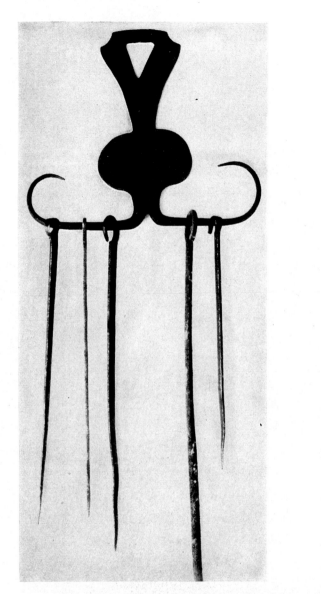

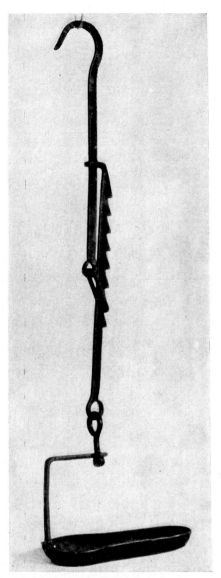

4075. Skewer Holder and Skewers. Such an Article Was Hung to a Nail on the Chimney Girt. Lately Several Fine Ones Have Come to Light. Wadsworth Atheneum.

4076-77. (Right.) Betty Lamp with Trammel. Very Rare. 18th Century. H. W. Erving.

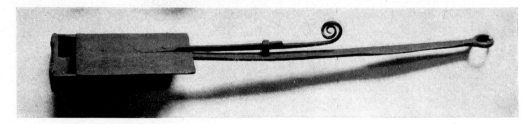

4078. Fire Carrier, in Which the Cover Slides Instead of Lifting. 17th or 18th Century. Fuessenich Collection.

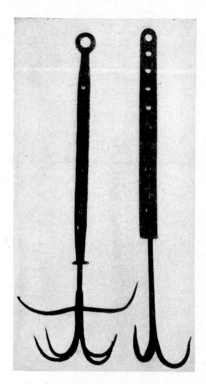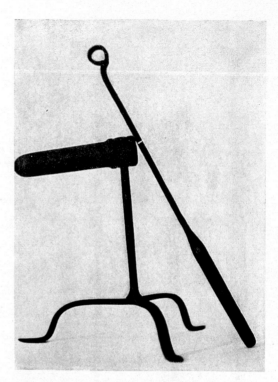

4079–80. Bird or Meat Trammels. 17th or 18th Century. Former: Dwight Blainey. Latter: Mrs. De Witt Howe.

4081. (Right.) A Gophering Iron.

The stick was heated red hot and placed in the sheath, which was then used for ironing ruffles by drawing them over it. The stick was so convenient for toddy that "the profane and the ignorant" have given it the name of a toddy stick. Of course, the toddy stick proper is never carefully rounded. The other name for it is a loggerhead. Yokels at a fireside getting into a quarrelsome discussion would seize these to maintain their positions, hence the expression, "at loggerheads."

4082–86. A Decorative Toaster, Copper Teakettle in Place on a Long-Handled Spider, the Handle To Rest in a Crotch in the Rear, a Charcoal or Invalid's Stove. The Top Lifted. The Pads Were To Hold a Large Dish. Betty Lamp on a Standard for Adjustment. Francis D. Brinton.

4087–88. Rare, Andirons. Late 18th Century. Rhode Island School of Design.

4089–91. Fire Frame, Brass Urns. Fireback: "F. Pleis." Andirons.
Bigelow Collection.

4092. Charcoal Broiler (Old Handle). 4093. Round Foot Stove. 18th Century. Wadsworth Atheneum.

4094. A Fire Carrier. A Common Convenience in Old Houses, before the Days of Matches. 18th Century. Wadsworth Atheneum.

4095–4100. Six Types of Shutter Fasteners, All Wrought. The Third and Fourth Are the Oldest. Those with Plates Attaching to the Wall Are the Latest, the Last Having a Spring, Being Used in the 19th Century.

4101. Pair of Excellent Shutter Fasteners. Similar Irons Were Used in the Walls of Brick Houses as Headers on Sustaining Rods. William B. Goodwin.

4102. (Right.) A Lantern with Feet and Gables for Ventilation. Sanderson Collection.

4103–05. Ship Lanterns or Binnacles. The First Is Made with Lighthouse Glass. That Is, the Shape Is Designed To Magnify the Reflections. Sanderson Collection.

Since the clipper ship and the sailing ship have gone out of use, ship's lanterns are desirable for porches or doorways or dens, especially in seashore houses.

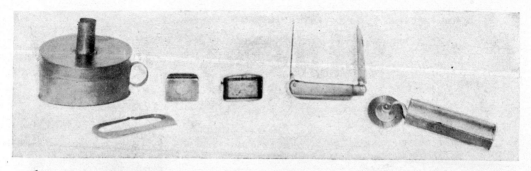

4106–10. A Series of Tinder Boxes or Sparkers. 18th Century. H. W. Erving. The Round Box Contains the Tinder, the Steel and Flint, and the Cover Is Used as a Candlestick. The Next Three Items Were To Carry in the Pocket. The Last One Generates the Spark by the Rapid Revolution of the Wheel. There Is a Pennsylvania Collection of These Articles Running into the Hundreds.

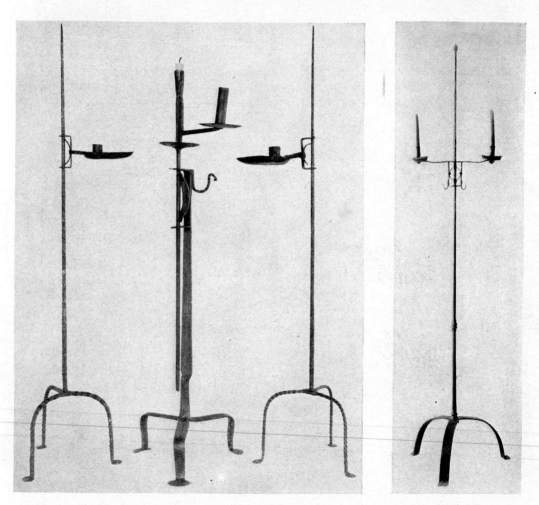

4111–14. A Pair of Iron Floor Standards for Betty Lamps, and in the Center a Rare and Quaint Example for Two Candles. J. Stogdell Stokes. The Last Number Has Brass Mounts. Formerly the Author's.

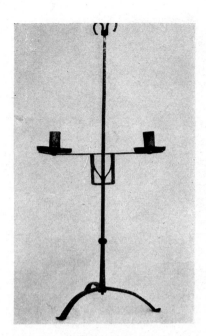 

4115. RARE TABLE CANDLE STAND, ADJUSTABLE. WADSWORTH ATHENEUM.

4116. (Right.) SQUARE IRON STANDARD ON A WEIGHTED TIN BASE. CANDLESTICKS AND HOOD
IN TIN. FORMERLY THE AUTHOR'S.

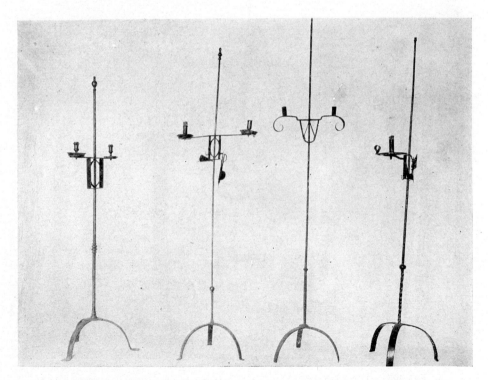

4117–20. FOUR STANDS WITH BRASS MOUNTINGS. THE LAST FOR A SINGLE CANDLE.
18TH CENTURY. FORMERLY THE AUTHOR'S.

4121–27. Sconces. The Upper Pair Carry Three Lights Each. The One in the Center Is Very Odd. Those at Each Side Are Also Unusual. All of Tin. Mrs. J. Insley Blair.

4128–35. The First Is Extremely Rare, a Screw Standard for Two Betty Lamps. That with the Trammel Had Two Candles. The Second in the Foreground Is a Cast Betty. The Next to the Last in the Background Is a Wooden Standard for a Betty.

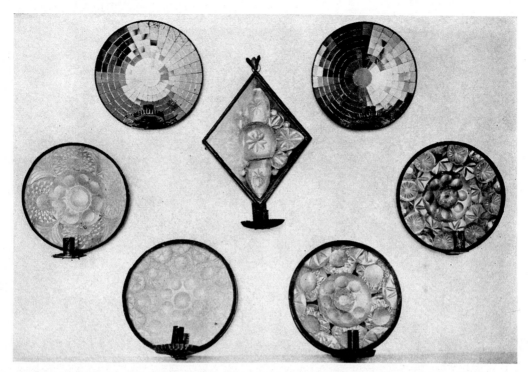

4136-42. Sconces of Small Sections of Mirror Glass or of Bits of Pewter as Thin as Tin Foil. A Very Rich Collection of Rare and Much Sought Pieces. Mrs. J. Insley Blair.

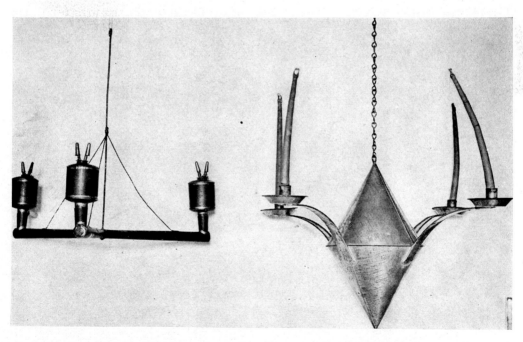

4143-44. Chandeliers. Left: for Sperm Oil. Right: A Diamond-Shaped Double Cone with Arms for Candles. Mrs. J. Insley Blair.

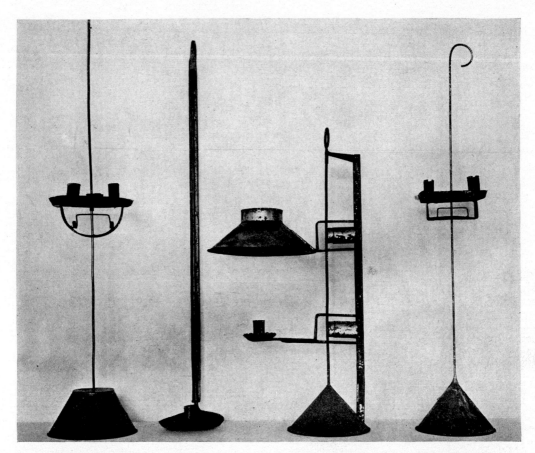

4145–48. Set of Four Standards, Three with Conical Tin Bases Filled with Sand. The Third Is Perhaps Unique. The Second Has a Trammel and Is Sometimes Called a Loom Light.

4149–50. Pewter and a Glass Sconce. All on This Page. Mrs. J. Insley Blair.

4151–53. Five, Six, and Four-Sided Lanterns. The Cut-Outs on the Center One Are Very Laboriously Done, and the Pattern Is Good. The Third Was To Hang against the Wall. Wadsworth Atheneum.

4154–55. Large Ship Lantern and a Lantern with a Reflector Within. Wadsworth Atheneum.

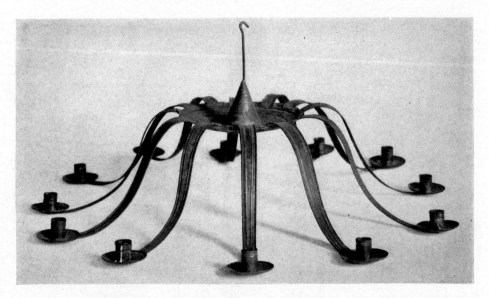

4156. Twelve-Candle Central Light Sconce or Chandelier. This Has More Grace Than Most of the Sort and Presents No Uncouth or Doubtful Lines. The Tin Is Strengthened at the Sides by Being Rolled over Wires. Fuessenich Collection.

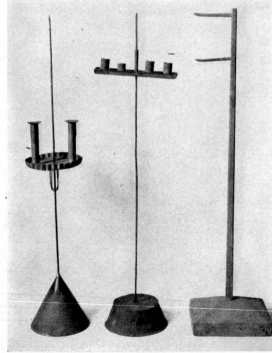

4157. A Unique Iron Chandelier with Odd Motives at the Top, Where Presumably Two More Candles Were Carried. Important. J. Stogdell Stokes.

4158-60. Two Tin and One Wood Stand, the Second for Four Candles, and the Last for Hooking on the So-Called Hog-Scraper Candlestick. Fuessenich Collection.

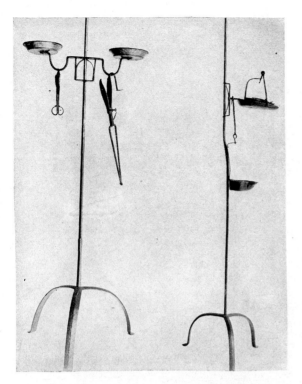

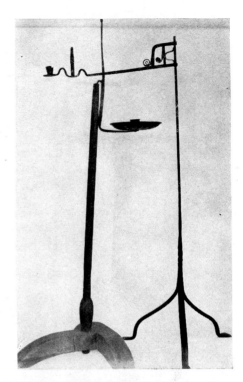

4161-62. Floor Stands, That at the Right for a Betty. The Curving Foot Is Beveled Both Ways. Edward C. Wheeler, Jr., Boston.

4163-64. (Right.) Rare Stand with a T Base Mortised, To Carry a Candle, Which Can Be Lifted from the Socket and Used as an Ordinary Carrying Candle. The Other Example Has a Very Fanciful Arm and Is Probably Unique. Both: 17th or 18th Century. J. Stogdell Stokes.

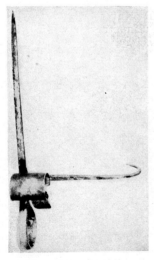

4165. Miner's or a Cooper's Candle with a Spring Catch. The Hook and the Point To Drive into the Wall. Should Be Shown with the Long Line at the Base.

4166-67. (Right.) Lantern and a Sconce. That at the Left Folds, as a Dark Lantern, That at the Right Has a Concave Reflector. H. W. Erving.

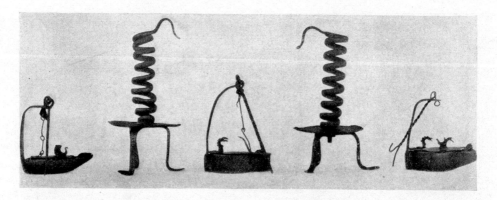

4168-72. Three Rare Bettys, the Left a Rooster, the Middle a Griffin, the Right a Rooster and Griffin. The Pair of Spiral Stands Are Found Abroad, and Perhaps Here Also. J. Stogdell Stokes.

4173-74. Rare Sconce Heads To Be Attached to Shaft. Both Have a Feature We Have Seen But Once Before, Namely Contrivances for Pushing up the Candle as It Burns. Fuessenich Collection.

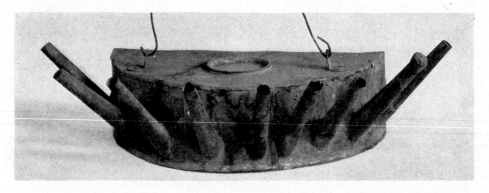

4175. Semicircular Lamp with Nine Outlets for Wicks. Rare or Unique. Fuessenich Collection.

4176–79. Four Rare Pieces. That at the Left Is a Standard for a Betty, and That at the Right Is a Rest for Two Bettys, Adjustable. The Central Pair Remind One of a Fleur-de-Lis. These Are All Pennsylvania Examples. J. Stogdell Stokes.

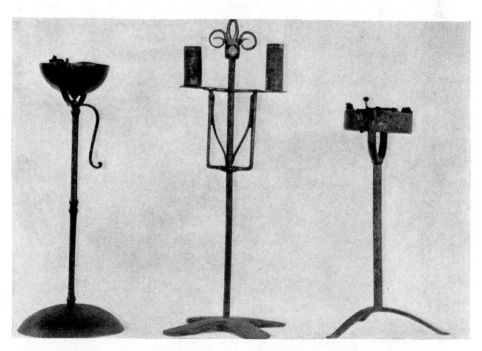

4180–82. Most Interesting Betty with a Turned Standard and Swivel, a Scroll Handle, and Reverse Saucer Base. The Second Has an X Stretcher Base and Top Decoration. At the Right Is a Swivel Betty. J. Stogdell Stokes.

4183-86. THREE OF THESE ARE UNIQUE, AND THE HANGING LOOM LIGHT IS RARE. FAT WAS BURNED IN A BETTY. A. H. RICE, BETHLEHEM. NOW SOLD TO MR. STOKES.

4187-89. THREE RARE LANTERNS, THOUGH THE SECOND IS PERHAPS EARLY 19TH CENTURY, FOR HANGING IN A HALL. THE OTHERS ARE OCTAGON, THAT ON THE RIGHT BEING EXTREMELY QUAINT. RUDOLPH P. PAULY.

4190-93. RARE PAIR OF CANDLESTICKS, AND TWO DOUBLE WALL SCONCES OF TIN. FLAYDERMAN & KAUFMAN.

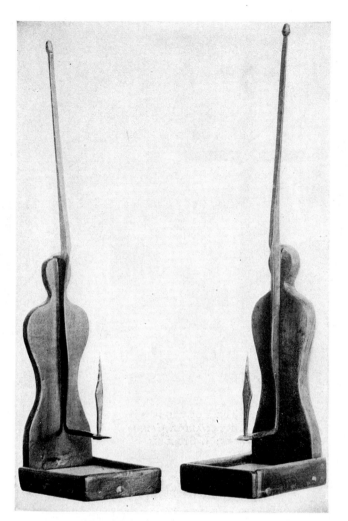
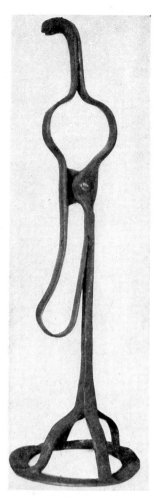

4194-95. Double Purpose Sconces To Remain or To Take Off. E. B. Leete Company.

4196. (Right.) Rare Iron Standard. Benjamin A. Jackson, Wickford, Rhode Island.

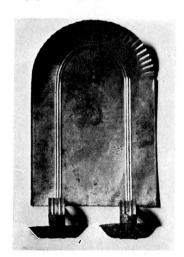

4197. A Double Wall Sconce of Tin. Fuessenich Collection.

4198-99. (Right.) A Wooden Bracket To Carry a Tin Lamp, and a Unique Betty, with a D Handle and a Swivel. J. Stogdell Stokes.

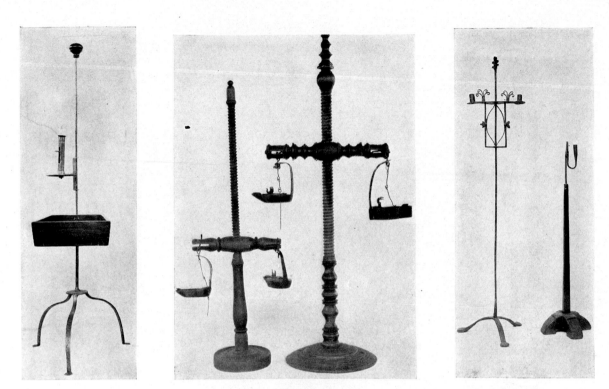

4200–04. The First Is an Adjustable Stand with a Box for Yarn or Other Work. The Screw Stands Are for Attaching Bettys, and Are Rare and Quaint. The Fourth Is a Good Floor Stand of Iron. The Last Is an X Base Wooden Standard for a Rush and a Candlestick. Fourth and Fifth: Owner Unknown. The Others: J. Stogdell Stokes.

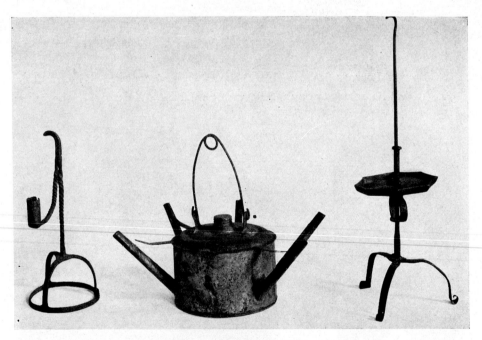

4205–07. A Rare Combined Rush and Candle Standard. A Camp-Meeting Lard Oil Lamp, and a Finely Wrought Standard for Wicks. Fuessenich Collection.

4208. An Elaborate Wrought-Iron Table Sconce with a Ring Carrier, and a Snuffer.

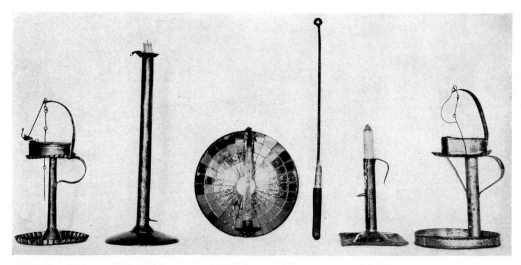

4209–14. Six Lighting Fixtures, the Second Being a So-Called Hog Scraper, and the Fourth a Loom Light. The Fifth Is a Square Base Candlestick.

4215. Combined Wooden and Tin Chandelier. 18th Century. Rare. Anthony T. Kelly, Springfield, Massachusetts.

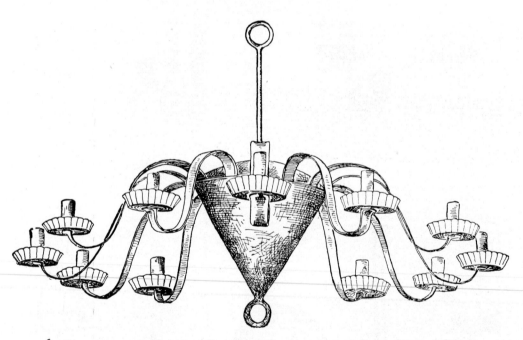

4216. Chandelier of Tin with Scalloped Saucers, and a Cone Center. Drawn by Strickland & Law, Boston, Who Are Acquainted with the Original.

4217. Swinging Wall Bracket for a Beacon.
4218. Camp-Meeting Lamp with Four Reflectors, "Giving Light to Every Quarter."
Both: Formerly the Author's.

4219–20. Left: North Carolina Carved Standard with a Shelf or Stick Light. Right:
Remarkable Fine Betty with a Brass Escutcheon, Bearing the Maker's or the
Recipient's Initials. This Has a Wick Pick. Both: Formerly the Author's.

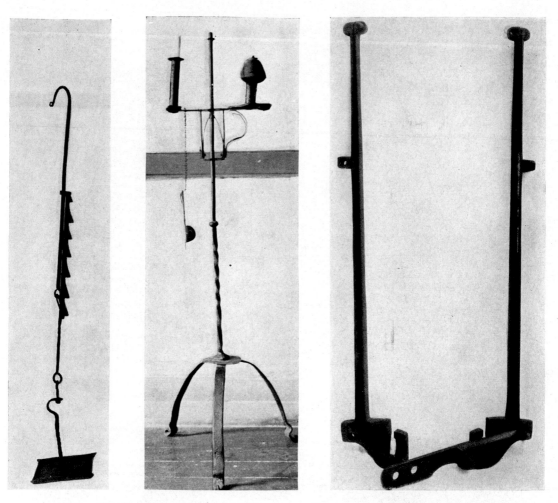

4221. Fat Lamp with Trammel. Fuessenich Col.   4222. Lamp and Candle.
4223–24. Iron Molds for Church Warden Pipes. Joe Kindig, Jr., York, Pennsylvania.

4225. Four-Wick Brass. Morristown. 4226–27. Cast Lanterns. Clifford R. Weld, Rock.

4228–30. Sconce with a Glass. Rare or Unique. Above, a Sconce with Blacksmith's Insignia. Unique. A Tin Sconce Decoration. J. Stogdell Stokes.

4231. (Right.) Betty Lamp of the Usual Pattern with Twisted Hook, Which May Be Placed over a Chair Ear or Jabbed into the Wall. Dr. and Mrs. J. M. Birnie.

4232. Lantern of Unusual Design with Ventilators So Arranged As To Prevent Blowing Out the Light. Sanderson Collection.

4233. Sconce with Imbricated Daisy Reflectors of Very Thin Pewter. Author's Collection, Wadsworth Atheneum.

4234-35. UNIQUE WALL SCONCES, QUAINT DESIGN. FUESSENICH COLLECTION.

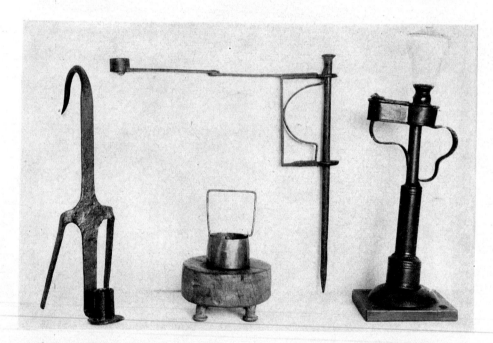

4236-39. SCONCE WHICH COULD BE PLACED OVER AN OPEN BARREL, OR ANY EDGE LIKE A
CHAIR BACK, OR HOOKED. THE SECOND IS A LOW STANDARD LAMP. THE THIRD, A JOINTED
SCONCE FOR A READING CHAIR OR SUCH PURPOSE. THE LAST IS A RARE BETTY.
MRS. J. INSLEY BLAIR.

Dates are not named, as a rule, because many of the lights like the Bettys were made
continuously in the 17th, 18th, and even the 19th centuries, up to 1857. Almost uni-
versally, however, the specimens are of 18th century.

4240. An Amusingly Intricate Church Chandelier with So Many Lights that One Would Be Weary of Counting. Unique. Fuessenich Collection.

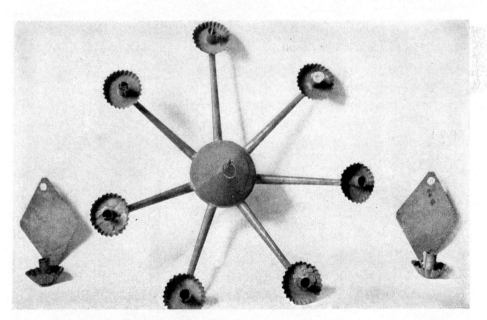

4241–43. Pair of Small Diamond Sconces and a Central Sconce for Seven Lights. Fuessenich Collection.

This collection and the Stokes collection with that of Mrs. J. Insley Blair include many hundreds, perhaps thousands of the rarest and best wrought iron and tin found in America.

It has been thought by some that no rush lights are native. It is hardly believable that simple lights of this kind were not made in the 17th Century in America. Of course, of late, many are brought in from Ireland, France, and Italy.

4244-48. At the Ends is a Pair of Graceful and Perhaps Unique Sconces. An Odd Betty. A Wall Toggle Light for Two Candles. A Spiraled Gophering-Iron. J. Stogdell Stokes.

4249-53. Lamps for Whale Oil or Lard Oil. James Davidson, New London.

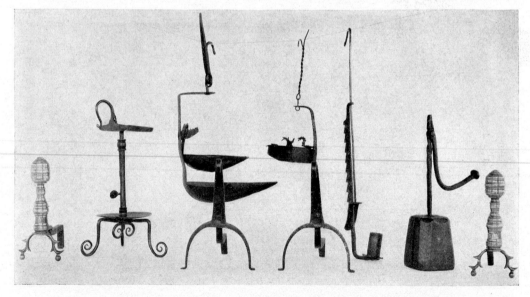

4254-59. At the Extremes a Pair of Doll's Brass Andirons. The Second is a Rare Betty Stand. The Third is a Double Betty. The Fourth for a Single Betty. The Fifth, a Loom or Ceiling Light, and Last a Wooden-Base Rush Light. J. Stogdell Stokes.

4260–61. THREE-CANDLE GLASS SCONCE, UNIQUE TO THE AUTHOR. FUESSENICH COLLECTION. THREE-CANDLE COMBINED GLASS AND TIN SCONCE, VERY EFFECTIVE. CHESTER E. DIMICK, GALES FERRY, CONNECTICUT.

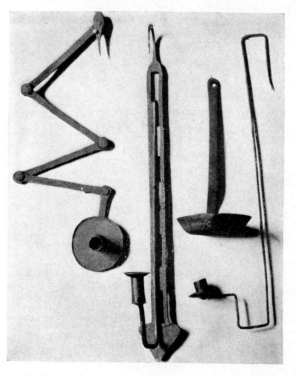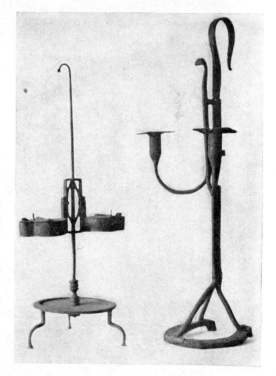

4262–65. RARE OR UNIQUE TRAMMEL CANDLE. THE OTHER SPECIMENS ARE VARIANTS. THE FIRST, HOW-EVER, HAS A BRAD WHICH MAY BE DRIVEN INTO THE WALL. FUESSENICH COLLECTION.

4266–67. (Right.) A UNIQUE DOUBLE BETTY STANDARD AND A HORSESHOE BASE, DOUBLE SCONCE, THE ANCESTRY OF THE LATTER BEING OBSCURE. WILLIAM F. HUBBARD, HARTFORD.

4268–71. Four Lanterns, the First Being Called Erroneously Paul Revere, the Second a Tin Dipper, Pierced, for a Candle. Perhaps Unique. The Other Two Are Variants of the Barred Lanterns. All: Rudolph P. Pauly.

4272–77. A Heart Waffle Iron. Below It a Three-Way Pair of Snuffers, Perhaps Unique. They Work Like Scissors. The Two Central Lamps Are of Tin for Whale Oil or Camphine. At the Right Is the Ordinary Brass Candlestick. Wadsworth Atheneum.

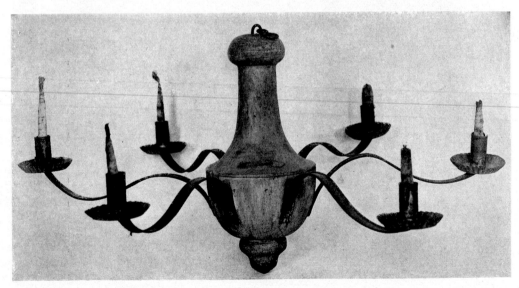

4278. Rare, Fine Six-Branch Chandelier with a Wood Hub. Present Owner Unknown.

4279. FOUR-ARMED TIN SCONCE WITH A GLASS GLOBE AT THE CENTER. 18TH CENTURY. PRESENT OWNER UNKNOWN.

4280. PIERCED TIN LANTERN. IT GAVE LITTLE LIGHT. PAUL REVERE COULD NOT HAVE SIGNALED WITH IT.

4281. (Right.) DECORATIVE LANTERN TO BE PLACED ON A POST. AN EXCELLENT PATTERN. BOTH: FORMERLY THE AUTHOR'S.

4282–85. Two Pairs of Sconces, All Tin, the Second Pair Perhaps Unique. They Now Contain Bayberry Candles, Such as the Pilgrims Made from Berries Growing among the Sands. Owners Unknown.

4286–90. Piggin, Reading Glass, Triple Sconce, Swivel Pewter Lamp, and Flint and Steel Candlestick. Owners Unknown.

4291–92. Pair of Odd, but Simple Hanging Sconces. Wadsworth Atheneum.

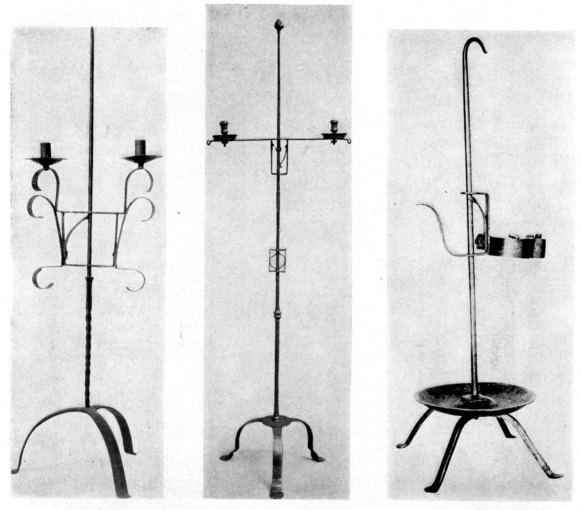

4293-95. The First Is a Very Good Floor Stand. Flayderman & Kaufman. The Second Is a Beautifully Wrought Iron Standard Mounted with Brass, the Top Being Spiraled. Metropolitan Museum. The Third Is a Unique Betty with Four Legs, and Drip Saucer. Wadsworth Atheneum.

4296-4301. Horn Lantern, a Scrolled Spring Stand, Two Sparkers, One Being a Pistol, a Swivel Betty, and a Bull's Eye. Former Ives Collection.

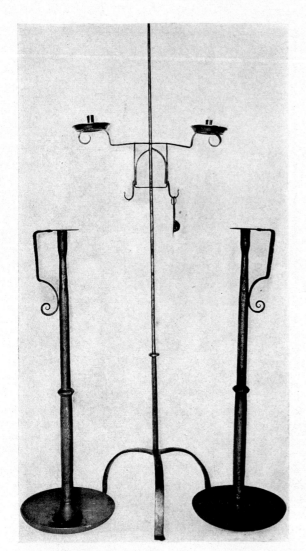

4302–05. PAIR OF CANDLESTICKS, FOUND IN THE RUINS OF A CHURCH AT MANHEIM, PENNSYLVANIA. A FLOOR STAND AND A DOUBLE CHANDELIER WITH BATTLEMENT OR CROWN ORNAMENTATION. ALL: MRS. J. INSLEY BLAIR.

4306–11. THE FIRST AND THE FIFTH ARE RUSH HOLDERS, THE FIRST ALSO CARRYING THE CANDLE. THE SECOND AND LAST ARE TIN LAMPS. THE THIRD IS A FINE SCONCE. FORMERLY ANTHONY T. KELLY'S.

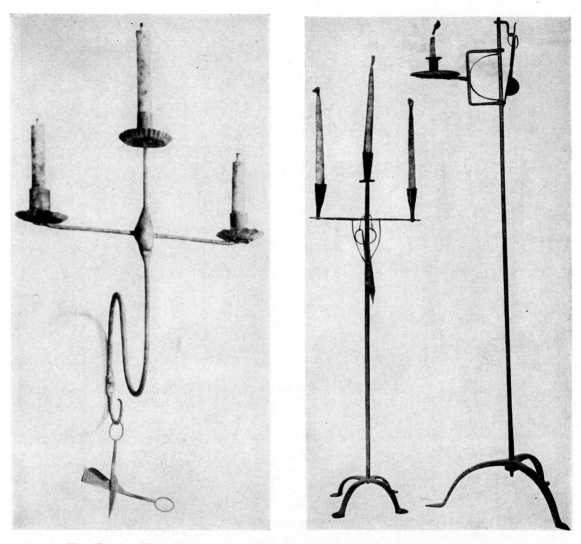

4312-15. THE FIRST A WALL SCONCE, SUSTAINING WROUGHT-IRON SNUFFERS. PAIR OF RARE STANDS AT THE RIGHT. PRESENT OWNERS UNKNOWN.

4316-24. FORMERLY THE AUTHOR'S, NOW WADSWORTH ATHENEUM. THE FIRST A RARE BOX LIGHT, THE THIRD, A COOPER'S LAMP, THE FOURTH A WOODEN STANDARD FOR A BETTY, THE NEXT A MAID'S OR HIRED MAN'S LIGHT TO CARRY TO ONE'S ROOM AT NIGHT. IT LOOKS LIKE A MINIATURE PITCHER. THE NEXT WITH A SNOUT, IS A WHALE-OIL LIGHT. THEN A LARGE SAUCER-BASE CANDLESTICK, AND A MINIATURE DOUBLE CANDLESTICK.

4325-27. The First and the Third Are Standards of Wood, Very Quaint. The Second Is the Usual Floor Candlestick. Formerly the Author's.

4328-29. (Right.) Floor Standards, the Former with a Wooden Base, from Davis Antique Shop, Old Lyme, Connecticut.

4330-32. An Odd Stand Perhaps for the Table. The Second and Third Are Table Stands of Quaint Design. J. Stogdell Stokes.

4333-36. GOOD SIX-SIDED LANTERN, A RARE LANTERN OF WOOD, A SCONCE LANTERN OF TIN, AND A WALL SCONCE WITH REFLECTOR MISSING. RUDOLPH P. PAULY.

4337-42. SIX LANTERNS, THE FIRST TO CARRY ABOUT THE HOUSE, THE FOURTH WITH A FRAME OF WOOD, THE FIFTH FOR A SHIP, AND THE LAST WAS COMMON FIFTY YEARS AGO. WADSWORTH ATHENEUM.

4343-49. CYLINDER CANDLE WITH FOUR LIGHTS, A REFLECTOR, THREE LARD LIGHTS, A WALL LAMP, AND A RARE, FOUR-SIDED GLASS SCONCE. ANTHONY T. KELLY, SPRINGFIELD.

4350–51. Pennsylvania Swivel Betty Lights. Hundreds of Designs Are Known, and Scarcely Any Two Alike.

4352–53. (Right.) Single Standards, One with a Toggle Joint, and the Other with the Usual Adjustable Standard, and the Large Base with Balls. All Four Formerly the Author's.

4354. A Table, Probably Unique. Two Drawers, One in Each End, with a Knot. Cherry, Found in Virginia. The Author Has Not Had Opportunity To Examine the Piece, but Believes It To Be of Great Importance. Mrs. Beryl DeMott, Millington, New Jersey.

4355. HALL LANTERN
WITH CUT-GLASS
GLOBE. CAREFULLY
WORKED-OUT DESIGN.
BRONZE MOUNTS.
FLOWING RIBBON
BAND. BIGELOW COL-
LECTION.

4356. A GATE LATCH
AND LOCK. RARE.
WADSWORTH
ATHENEUM.

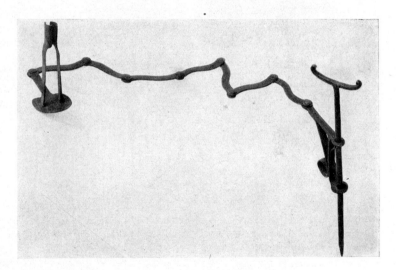

4357. RARE STANDARD WITH SERPEN-
TINE JOINTED ARM AND SPRING CANDLE-
STICK. 18TH CENTURY. FLAYDERMAN
& KAUFMAN.

4358-59. (Below.) UNIQUE TULIP BUD
DOOR SET. 18TH CENTURY. THE ORIG-
INAL HANDLE SUPPOSED TO BE SHOWN
HERE HAS NOW BEEN FOUND, AND IS
BETTER THAN THIS. WADSWORTH
ATHENEUM.

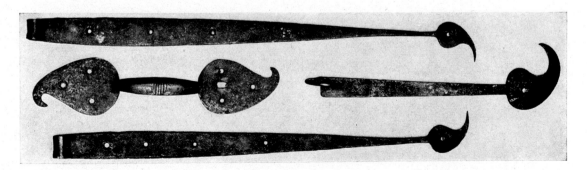

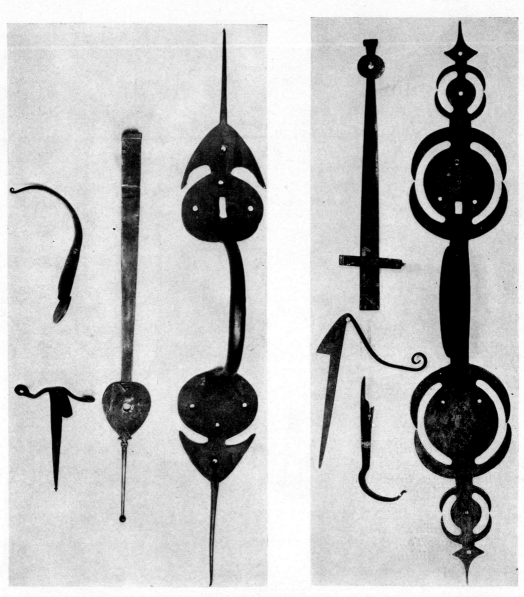

4360–62. Sword Fish Pattern with One of the Two Best Latch Bars Known. Heart Motive. Irving P. Lyon, M.D., Buffalo. Also a Double Brace Wrought Catch.

4363–64. (Right.) Decorative Latch, Spear and Ball Pattern. Latch Bar with a Flat Curled End. Wadsworth Atheneum.

4365–71. Seven Latches. Palmer-Metropolitan Museum Collection. A Part in Brass. Those at the Right Are Later.

4372. Remarkably Good Cupboard Latch, Wrought Iron, Drop Spring Handle.
Wadsworth Atheneum.

4373-74. (Right.) Ancient New London Jail Lock and Hand Cuffs. James Davidson.

4375. Conestoga Wagon and Tool Box Lid, with Dutch Tulip
Design, and Hasp and Hinges. Philip Meredith Allen, Broad Axe,
Pennsylvania.

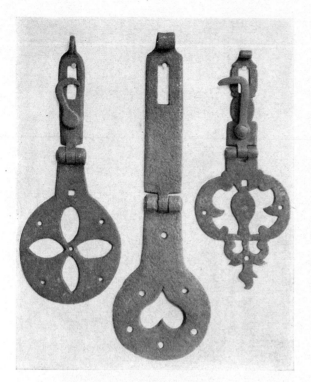

4376–78. The First Three Numbers Are Remarkably Fine Hasps. Probably Pennsylvania-Moravian. William B. Montague, Norristown.

4379–83. (Right.) Four Latches and a Unique Latch Bar. Pennsylvania. It Is Only There That We Find the Latch Handle with a Single Plate, the Bottom Having a Clinch Spur. Same Owner.

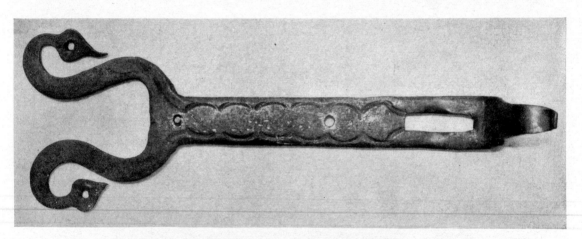

4384. A Scrolled and Stamped Hasp. Late 18th Century. Wadsworth Atheneum.

4385–86. Square Plate Spring Latches. 1750–90.

4387–91. Five Latches, the Center One Very Fine. All Wrought. Palmer Collection. Metropolitan Museum.

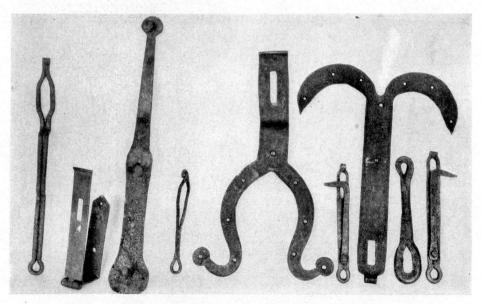

4392–4400. Series of Hasps, All Wrought, Mostly from Pennsylvania Wadsworth Atheneum.

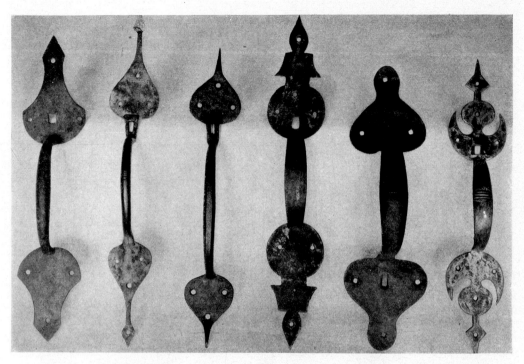

4401–06. Six Latches, the Second and Last Being Very Fine. 18th Century.
Wadsworth Atheneum.

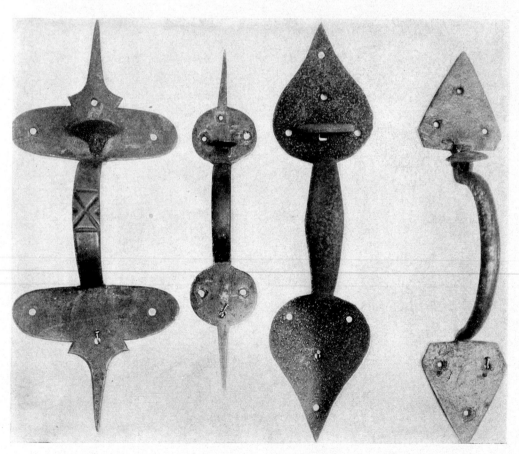

4407–10. Four Latches, the Finest Being the First. 18th Century.
Wadsworth Atheneum.

4411–12. MOLDED BRASS BOX LOCK. 1730–60. THIS IS THE ELEGANT LOCK OF THE BEST HOUSES IN THE 18TH CENTURY. NORTH SHORE, MASSACHUSETTS. FORMERLY THE AUTHOR'S. ANOTHER IN THE METROPOLITAN MUSEUM.

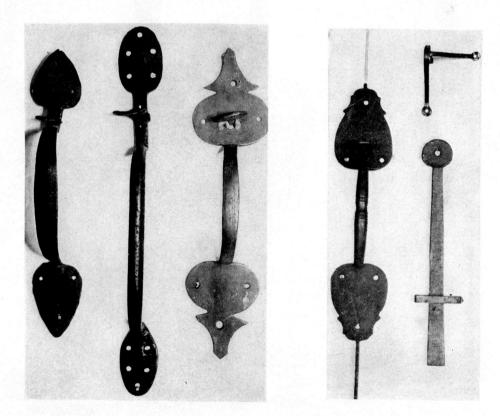

4413–17. THE SECOND WAS INTENDED FOR A VERY NARROW STILE. HEART SHAPES OR A MODIFICATION IN LATCHES PREVAIL. AT THE RIGHT TOP IS A DOUBLE-BRACED CATCH. A LATCH CONSISTS OF FIVE PARTS: HANDLE, THUMB PIECE, LATCH BAR, GUARD, AND STRIKER. WADSWORTH ATHENEUM.

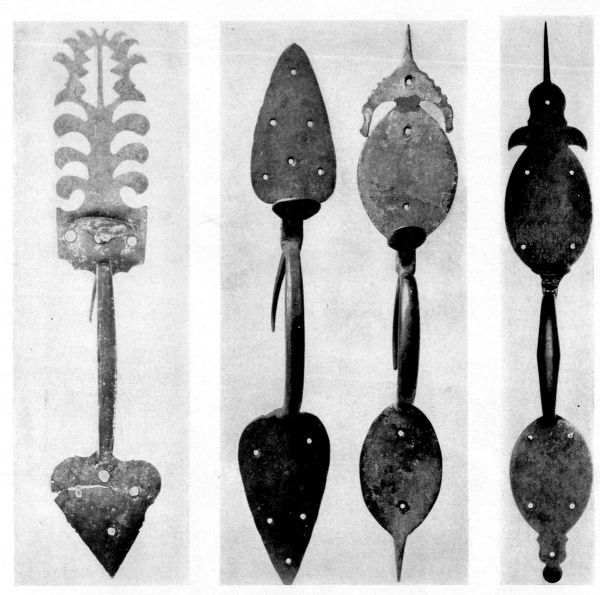

4418-21. Unique Flower Blossom Latch, and Three Church Door Latches. 18th Century.
Wadsworth Atheneum.

4422-26. Pennsylvania Locks, All with Springs Except the Middle One. The Last Are
Also Found in Germany. Wadsworth Atheneum.

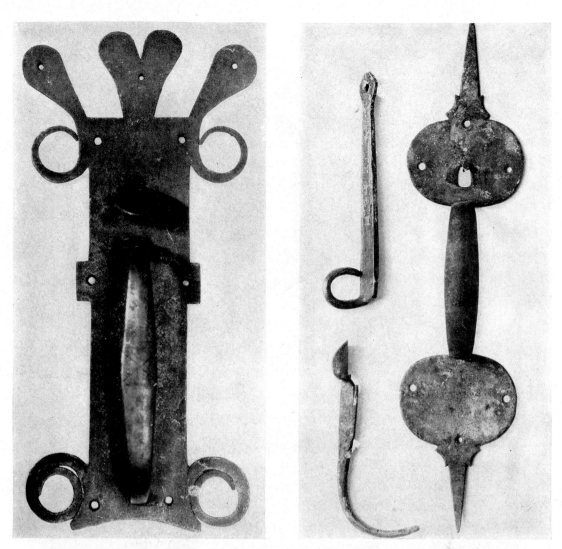

4427. LARGE LATCH, ONE OF TWO FOUND IN CONNECTICUT. WADSWORTH ATHENEUM.
4428. (Right.) BALL AND SPEAR PATTERN WITH ROUNDED THUMB PIECE. L. P. GOULDING, SUDBURY.

4429-36. EIGHT LATCHES, TRIANGLE, HEART AND BALL MOTIVES. 1810. WADSWORTH ATHENEUM.

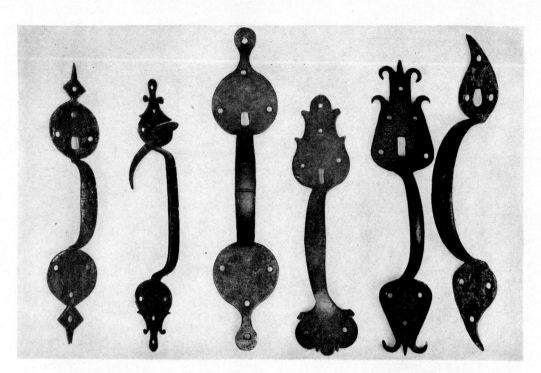

4437-42. Six Latches, the Next to the Last Being a Tulip, and the Last a Tulip Bud. New England and Pennsylvania. Wadsworth Atheneum.

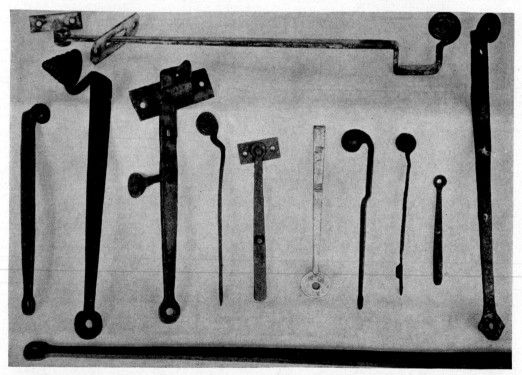

4443-54. Twelve Latch Bars. The Top One and the Second Vertical One Being Unique. The Latter Has a Spiral in the Form of a Cone. Those with the Plate of Early 19th Century. The Others, 18th Century. Wadsworth Atheneum.

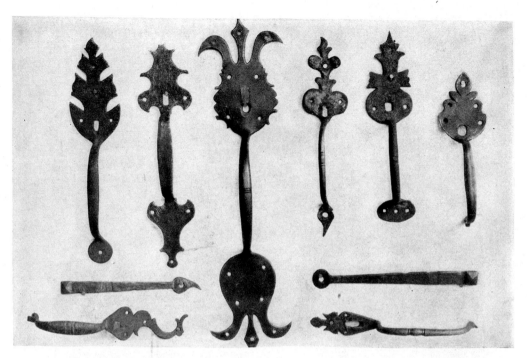

4455-64. COLLECTION OF WILLIAM B. MONTAGUE, NORRISTOWN. SEVERAL ARE UNIQUE. THE LARGEST IS THE BEST TULIP LATCH KNOWN TO THE AUTHOR. THE FIRST IS A LEAF PATTERN BETTER UNNAMED.

4465-67. THE FIRST A BALL AND SPEAR. L. P. GOULDING. THE OTHERS, A RARE LATCH WITH ALL ITS PARTS, AND AN ODD BETTY LAMP. H. W. ERVING.

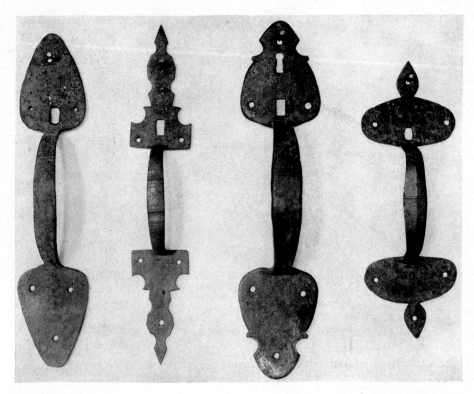

4468-71. Four 18th Century Latches. Wadsworth Atheneum.

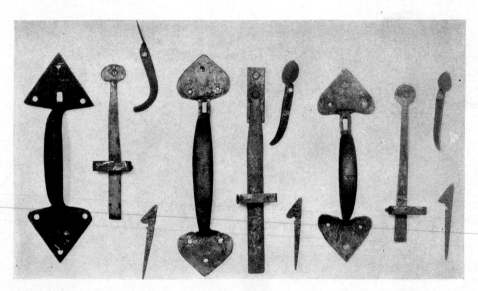

4472-74. Three Latches with All Their Parts. The Triangle, the Heart, and the
Fully Formed Heart Patterns. It Shows the Usual Plain Catch.
Wadsworth Atheneum.

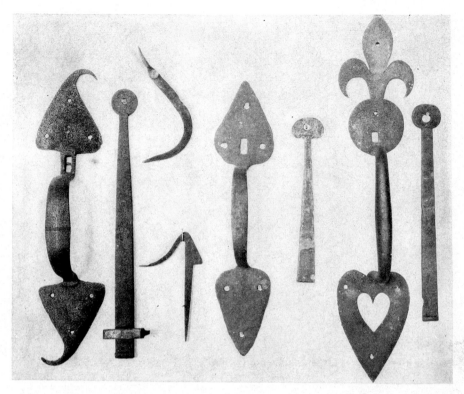

4475–77. THREE LATCHES, THE FIRST A CURVED TRIANGLE, THE LAST A HEART, BALL, AND FLEUR DE LIS, WITH AN INCISED HEART. THESE AND THOSE AT THE BOTTOM OF THE PAGE, WADSWORTH ATHENEUM.

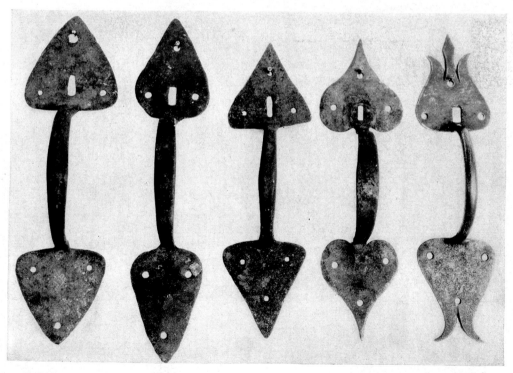

4478–82. THE NEXT TO THE LAST IS A FINE HEART SHAPE, AND THE LAST IS A TULIP LATCH.

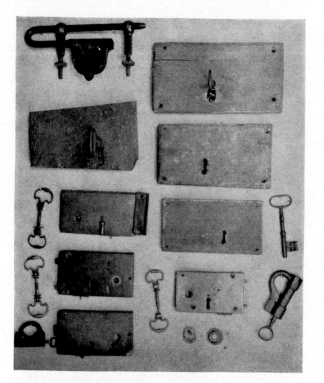

4483–94. Iron, Brass, and Wood Locks. Some of These Are To Be Attached to the Wood by Bolts, and Others by Screws. Interesting Padlocks and Two Early Door Escutcheons.
4495–96. (Right.) A Huge Round Plate Latch with Scalloped Edge. A Bar for a Large Door.

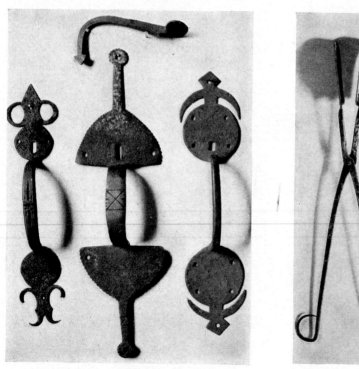

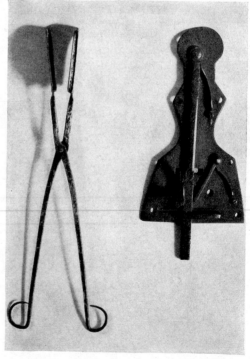

4497–99. Three Very Odd Latches. Fuessenich Collection, Torrington.
4500–01. (Right.) An Odd Curling Iron, and Good Pattern of a Spring Plate Latch.
George S. Palmer, New London.

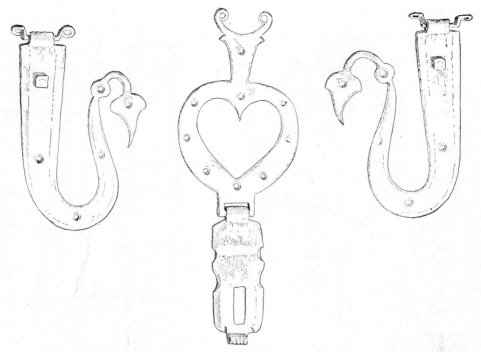

4502–03. Pair of Chest Hinges with Tulip Bud, and a Fine Heart Hasp, Forming a Set. Pennsylvania. Wadsworth Atheneum.

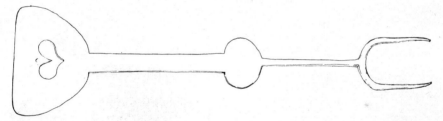

4504. Double Ender with Heart Motive on the Cake Turner, and a Ball at the Center. Pennsylvania. Wadsworth Atheneum.

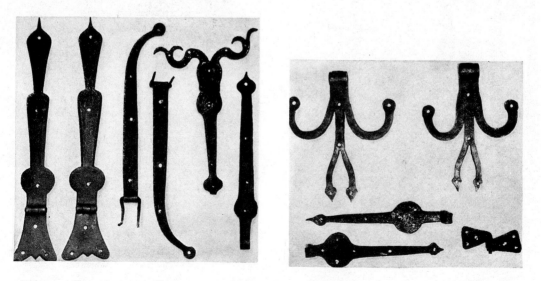

4505–11. Pennsylvania Hinges, except the Last Little Oxshoe Hinge. All Wrought. 18th Century. Wadsworth Atheneum.

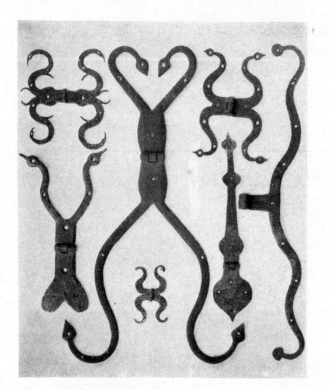

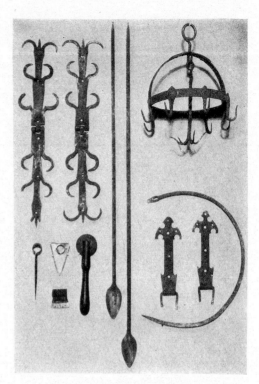

4512–29. Hinges, Stick Candleholder, Triangular Candlestick, Minute Candle Ring, a Pie Cutter, Two Thatching Needles, a Unique Meat Hanger, or Spit, a Curved Thatching Needle, and a Pair of Scrolled Hinges. The Thatching Needles Are Very Rare in America. All Owned by William B. Montague, Norristown, Pennsylvania.

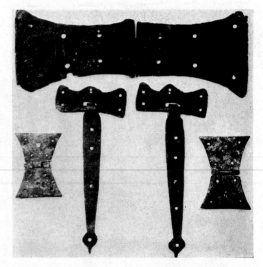

4530–33. Rare or Unique Hinges, One Being a Tulip Blossom. William B. Montague, Norristown.

4534–36. (Right.) An Immense Butterfly Hinge a Foot Long, Two Sizes of Conventional Butterflies, and a Pair of 17th Century Butterfly and Strap. Wadsworth Atheneum.

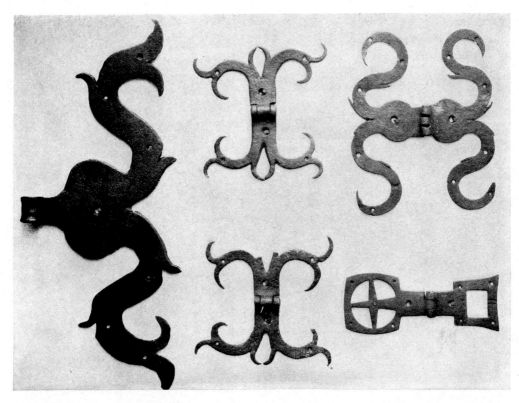

4537-40. MORAVIAN HINGES AND A HASP OF THE SAME ORIGIN, 17TH AND 18TH CENTURIES.
WADSWORTH ATHENEUM.

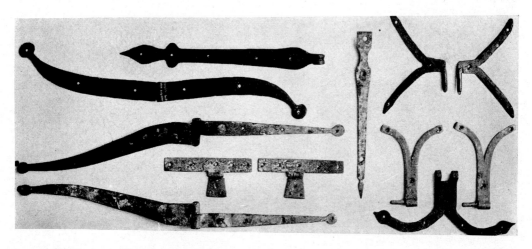

4541-48. UNUSUAL HINGES. THE T PAIR AND THE V SCROLL BEING NEW ENGLAND AND THE REST
PENNSYLVANIA. WADSWORTH ATHENEUM.

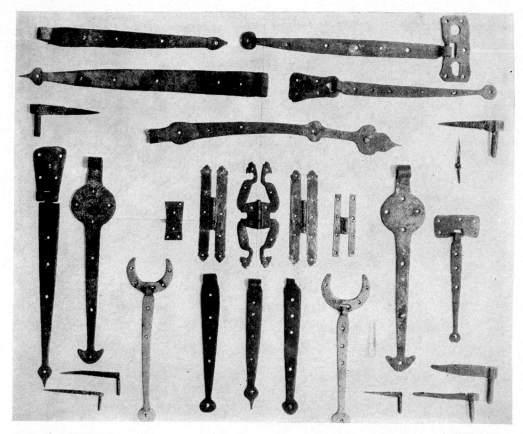

4549-69. SHEET OF HINGES AND GUDGEONS. AMONG THEM THE ONLY CURVED OR FISHTAIL HINGE SHOWN. AT THE CENTER A COCKSCOMB, THE BEST AMERICAN HINGE AND COPIED FROM THE ENGLISH, NO DOUBT. TWO OFFSET STYLES, A RAGGED, A SCREW, AND A CLINCH GUDGEON. THE DOUBLE COTTER-PIN HINGE FOR CHESTS, A SPEAR-HEAD PAIR, AND A HORSESHOE AND STRAP PAIR, AND SOME OTHER VARIETIES. THIS SHEET AND THE FOLLOWING: WADSWORTH ATHENEUM.

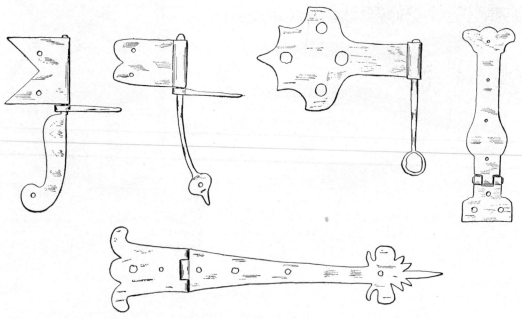

4570-74. PENNSYLVANIA CUPBOARD HINGES, EXCEPT THE LAST, WHICH IS NEW ENGLAND. THE SECOND IS THE DEVIL TAIL. WADSWORTH ATHENEUM.

4575–78. A Door Set with Open Heart Motive. Latch Found in New England and Hinges in Pennsylvania; About 1700. Wadsworth Atheneum.

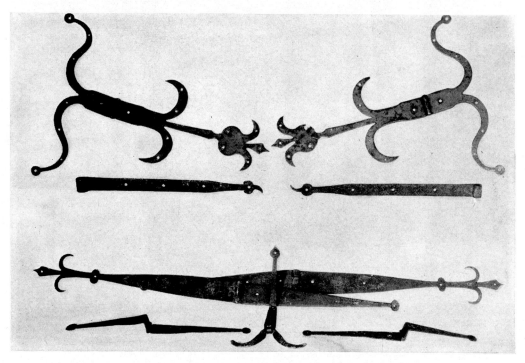

4579–85. Tulip and Scroll, Tulip Bud, Attenuated Tulip, Ram's Horn and Strap, and Simple Chest Hinges. Wadsworth Atheneum.

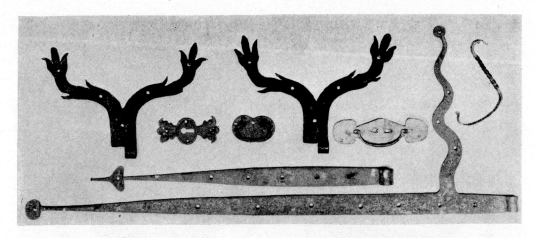

4586-92. A Scroll Pair, a Fine Escutcheon, Two Chest Handles, a Twisted Kettle Lifter, a Heart Hinge, and a Serpentine. Wadsworth Atheneum.

4593-4602. Minute Blind Fastener and Two Other Styles. The Others Are Pennsylvania Type, Except a Pair Which Look Like T Hinges, That Are Wrapped Joints, and 17th Century. Wadsworth Atheneum.

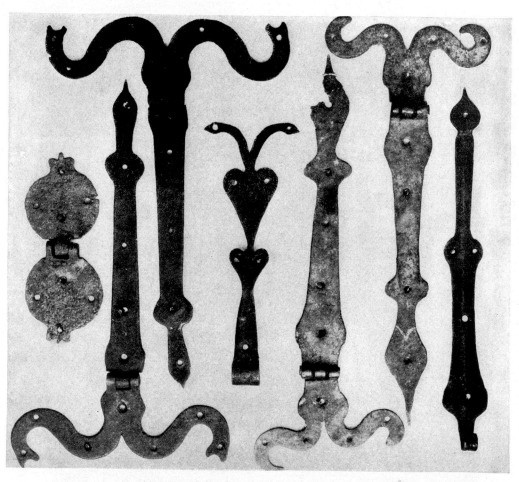

4603–08. LATE 17TH AND EARLY 18TH CENTURIES. PENNSYLVANIA HINGES, THE FIRST BEING IN THE FORM OF TWO DISCS. WADSWORTH ATHENEUM.

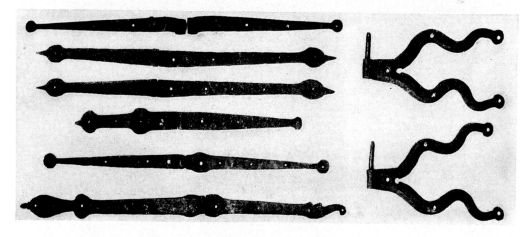

4609–15. PENNSYLVANIA CHEST AND DOOR HINGES, 18TH CENTURY. WADSWORTH ATHENEUM.

4616. FULLY SCROLLED HINGES, MORAVIAN. PHILIP MEREDITH ALLEN, BROAD AXE, PENNSYLVANIA.
4617. (Right.) WROUGHT CHEST, ELABORATE LOCK. USED AS SAFE. JOE KINDIG, JR., YORK.

4618-21. PAIR OF SPLENDID HINGES, ESCUTCHEON, HASPS WHICH BAND THE TRUNK,
AND LIFTERS AT THE END. FOREIGN. 16TH CENTURY. PHILIP MEREDITH ALLEN.

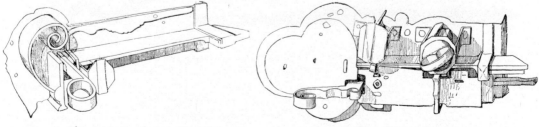

4622-23. DETAILS OF TWO FINE PENNSYLVANIA LOCKS, WADSWORTH ATHENEUM.

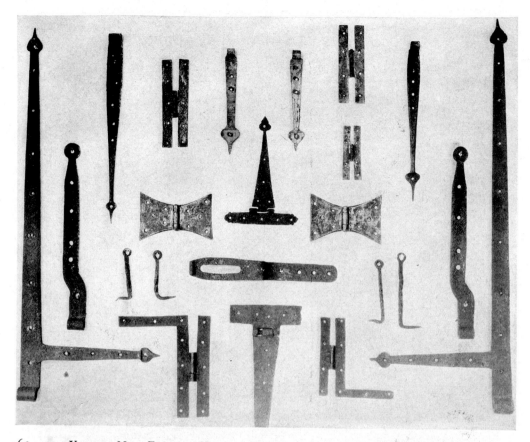

4624-39. Various New England Hinges. The Outside Pair Are Hammered L, as Distinct from the Inside H Hinges, Which Are Cut Out. A Pair of Very Fine Pointed Heart Hinges, a Scrolled T Specimen. An Offset Pair, a Pair of Butterflies, a Common T, Two HLs, and Five Hasps.

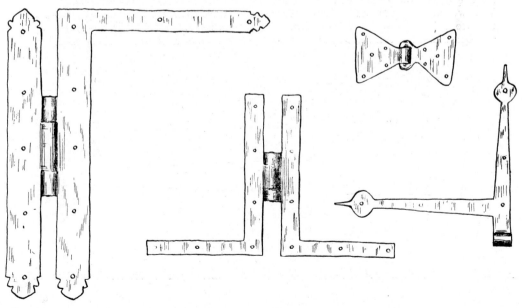

4640-43. Four Rare Hinges. The Scroll HL, and the LL Hinge Are the Rarest, but the Butterfly with the Wrapped Joint Is 17th Century. Present Ownership Unknown.

4644-51. Church Door Set Arranged by Morgan B. Brainard, and Presented to Wadsworth Atheneum. The Large Wrought L Hinges Have a Pointed Heart Termination. The Long Bolt Has a Curve To Free the Lower Sector for the Hand, the Other Bolt Is for the Floor. A Remarkably Fine Set. Made by Hall, an East Haddam Blacksmith.

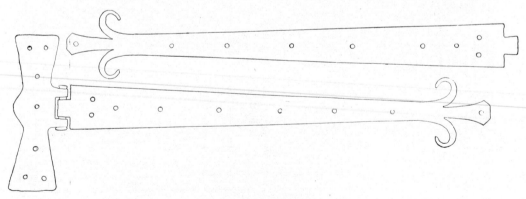

4652. Pair, Butterfly and Strap, Fleur de Lis Ends. 17th Century. The Author's.

4653-57. Court Cupboard Pillar Turnings. The First Is That of the Parmenter Cupboard, the Second and Fourth Are on a Pine Cupboard, the Third Is the Prince-Howes Cupboard, and the Last Is the Sunflower and Tulip Connecticut Court Cupboard.

4653, 20⅛ x 4; 4655, 17¾ x 4⁷⁄₁₆; Smallest Diameter 1⅜; 4657, 3⅞ Diameter.

These turnings are always in one piece and are never built up. They are doweled at both ends to fit into the cupboard shelf below and the cornice above. It will be noticed that the middle one is reversible. The material may be maple, or any semi-hard wood like basswood. The smaller turnings have been found in cherry. These large sections often cracked open. They were always painted black, which in process of time has acquired a green tint.

The other court cupboard turnings are, in the case of the urn shape, important, but they are fairly obvious; we show three others. About fifty-four court cupboards have been tallied, and most of them pictured by the author. The greater part are now in museums, and the balance in the hands of collectors or original owners.

4658–60. The Walnut Post of the Durham Cupboard, the Court Cupboard Table Leg, 3½ Inches Diameter, and the Virginia Cupboard, the Central Section of Which Is 6 x 8.

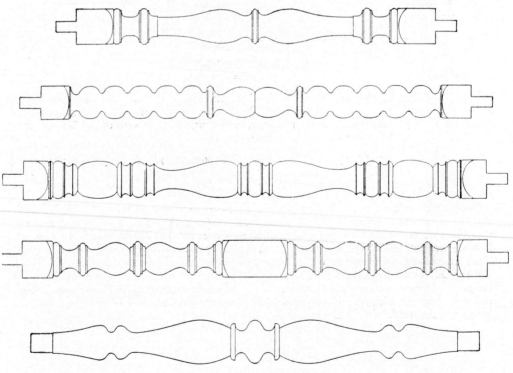

4661–65. Table and Chair Stretchers, Late 17th and Early 18th Centuries.

4666–69. GREAT 17TH CENTURY TABLE LEGS. THE THIRD AND THE FOURTH REPRESENT COMMUNION TABLES. THE FIRST IS THE BULBOUS LEG OF THE GREAT ANDOVER TABLE, 31¾ x 4⅛. NOTE THE EXTENSION AT THE TOP, THE TENON ENTERING INTO THE MORTISE OF THE TOP, WHICH IS LEFT LOOSE. THE LAST BELONGS TO THE FAMOUS SALISBURY TABLE, THE FIRST GREAT COMMUNION TABLE, SHOWN UNDER TABLES.

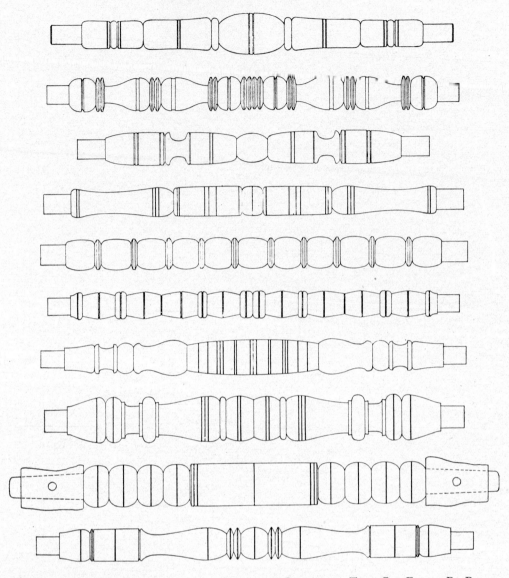

4670–79. Chair Stretchers, 17th and Early 18th Centuries. They Can Easily Be Picked Out From Our Pictures, of the Brewster, Carver, and Other Early Chairs.

These turnings are usually in maple, altogether the best material except birch which is just as good. Ash is slivery and wholly unsuited for intricate turnings. There is no objection to beech.

The period of a chair may be roughly estimated from the size of the turnings. In the earliest examples some of the chairs run to a diameter of 2½-inch posts. Broadly speaking anything less than 2 inch may be set near the close of the century. The author has pointed out what has now become a recognized principle of collectors, that other things being equal, the larger the post, the greater the value. At least one hundred dollars may be allowed for every eighth of an inch up or down of diameter.

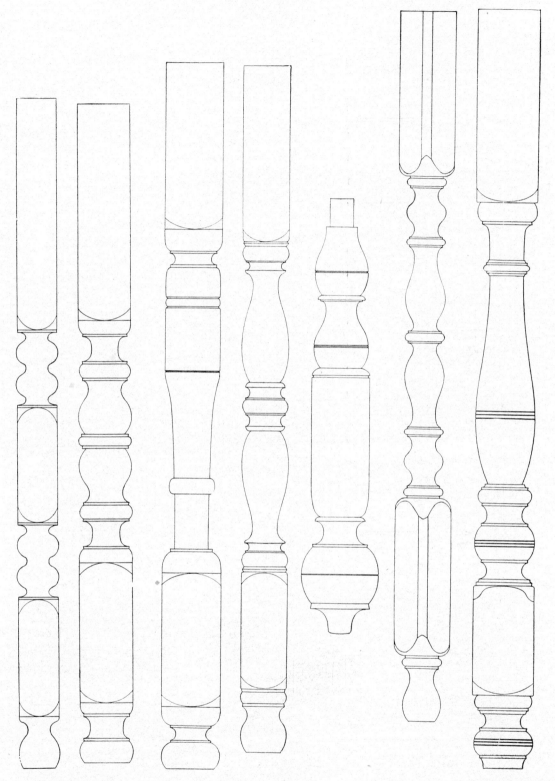

4680–86. 17TH CENTURY TABLE LEGS WITH ONE COUCH LEG. ALL THE LEGS SHOWN ARE FROM PIECES IN THIS WORK.

4687-91. 17th Century Chair and Table Legs. All Shown in This Work.

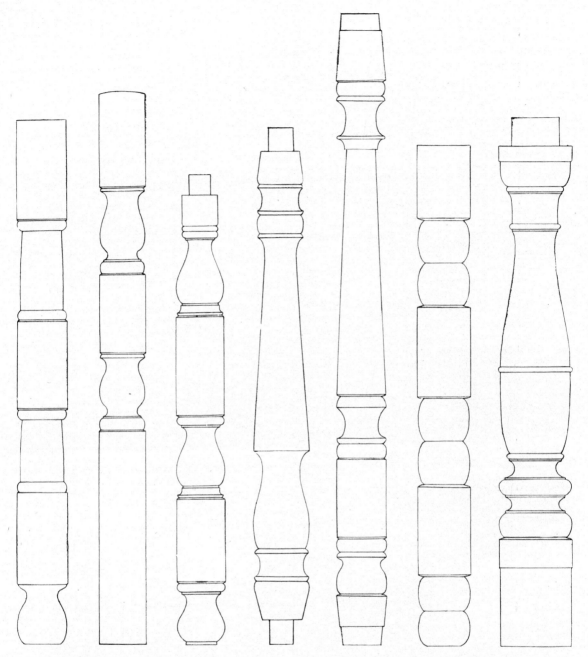

4692–98. First, Fruit-Wood Leather-Seat Chair; Second, Spanish Foot Chair; Third, a Corner Maple Chair; Fourth and Fifth, Banisters from a Carved Banister Back; Sixth, Cromwellian Chair Leg; Seventh, the Shaft of a Simple Maple Table. Richer Tables Shown Elsewhere. The Earliest of These Is the Cromwellian.

We point out again that the banisters must, in the best style, be precisely identical with the back posts. One should note also that the Cromwellian chair is ordinarily made with a right-angle seat, no wider at the front than at the back. The earliest turnings are always the simplest. Elaboration increases as periods grow later. The earliest chairs have no turnings whatever below the seat.

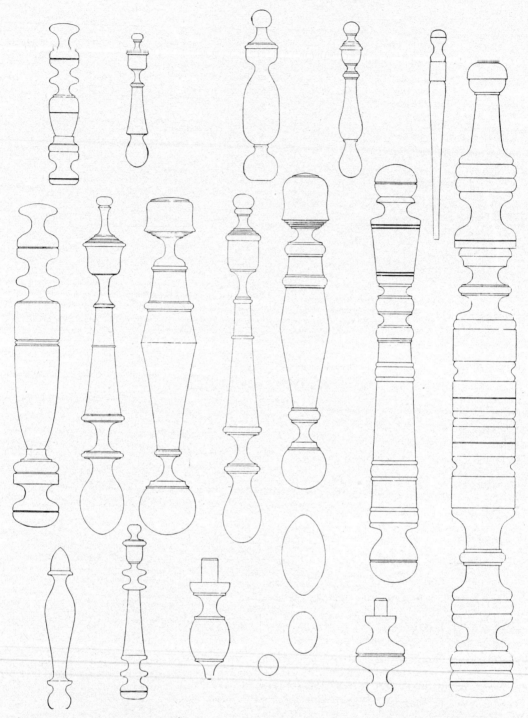

4699-4717. Split Spindle Ornaments Otherwise Called Drops or Bosses on Oak Chests. The Finer Ones with Bolder Turnings Belong to the Connecticut Sunflower. All the Pieces Appear in This Work. At the Bottom the Third Piece from the Left Is the Drop from the Cornice of the Sunflower Chest. The Circle and Ovals Are Outlines of the Bosses on the Same; and the Last Small Drop Is on the Great Concord Table.

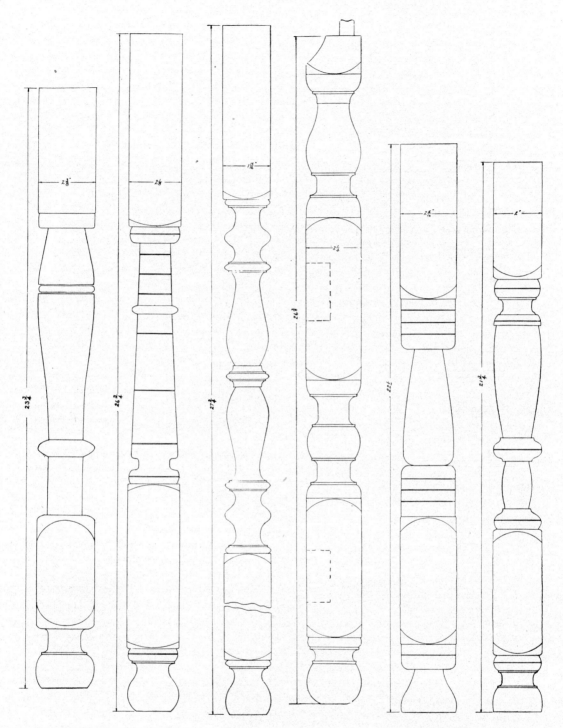

4718-23. 17TH CENTURY LEGS OF TABLES SHOWN ELSEWHERE. AMONG THE EARLIEST ARE THE
SECOND AND THE FIFTH.

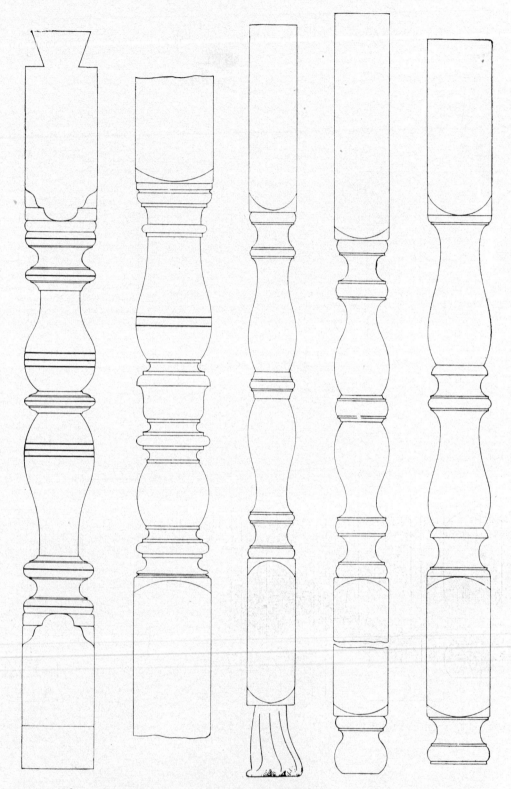

4724–28. 17th Century Table Legs. The First Is the Cherry Post of a Trestle Gate Leg. The Other Turnings on This Plate Are Gate Legs Beyond the First Two. The First Post Is 26 x 2⅝.

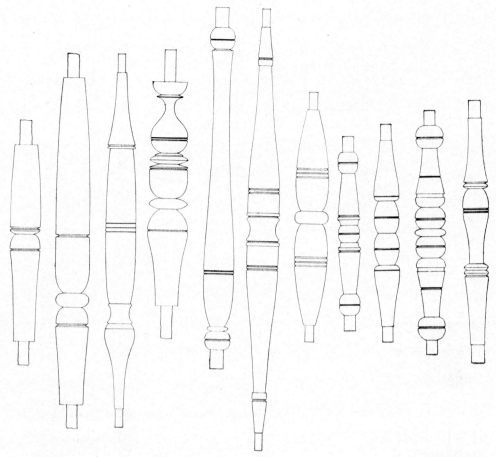

4777–87. 17TH CENTURY CHAIR SPINDLES, ALL BREWSTER OR CARVER. WADSWORTH ATHENEUM.

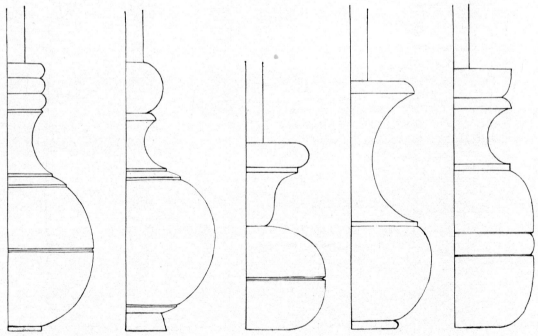

4788–92. FIVE BALL FEET AS FOUND ON OAK CHESTS OF DRAWERS OR CHESTS. ALL 17TH CENTURY.

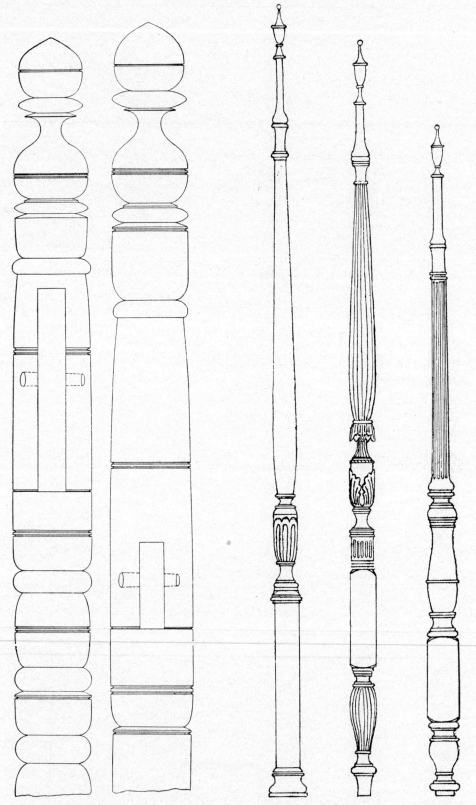

4793–97. Five Bed Posts. The First and Second the Best 17th Century Bed.
The Other Three Are: the First, Carved Maple, 1780; the Second, Carved
Mahogany, 1800; and the Last, Fluted Maple, 1790.

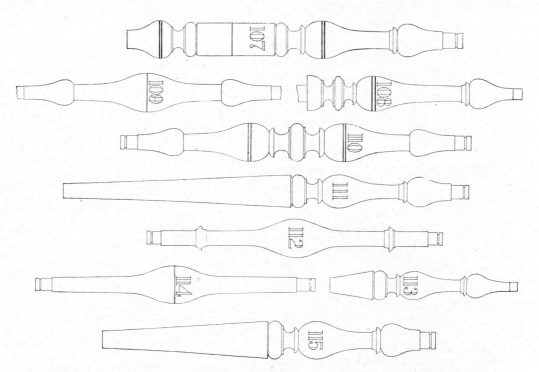

4798-4806. Windsor Chair Turnings. The Numbers Were in a Former Edition. The Four Near the Top Are Pennsylvania Windsors, Front Posts and Stretchers. The Others Are Taper-Turned Windsors, High Chair, Stretchers, Short Posts, and Leg.

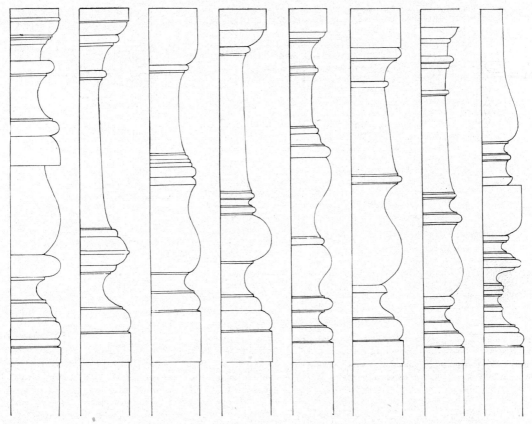

4807-14. Half Posts of Mahogany Tip and Turn Table Shafts. 1750-75. They Range from 4⅛ Inches Down, That Being the Largest Diameter of the Bowl of the Base. All Carved.

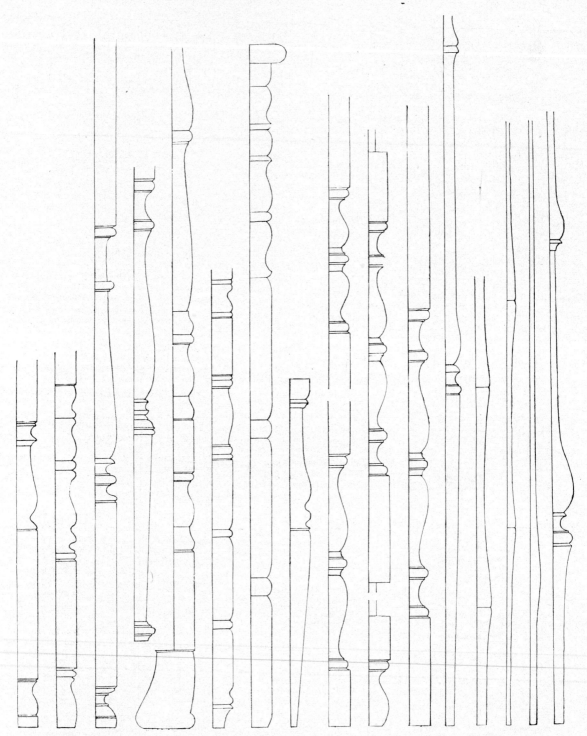

4815–30. Turnings to Centers. On the Left, Back and Small Spindles of Windsors and Stretcher of Bamboo Windsor, and a High-Chair Leg. The Three Following Are from a Turned Crane Bracket, Then the Short Front Spindle of a Windsor Arm. The Next, a Tall One, Is a Mushroom Post. The Rest Are Chair or Table Legs of About 1700. The Diameter of the Large Bulb on the First at the Right Is Two Inches, from This the Others May Be Gauged.

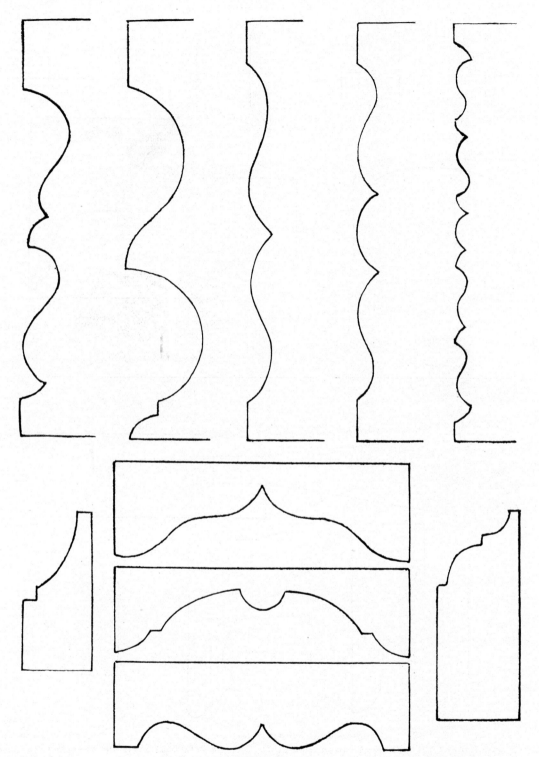

4831–40. The Upper Section Shows the Contour of Desk Cabinet Divisions. At Right and Left Are Base Moldings of Desks, at the Center Are Contours of Three Small Cabinet Drawers.

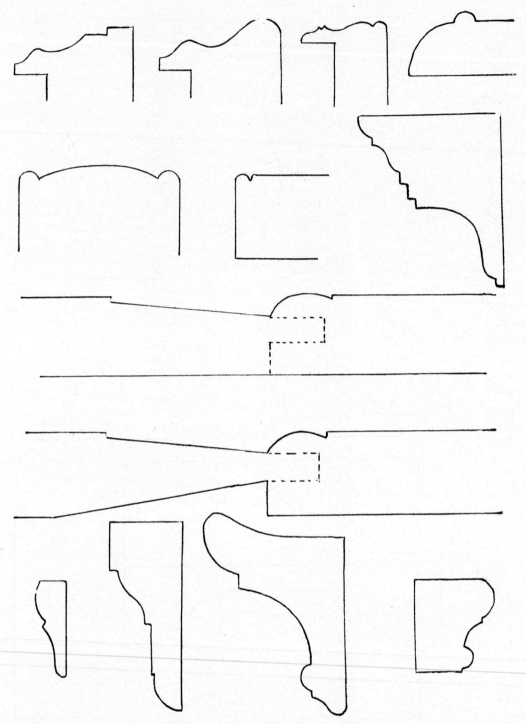

4841–53. THE TOP LINE SHOWS LOOKING-GLASS MOLD, NEXT LINE LEFT, MOLDED DUTCH
CHAIR BACK; THEN A BEAD, AND THE CLOCK MOLD. THE TWO MATCHED PORTIONS SHOW PANELED
SHEATHING. AT THE BOTTOM, FIRST, AN APPLIED CHEST MOLD; NEXT, PINE CUPBOARD MOLD;
THIRD, MAHOGANY DRESSING TABLE; FOURTH, OAK MOLD ABOUT SUNFLOWER CHEST.

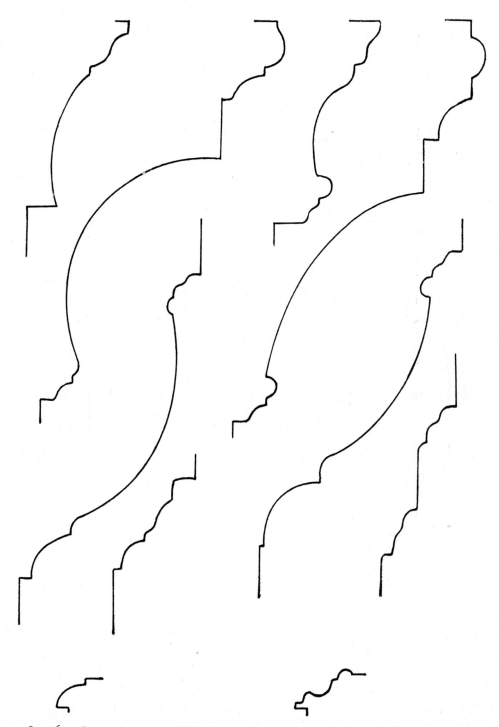

4854–63. Chippendale Period Highboy Moldings, Showing Two Complete Highboys. The Flat Sections Are Called Fillets. The Quarter Round Is Self Explanatory. The Ogee Is a Combination of Concave and Convex Mold. The Astragal Is a Very Small Quarter Round. The Great Single Concave Is Called a Cove.

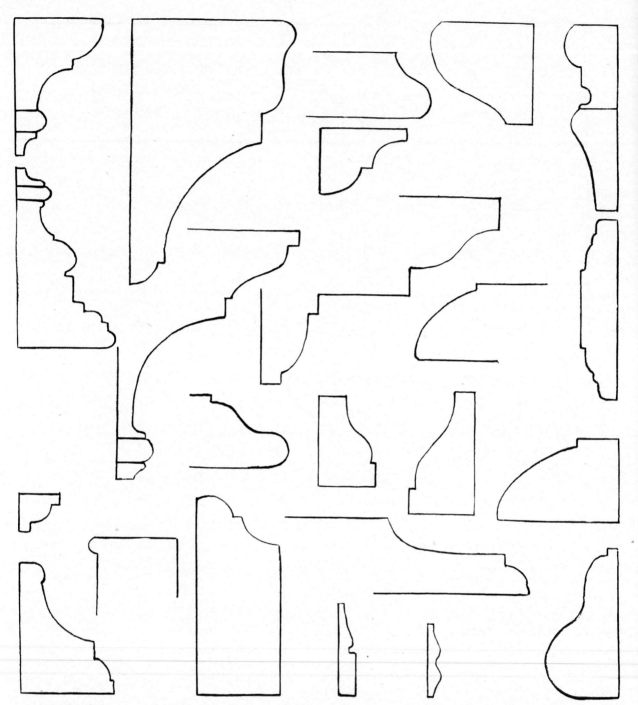

4864–86. Top Left and Thence Downward Are an Upper and Base Desk Mold. A Silver Cabinet Top and Base Mold. Again at Top, the Large Mold Is a Secretary; Next Below, a Maple Secretary, a Mahogany Chest of Drawers Top, and Finally a Mahogany Desk Base Mold. At the Top Again, the Block-Front Chest of Drawers, and under It a Supporting Mold. The Next, Very Large, Is a Dresser Mold, Followed by a Small Base Mold. The Large Horizontal Mold Is on the Splice of a Windsor Chair Arm. Two Small Ones at the Bottom Are a Lining Mold and Channel Mold on the Oak Chest. At the Top Again, Next to the Last, Is an Oak Looking-Glass. At the Extreme Right Top and the One Beneath It Are Oak Molds on a Small Chest-on-Frame. The Third in Line Is an Oak Chest of Drawers Top, and at the Base Is an Oak Bottom Mold on the Same.

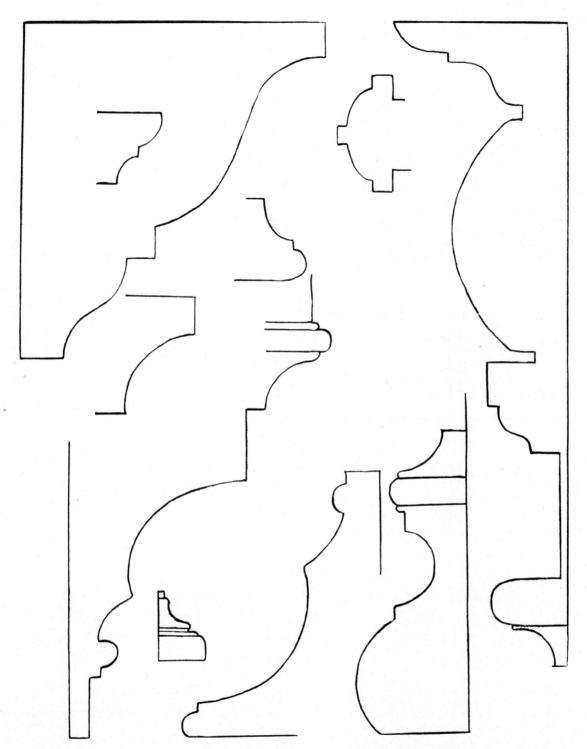

4887–96. The Top Left, Corner Cupboard Mold and Shelf Edge. Small Mold Next at Right Is the Edge of the Small Shelf on the Same Cupboard, and Below at Left a Simple Clock Top, Followed by the Very Large Mold Showing the Full Details of the Elaborate Clock Top. The Little Mold Below Runs Around under the Hood. At the Top the Great Mold Is the Inside of the Corner Cupboard Mold, the Small One at Left Is the Section of a Muntin of This Same Cupboard. At the Bottom the Section at the Right Is the Base of the Pillar of the Corner Cupboard, and Next Left Is a Clock Base Mold.

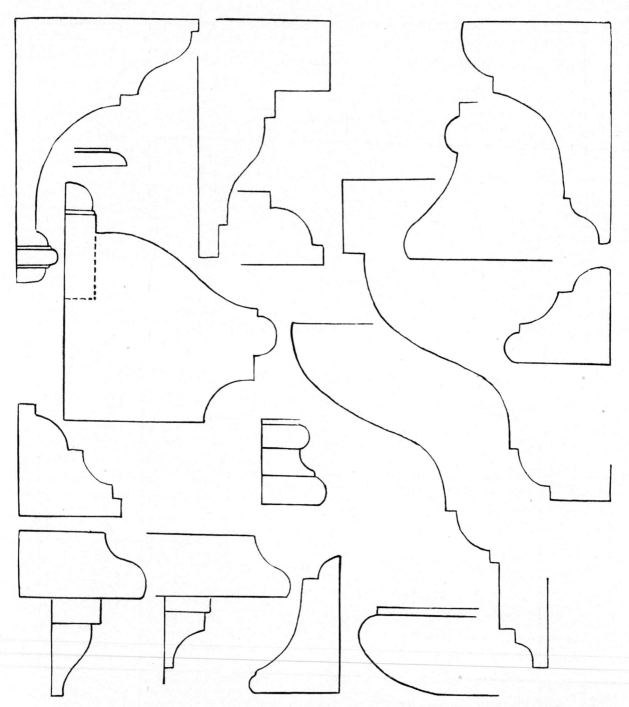

4897–4906. TOP LEFT, MAHOGANY CHEST-ON-CHEST TOP MOLD, THEN THE THUMB-NAIL EDGE OF DRAWER. THE NEXT WITH THE DOTTED LINE SHOWS THE MIDDLE SECTION MOLD, AND BELOW IS THE BOTTOM MOLD. BOTTOM LEFT IS A WALNUT SIDEBOARD TABLE, AND NEXT LEFT A MAPLE LOWBOY. AT THE TOP AGAIN, THE SECOND IS A DRESSER-TOP AND BOTTOM MOLD. BELOW THE SMALLEST MOLD IS A SUNFLOWER CHEST BAND BETWEEN THE DRAWERS OF OAK. AT THE BOTTOM, THIRD FROM LEFT, IS A BASE MOLD OF A SMALL TABLE DESK. TOP RIGHT, A SMALL HIGHBOY TOP MOLD, FOLLOWED AT THE LEFT BY A CHEST-OF-DRAWERS BASE OF THE PINE PERIOD. SECOND FROM TOP, AT RIGHT, IS THE CENTRAL MOLD AT THE DIVISION OF A MAHOGANY HIGHBOY. THE TWO GREAT MOLDS NEXT FOLLOWING ARE THE NEW ENGLAND DRESSER TOP AND THE WELSH DRESSER TOP; AND FINALLY THE MOLD ON THE SHELF OF THE WELSH DRESSER.

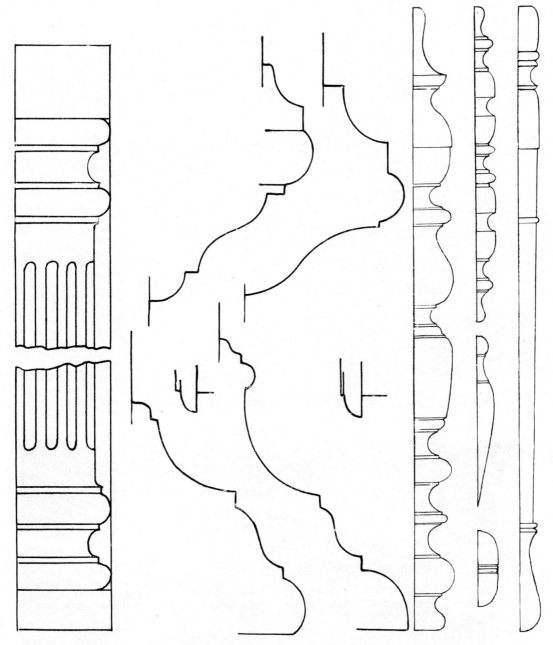

4907-13. At the Left Is a Mahogany Quarter Column, Fluted, Next Are the Upper and Middle Sections of Two Highboys; and the Thumb-Nail Drawer Edges.

4914-18. (Right.) Half Spindles from the General Payne Court Cupboard, and Chest. The Little Double Boss Probably Unique.

Of course, no one contends that all, even of the most ancient turnings, are in perfect taste. They have a charm arising from their quaintness and their striving after beauty which, in a remarkable number of instances, they attain. The chief criticism from our modern viewpoint is that they are somewhat too ornate.

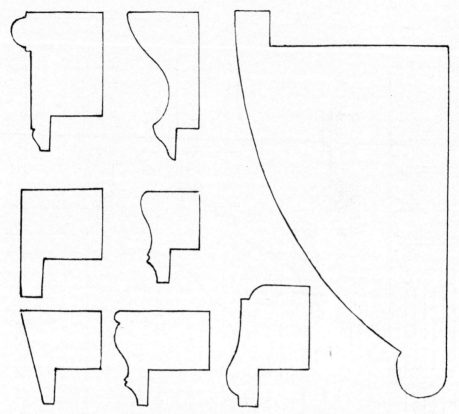

4919-26. Looking-Glass Molds, Largest Being Walnut on Pine, 17th Century. The Other Walnut and Mahogany.

4927-40. Nine Fine Bandboxes, Hat Trees, Twelve Early Poke Bonnets, and a Half Dozen Caps. The Fireplace Molds and Cornice Are 1782. On the Mantel Is a Bronze and Crystal Lighting Set. Old Bonnet Show Stands.

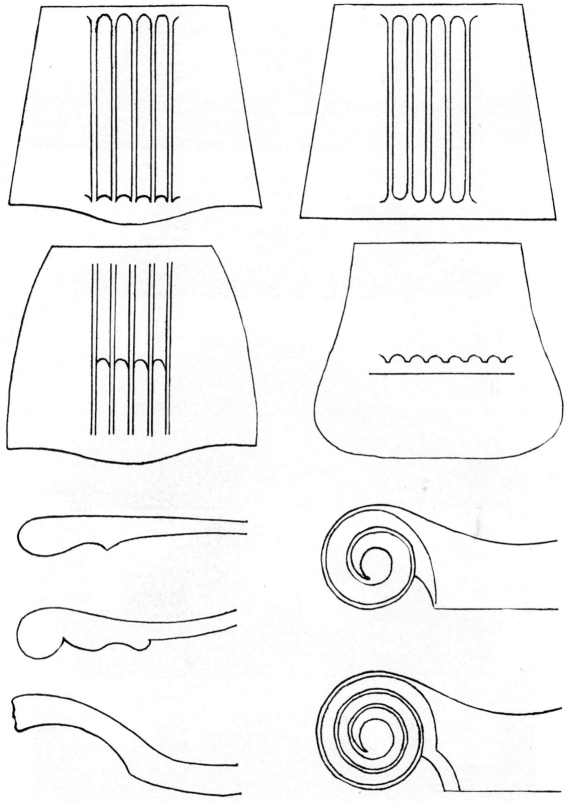

4941-53. At the Top Chippendale Chair Seats, Followed by a Hepplewhite and Dutch Seat, Inside Them Are Shown the Various Forms of Flutes, and the Last Shows a Reeding. The Five in the Lower Half Show Five Chippendale Arms or Ears.

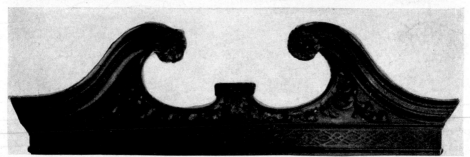

4954–58. THE HEADS OF FOUR SECRETARIES. BEGINNING AT TOP, BIGELOW COLLECTION, FIRST, SECOND, AND THIRD. THE FOURTH FROM SAMUEL WINECK. THE LAST A SECTION OF A FRAME, RHODE ISLAND SCHOOL OF DESIGN.

4959–63. Two Chair Backs, Rhode Island School of Design; the Unusual Termination of Blocking on a Desk Front; a Shell on a Knee-Hole Desk, J. K. Beard, and a Chippendale Chair Back. Probably Metropolitan Museum.

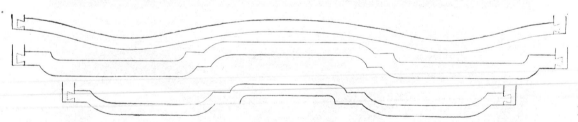

4964–69. Top: Secretary Cornice with a Carved Bird and Inlays. This Represents the Last Type in Good Secretaries. J. K. Beard, Richmond, Virginia. The Next Is the Top of a Highboy Showing Dentils on the Straight Cornice and Also on the Scrolled Arch. The Open Fret Is Always Attractive. Morris Schwartz, New York. There Follow Details from the Frame of a Glass Door. Rhode Island School of Design. At the Bottom Are Three Drawer Fronts. The Dovetail Should Not Show, as They Run in from the Side. First Is the Oxbow, Secretary or Chest of Drawers; the Second Is the John Goddard Secretary in the Full Form; the Last Is from the Small Plain Blocked Chest of Drawers.

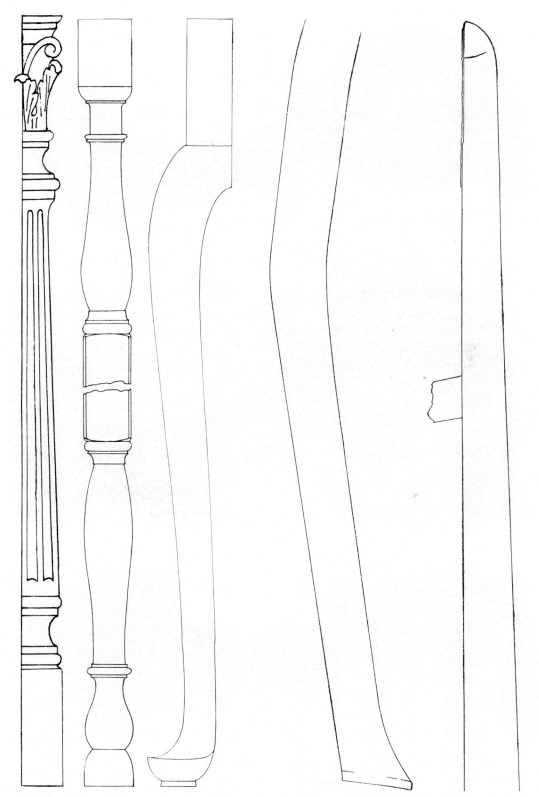

4970-74. Side of a Half Column on Front of Document Drawer, Helen T. Cooke; the Leg of a Spinet, of a Dutch Table, and the Two Sections of a Back Chippendale Leg. The Author's.

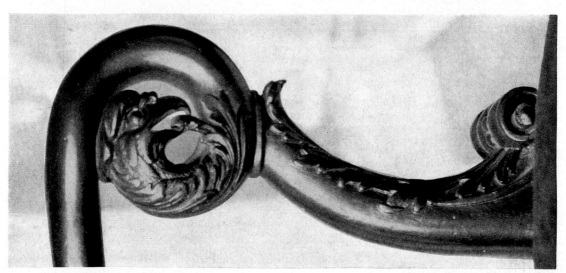

4975-77. Details of Various Angles from the Arm of the Grinling Gibbons Settee, Rhode Island School of Design.

4978–80. Leg of a Sheraton Chair, Estate of H. W. Weeks; Barometer, and Gibbons Chair Post.
Rhode Island School of Design.

4981–83. Spoon Racks, Hudson and Delaware Valleys. Knickerbocker or Pennsylvania German. Above Are the Best So Far Discovered. The First and the Last Bought by the Author Near Hackensack. The Middle One Combines a Knife Box with the Rack, Stars, and Spiral Wheels. The Third Has Most Delicate Tracery in the Central Panel. Also the Inevitable Tulip Above. Dated 1745. Wadsworth Atheneum.

4984. Two Fashions of Wheels, Alternating. Knife Box, Rack Bars Slotted, Not Pierced; Mrs. George R. Fearing, Jr.

4985. Top as if the Kas were Represented. Wadsworth Atheneum.

4986. Very Fully Carved, Morris Berry. The Maker Indulged Himself in Four Fashions of Wheels, Which He Probably Got Out of His Head. There Is Also a Herringbone Carving.

4987. From A. H. Rice, Bethlehem, Found in Delaware Valley. A Runic Motive.
4988. (Right.) There Are Four Star Wheel Motives. Mrs. Geo. R. Fearing, Jr.

4989. Star and Swastika. The Other Name for a Spoon Rack Was Lepel Bortie. E. B. Leete Co.
4990. (Right.) An Elaborate Pattern, Doubled Heart, and Tulip. 1775. A. H. Rice, Bethlehem.

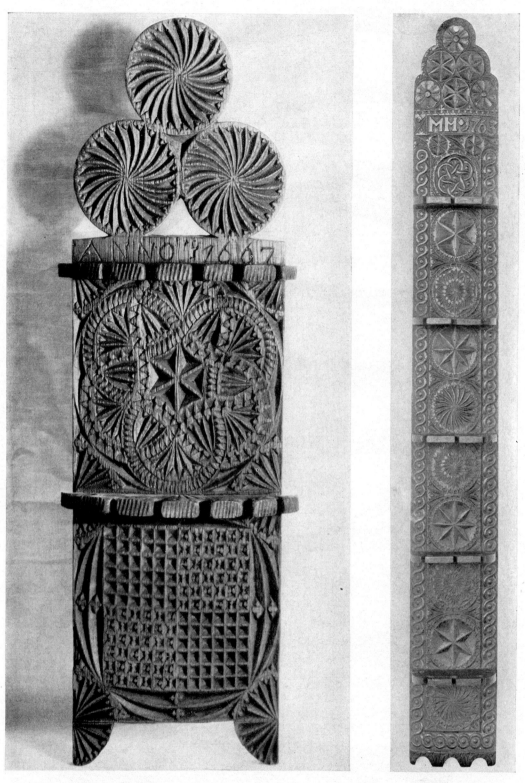

4991. "ANNO 1667." THIS SEEMS TOO CRUDELY DONE, BUT MAY BE CORRECT. THE RACK ITSELF
IS IN A PATTERN QUITE DIFFERENT FROM ANY OTHER, AND MOST INTERESTING. 5 x 17½. P. S. BRIGGS,
RADNOR, PENNSYLVANIA.

4992. (Right.) "MH-1763." A PATTERN UNIQUE TO THE AUTHOR. INTRICATE AND CAREFUL CARVING.
TWELVE DESIGNS OF WHEELS, AND A GOOD ENDLESS BAND. VERY LONG. J. STOGDELL STOKES.

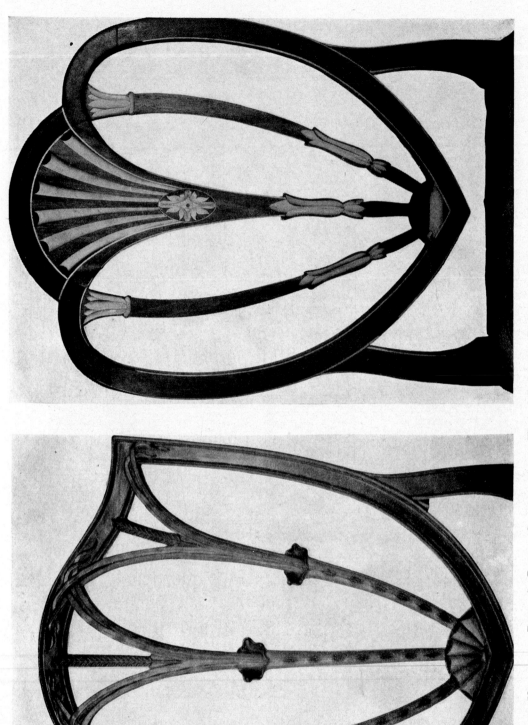

4993. Hepplewhite Back. Unusual in Being So Richly Carved. Three Wheat Ears, and Banisters Appearing To Rise from Petals. 1780–85. Rhode Island School of Design.

4994. (Right.) Finely Inlaid Back, Hepplewhite. J. K. Beard, Drewerys' Mansion, Richmond, Virginia.

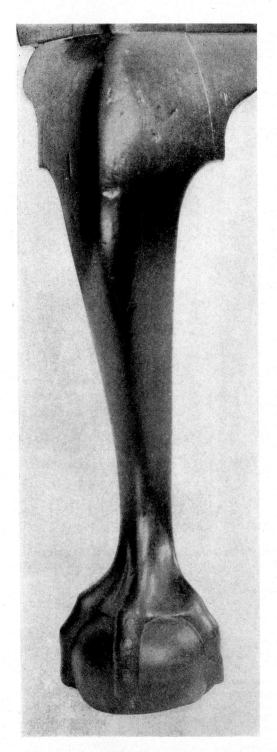 

4995. Leg of Chippendale Chair. 1750–70. Sanderson Collection.
4996. (Right.) Corner Detail of Half Column Set on Chamfer of a Serpentine Chest of Drawers. One Other Known, Apparently a Mate to This. Charles P. Cooley, Hartford, 1750–75.

4997. Leg of a Tripod Table. Courtesy of "Antiques." 1800–20. Metropolitan Museum.

4998. (Right.) Satyr Head on Hip. It Is Unusual in Running up onto the Frame. Tassel and Acanthus Carving. A Four-Toed Foot. 1720. Rhode Island School of Design.

It will be noted that the caster comes in with the 19th century, and that at first it was applied to a turned or decorative brass casting, like that in the Phyfe table above. The presence of casters before late Sheraton or Empire is quite conclusive that the piece originally did not have them. It was very much later that casters were applied directly to the wood. That method belongs to degraded Empire time. The four-toed foot referred to above is often called an animal foot as distinct from the bird, dragon, or rat foot which is more generally found and preferred. The term "rat foot" is used to designate a narrow, very long ball. The ball-and-claw motive is supposed to have come from China, at least there is a chair in China with such a foot, dated from the 8th century.

NOTE: Two errors in numbers are compensated by insertion of many a, b, c, numbers. The total number of objects is much above 5000.

4999. EFFECTIVE HEAD. BASE OF LOOKING-GLASS. THE STAR ABOVE THE FOREHEAD, THE HANDLING OF THE CONVENTIONALIZED HAIR, AND THE BACKING OF ALL WITH A SHELL IS VERY EFFECTIVE. RHODE ISLAND SCHOOL OF DESIGN. BELOW, DETAIL OF LOOKING-GLASS FRAME.

5000. SWAN ON NEST DETAIL. 1760–75. RHODE ISLAND SCHOOL OF DESIGN.

INDEX

The references are to numbers under the figures. The second volume
begins with 1774.

INDEX

INDEX

INDEX

INDEX

INDEX

INDEX

INDEX

INDEX

INDEX

INDEX

INDEX

Massachusetts Bay, 330

Mayereffer, Arcangelo, 3531

Mercer, Frederick W., 626, 628

Metcalf, Stephen O., 3520

Metropolitan Museum, 65, 198, 217, 269, 323, 325, 326, 328, 339, 343, 361, 364, 412, 423, 437, 448, 456, 467, 468, 510, 520, 524, 529, 629, 632, 634, 635, 686, 687, 711, 726, 737, 739, 744, 757, 781, 782, 829, 835, 851, 938, 956, 957-58, 1008, 1024, 1029, 1085, 1107, 1115, 1116, 1117, 1118, 1160, 1295, 1500, 1590, 1591, 1674, 1692, 1700, 1705, 2059, 2060, 2075, 2120, 2121-22, 2132, 2154, 2159, 2181-83, 2319, 2321, 2403-04, 2441, 2559, 2664, 2698, 2967, 3189-90, 3242, 3243, 3244, 3265, 3284-85, 3329, 3340-41, 3373, 3374, 4294, 4387-91, 4411-12, 4963, 4997

Miller, John M., 3240, 3241

Miner, Dr. Mark L., 1204

Mireau, Francis, 2556, 2704-05, 3270, 4029-38

Mirrors, *see* Looking-glasses

MolBrow, Henry G., 3280

Mold, cedar, 42

Molds, 4841-4926

Molds, channel, 1, 12, 14, 16, and generally where stiles are not carved

Molds, double arch, 79, 80

Molds, highboy, 346

Molds, of panels, 1, 3 ff; generally on chests, cupboards in oak and best pine

Molds, serrated, or sawtooth, 35-39

Molds, single arch, 78, 84, 91

Molds, thumb or thumb-nail, 23

Molds, tulip, 55, 56, 57, 59-76

Montague, William B., 1891, 1908, 2561, 3278, 3307, 3309, 3756, 3790, 4059-64, 4065-66, 4376-78, 4379-83, 4455-64, 4512-29, 4530-33

Montague, William E., estate of, 3330, 3332, 3333, 3371, 3380-83, 3385, 3391, 3404, 3413, 3455, 3551

Moore, T. G., 3519, 3560

Morson, C. R., 559, 1005, 1639, 1655, 1728, 1730, 2944, 2968, 2974, 3002, 3070, 3091, 3099, 3134, 3137, 3169, 3171, 3173

Mortar, 3787, 3791, 3795, 3797, 3807, 3810

Mulligan, W. L., 3260

Mulliken, S., 3425

Mummery, Dover, England, 3520

Musical instruments, 1577-85

Myers, L. G., 480, 863, 1224, 1297, 1615, 1843, 1938, 2399, 2408, 2757, 2776

N

"Nail heads" of wood, decorative, applied, 26

Nash, Chauncey C., 104, 108, 109 A, 329, 387, 593, 865, 870, 935, 1209, 1290, 1812-13, 2484, 2738, 2770

Needlework, 3262

New Hampshire, 10, 13, 26

New York, Long Island, 2

New York City, Washington table, 651

Newton, Herbert G., 2522-23

Norton, Malcolm A., 35, 36, 57, 270, 697, 1033, 1086, 1314, 2936, 3139, 3300, 3607-10, 3673-78

Nutting, Wallace, 206, 256, 257, 284, 569, 621, 653, 756, 779, 878, 983, 1047, 1048, 1051, 1104, 1109, 1120, 1194, 1402, 1412, 1578, 1622, 1909, 2066, 2068-69, 2124, 2171, 2250, 2264, 2393, 2447, 2454-55, 2464, 2485, 2502-04, 2529, 2811, 2953, 2986-87, 3082, 3379, 3387, 3431, 3672, 3878-86, 3904-16, 3960-62, 3982-84, 4652, 4971-74

Nutting, Wallace, former collection, 440, 479, 770, 773, 774, 778, 902, 912, 913, 1015, 1019, 1020, 1042, 1075, 1081, 1101, 1124, 1142-45, 1226, 1280, 1289, 1298, 1380-81, 1388, 1416, 1496, 1497, 1572, 1577, 1584-85, 1605, 1637, 1644, 1716, 1727, 1782, 1875-76, 1890, 1892, 1922, 1928-29, 2036, 2078, 2102, 2105-06, 2120, 2197, 2232, 2241, 2273-74, 2292, 2294, 2306, 2330, 2334-35, 2338, 2346, 2351-52, 2359, 2361-62, 2385, 2387, 2474-75, 2499, 2507, 2517, 2524-25, 2530, 2534-37, 2553, 2560, 2568, 2571, 2606-07, 2611, 2613, 2615, 2665, 2668-69, 2670, 2677, 2678-79, 2685, 2686, 2689, 2696-97, 2699, 2700-01, 2702-03, 2843, 2919, 2954, 2960, 3056-57, 3130, 3174, 3199, 3386, 3474, 3963-65, 4111-14, 4116, 4117-20, 4208, 4217, 4218, 4219-20, 4280-81, 4316-24, 4325-27, 4350-53

INDEX

INDEX

Reel, for table, 1425

Reel, to measure yarn, 3226, 3238

Reels, 3236, 3757

Reifsnyder, Howard, 99, 242, 243, 486, 506, 610, 619, 636, 738, 775, 837, 948, 1026, 1028, 1030, 1139–40, 1350, 1482, 1640, 1641, 1652, 1679, 1690, 1709, 1725, 1754, 1772, 1967, 2064, 2119, 2160–62, 2220, 2316, 2340, 2379–80, 2716, 2747, 2922, 2969

Rhode Island Historical Society, 3319

Rhode Island School of Design, 214, 432, 587, 916–917, 1484–85, 1567, 1628, 1648, 1658, 1660, 1694, 1773 A B C, 1946, 2157, 2158, 2196, 2710, 2887, 3167, 3250, 3308, 3359, 3360, 4087–88, 4958, 4959–60, 4966, 4975–77, 4978, 4980, 4993, 4998, 4999

Rice, A. H., 293, 294–96, 500, 570, 4987, 4990

Rice, Mrs. C. F., 702

Richardson Tavern, Millis, 800–02

Rimbeault, Stephen, 3523

Rittenhouse, Benjamin, 331

Rittenhouse, David, 3277, 3278, 3279, 3309, 3315, 3333, 3344

Robart, Frank A., 176, 177, 286, 353, 410, 540, 741, 855, 980, 1004, 1074, 1168, 1175, 1179, 1389–90, 1673, 1676, 1746, 2099, 2107, 2113, 2148–51, 2225, 2257, 2284, 2370–74, 2378, 2411–19, 2420–21, 2424–25, 2462–63, 2500–01, 2509–10, 2557–58, 2564–65, 2640–41, 2790–93, 2796–97, 2805–06, 3016–17, 3020–21, 3066, 3089, 3181–82, 3185–86, 3204, 3255–58, 3480–86, 3623–31, 3632–39, 3640–47, 3648–55, 3664–71

Robinson, Leonard M., 3259

Robinson House, Wethersfield, 509

Rogers, Mrs., 1588

Rollin, Sherwood, 499

Rooms, 670, 678, 894, 905, 971, 1054, 1131, 1281, 1422, 1458, 1464, 1472, 1475, 1544, 1592, 1663, 1736, 1747, 1760, 1858, 1884

Rose, Daniel, 3326

Rosenbach Company, Philadelphia, 3328

Rosettes, 55, 163

Royce, Lucy A., 493

Rush lights, 4196, 4204, 4205, 4258, 4306, and others

Russell, William G., heirs of, 3248

S

Sack, I., 261, 262, 266, 275, 277, 281, 288, 289, 297, 302, 305, 306, 313, 315, 319, 346, 347, 362, 375, 384, 400, 420, 433, 530, 533, 537, 560, 589, 600, 650, 655, 662, 669, 717, 736, 752, 754, 780, 815, 978, 994, 1006, 1018, 1063, 1108, 1169, 1171, 1479, 1486–87, 1596, 1657, 1695, 1697, 1745, 1889, 1986–92, 1995–2001, 2004–10, 2013–19, 2022–28, 2052, 2057, 2063, 2136, 2180, 2186, 2202, 2212, 2215, 2218, 2227, 2235, 2236, 2260, 2282, 2283, 2305, 2323, 2325, 2343–44, 2438–39, 2742, 2748, 2783, 2815, 2909, 2923, 2930, 2991, 2997, 3312, 3393, 3443, 3956

Safford, P. H., 3425

Salliday, D. H., 3332

Sampson, Mary M., Boston, 26, 75, 145, 356, 601, 643, 839–41, 881, 1286, 1311, 1333, 1349, 1374–75, 1681, 2579, 2709, 3427

Samson Collection, 2138

Sanderson, Edward F., 639, 652, 850, 1000–03, 1034, 1045, 1152, 1186, 1417–21, 1483, 1503, 1541, 1608–09, 1611–12, 1699, 1724, 1726, 1765, 1766, 2065, 2206, 2213–14, 2238–39, 2280, 2322, 2366, 2634, 2674, 2804, 2847, 3010, 3022, 3153, 3497, 4102–05, 4232, 4995

Sawin, John, 3388, 3392, 3398

Sawin & Dyar, 3370, 3374

Scales, 3784

Scallops on bases, 6, 40

Schmidt, John, 3563

Schwartz, Morris, 226, 309, 354, 403, 418, 428, 505, 605, 630, 685, 1258, 1309, 2110, 2279, 2436–37, 2628, 3136, 4965

Sconces, 4121 ff

Scrapers, 3798, 3799, 3826, 4052

Screens, 1399–1416

Scrimshaw ornaments, 1419

Secretaries, barrel roll, 728, 738

Secretaries, block-front, 687, 692, 693–712

Secretaries, desks with upper sections, 653–738

Secretaries, Hepplewhite, 562, 654–73, 726, 728, 732, 736, 738

Secretaries, John Goddard, 701, 708, and probably others

Secretaries, kettle base (bombé), 687, 717

INDEX

INDEX

INDEX

INDEX

INDEX

Wetherfield Collection, 3350–51, 3352, 3353, 3356, 3515–16

Wetmore, T. T., 2488

Wharton, Miss Susan P., 3517

Wheaton, Caleb, 3322

Wheeler, Ed. C., 96, 332, 337, 394, 495, 498, 515, 577, 594, 857, 866, 1214, 1216–17, 1233, 1254–55, 1372–73, 1603, 1981–82, 1994, 2033–34, 2035, 2037–38, 2041, 2043, 2092, 3224, 4161–62

Wheeler, Richard E., 3411

White, Peregrine, 3506

Whitewood, *see* Tulipwood

Wigon, Barker, 3303

Wilder, Joshua, 3295, 3320, 3336, 3429

Willard, Aaron, 3338, 3383, 3384, 3407, 3421

Willard, Aaron, Jr., 3263, 3390, 3432

Willard, Benjamin, 3260

Willard, Ephraim, 3247, 3253

Willard, Simon, 3287, 3316, 3337, 3366, 3367, 3368, 3371, 3372, 3379, 3387, 3402, 3417, 3434

Willard, Simon & Sons, 3361

Williams, Charles F., Collection of, 3294, 3402

Williams, David, 3271, 3321

Williams House, 532

Willis, H. P., 2101

Willson, Joshua, 3353

Window seats, 1727–34 B

Windsor, Connecticut, 1

Wine cooler, 772 A, 1758, 1759

Wineck, Samuel, 180 A, 181–83, 608, 1031, 1181, 1691, 2427, 2452, 2838–39, 2966, 3187, 3215, 4957

Winkley, John, 3397

Winthrop, Ed. Dwight, 464

Wolf, S., 280, 1722

Wood, David, 3373, 3389, 3430, 3435

Worcester Antiquarian Society, 2468

Wright, Alan, 1088, 1154, 3008

Y

Yale University, 449, 454, 1789

Yarn holder, 1869

Yarn reel, with clicking counter, 3225

York Jail, Maine, 1447, 3834